Brazil

LATIN AMERICAN HISTORIES

Thomas E. Skidmore, Series Editor

Brazil

Five Centuries of Change

Thomas E. Skidmore

New York • Oxford
OXFORD UNIVERSITY PRESS
1999

Oxford University Press

Oxford   New York
Athens   Auckland   Bangkok   Bogotá   Buenos Aires   Calcutta
Cape Town   Chennai   Dar es Salaam   Delhi   Florence   Hong Kong   Istanbul
Karachi   Kuala Lumpur   Madrid   Melbourne   Mexico City   Mumbai
Nairobi   Paris   São Paulo   Singapore   Taipei   Tokyo   Toronto   Warsaw

and associated companies in
Berlin   Ibadan

Published by Oxford University Press, Inc.,
198 Madison Avenue, New York, New York 10016
http://www.oup-usa.org

Oxford is a registered trademark of Oxford University Press

Library of Congress Cataloging-in-Publication Data
Skidmore, Thomas E.
   Brazil : five centuries of change / Thomas E. Skidmore.
      p.   cm. — (Latin American histories)
   Includes bibliographical references (p.   -   ) and index.
   ISBN 0-19-505809-7 (hardcover). — ISBN 0-19-505810-0 (pbk.)
   1. Brazil—History.   I. Title.   II. Series.
F2521.S54   1999
981—dc21   98-23122
                                                       CIP

9 8 7 6 5 4 3 2
Printed in the United States of America
on acid-free paper

Contents

List of Exhibits

Acknowledgments

Writing a one-volume history of any well-established country is inevitably a collective enterprise, no matter what the title page may say. My greatest debt is to many Brazilians who over the last three decades have been unfailingly generous with their historical knowledge and their hospitality. Alberto Venancio Filho and Paulo Sergio Pinheiro, both friends of many years, read a draft manuscript and made valuable suggestions, although neither saw the final version. A number of American colleagues gave similar help; they include Dain Borges, Todd Diacon, Frank McCann, Steve Topik, and Joel Wolfe. Final responsibility is, of course, mine.

A series of excellent research assistants include Joel Karlin, Helan Gaston, Nelly Letjer, Lisbeth Pimentel, Chi Watts, Telia Anderson, and Barbara Martinez. Logistical support was offered by Ron Rathier. Sheldon Meyer, formerly senior editor at Oxford University Press and my long-time friend, furnished that knowing encouragement which has been so important to so many American historians.

I owe a special debt to my wife, Felicity, who once again demonstrated her formidable skills as a book midwife. With her left hand she edits and with her right hand she tends the heart. What more could a spouse ask for?

Introduction:
Why Read About Brazil?

Brazil has created, beneath a facade of harmony, a contradictory society. The contradictions have several sources. They are a product of the mixture of peoples—indigenous, European, and African—and the Portuguese-derived culture that binds Brazil together. The contradictions are also produced by past promises of opportunity, which are negated by the present realities of discrimination, violence, and widespread poverty. The ultimate contradiction is between Brazil's justifiable reputation for personal generosity ("cordiality") and the fact of having to live in one of the world's most unequal societies. In a word, Brazil exemplifies all the problems of capitalism in the developing world.

Brazilian society has proved to be varied yet remarkably integrated, not on egalitarian but on hierarchical terms. The culture inculcates a sense of intimacy along with a sense of distance, thus allowing the elite to dominate society with little fear of challenge. Our main task is to ask how this society emerged and what keeps it from becoming more open and egalitarian—which has been the declared aim of national leaders at least since the proclamation of the Republic in 1889.

There are many other themes to explore. The first is the question of how Portugal held together such a huge territory—modern Brazil is larger even than the continental United States—while Spanish South America fragmented into the many contemporary nations. Meanwhile, Brazil cohered not only culturally but politically. This is one of the more stunning accomplishments of nation-building in the modern world.

Brazil is also a relatively successful multiracial society. It houses the largest population of African descent outside of Africa. It has one of the most richly varied indigenous populations. How have the three principal ethnic groups—plus later immigrants, including Asians—mixed to produce a nation which has long lacked legally defined racial barriers? What legacy has this created for a semi-modern, increasingly urban, partially industrialized society?

In terms of politics, one must marvel at how a relatively small political elite has been able to defuse and deflect popular protest. Again and again, the threat of revolution has been averted by shrewd conciliatory and co-optive moves by those in power. The result has been a remarkable continuity in the hierarchical social structure and in the distribution of power.

Brazil has led in one department that has not been a forte in most of Latin America: industrialization. Southeastern Brazil succeeded in building the largest industrial park in the Third World by the 1970s. Industrialization has also created a dilemma: how to raise mass living standards in a labor-surplus economy.

Finally, what national identity has Brazil developed? Brazilians see themselves as very different from all other New World societies and claim to have produced their own civilization. Yet the inequalities and vulnerabilities remain. Only one thing is certain: Their future will depend not only on their past but also on their vision of the future.

Brazil

1 Birth and Growth of Colonial Brazil: 1500–1750

Only four countries in the world—Canada, Russia, the People's Republic of China, and the United States (if Alaska is included)—are larger than Brazil. This chapter tells the story of how Portugal, a country far smaller than almost all of its competitors in the race for colonial territory, imposed its authority and culture on a country that spans more than half of South America.

The focus of this chapter is on key themes that dominate Brazilian colonial history and help explain Brazil today:

- Portuguese origins
- Contact and clash with indigenous peoples
- Forced importation of millions of African slaves
- Creation of a multiracial society
- Consolidation and expansion of Portuguese-ruled territory
- Establishment of an export-based economy
- Beginnings of an independent Brazilian cultural and political consciousness

A brief overview of Brazil's current scale, climate, and geography provides the context for the story. (See exhibit 1-1 for the extraordinary contrast between Brazil's place in South America and Portugal's place in Europe.)

The Country the Portuguese Created in the New World

Present-day Brazil covers 3,286,488 square miles. It extends for almost 2,700 miles from north to south, and roughly the same distance from east to west. By the 1991 census it numbered 146.8 million inhabitants, 52 percent white, 42 percent mulatto, 5 percent black, 0.4 percent Asian, and 0.2 percent Indian. As we shall see, these racial categorizations are much less rigid than in the United States. And Brazil boasts virtually

Exhibit 1-1. Comparative size of Brazil. From E. Bradford Burns, *A History of Brazil*, 3rd ed. (New York, 1993), p. 14.

every mineral needed for a modern industrial economy, with the conspicuous exceptions of coal and petroleum (although offshore wells are now helping to produce 60 percent of domestic needs).

Brazil's climate has been much maligned. "Insalubrious" has been used historically to describe it, though public health precautions were all it took to subdue the hideous tropical diseases that so frightened chroniclers in the past. Although many areas are typically humid, the extreme cold temperatures afflicting North America and Europe are unknown, and the high temperature extremes are certainly no worse than those of the United States. Hurricanes and earthquakes are also unknown, although floods and drought are relatively common threats.

Present-day Brazil covers five major regions. (See exhibit 1-2.) The following description focuses on the twentieth-century features of these regions. Their characteristics in the colonial era will be discussed later in this chapter.

The North includes the states of Rondônia, Acre, Amazonas, Roraima, Pará, and Amapá. It also includes the Amazon Basin and is by far the largest region, accounting for 42 percent of the national territory. Enthusiasts, both Brazilian and foreign, have nourished illusions through the years about the agricultural potential of the greater

Exhibit 1-2. The five regions of Brazil. From E. Bradford Burns, *A History of Brazil*, 3rd ed. (New York, 1993), p. 11.

Amazon Basin—from Henry Ford's disastrous effort to grow rubber in the 1930s, to the Brazilian military dictatorship's decision to build the Trans-Amazon highway and offer a variety of tax incentives in the 1970s. The facts of the region contradict them. The great barrier to agricultural development of the Amazon Basin is and has always been the vast tropical rain forest. It makes overland travel impossible, leaving the rivers as the only mode of transportation in earlier eras (which air travel is added today). More fundamentally, because rain leaches the soil if the vegetable cover is cut down, these lands cannot be used for conventional agriculture, leaving the area with insufficient carrying capacity for intense human settlement.

The Northeast includes the states of Maranhão, Piauí, Ceará, Rio Grande do Norte, Paraíba, Pernambuco, Alagoas, Sergipe, and Bahia. This region, which covers 18 percent of the national territory, was the heart of the colonial settlement. Since the nineteenth century, however, it has been in economic decline, with its once-flourishing export agriculture no longer competitive in world markets. The result has been continuing poverty for the population, which now constitutes the largest pocket of misery in the Americas. Much of the coast is a humid strip (*zona de mata*) that has lent itself to plantation agriculture, especially cane sugar and cotton. Behind this relatively narrow humid zone lie two other zones that are less hospitable to agriculture: the *zona de agreste*, a semi-arid region, and the *sertão*, a larger region subject to periodic drought. These latter two regions were famous in the twentieth century for the Brazilian bandits, such as Lampião, immortalized in verse, song, and film. The Northeast is also notable for the effectiveness with which its politicians have represented the region's interests (historically synonymous with the landowners' interests).

The Southeast comprises the states of Minas Gerais, Espírito Santo, Rio de Janeiro, and São Paulo. This is the heartland of Brazilian industrialization, occupying 11 percent of the national territory. The state of Minas Gerais is growing rapidly, having recently succeeded in combining agriculture with industry. Present-day Espírito Santo relies primarily on agriculture, especially coffee and cacao. Rio de Janeiro was the political capital of Brazil until the 1960s. In 1960 it lost its premier status when the national capital was shifted to Brasília, a modernistic new city built from scratch in the interior. Since then it has been losing industry to surrounding states. São Paulo was an economic backwater until the second half of the nineteenth century, when it became the world's primary coffee-producing area. In the twentieth century, for reasons still not perfectly understood, it has become the industrial giant of Brazil, as well as the champion producer of non-coffee foodstuffs.

The South consists of Paraná, Santa Catarina, and Rio Grande do Sul. A temperate region, it was and remains a cattle and grain-growing area with only modest industrialization. It is the smallest of the regions, occupying only 7 percent of the national territory. Historically, the most important state in the region has been Rio Grande do Sul, primarily because it borders both Argentina and Uruguay. The residents (known as *gaúchos*) flirted with separatism in the 1840s and 1890s, but have since became known as among the most nationalistic of Brazilians. Like Espírito Santo in the Southeast, Rio Grande do Sul experienced a heavy inflow of German immigrants after 1890. Paraná was a marginal state until the 1950s, when the coffee culture moved south from São Paulo and touched off an agricultural boom. Paraná was also a prime destination for immigrants from Japan, Germany, and East Europe.

The final region, the Center-West, includes the states of Mato Grosso, Mato Grosso do Sul, Goiás, and the Federal District (greater Brasília). Traditionally underpopulated, this has become one of Brazil's fastest growing areas. It covers 22 percent of the national territory, including much of the *cerrado,* or interior farmland, which has become highly productive since the 1970s, especially of soybeans. The building of Brasília (inaugurated in 1960) was a great stimulus to growth in this region, bringing modern transportation for the first time, and thus the capacity to market products to the rest of Brazil.

HOW COULD THE PORTUGUESE DO IT?

Any explanation of Portugal's historic role in the Americas must begin with the link between the crown and overseas exploration. The discovery of Brazil fits squarely into that relationship. The series of events leading directly to the discovery of Brazil began in early March 1500, when King Manuel of Portugal attended a solemn mass in his capital city of Lisbon to celebrate the launching of a new ocean fleet. Larger than any of its predecessors, it was to include thirteen ships carrying a total of 1,200 crew and passengers. Barely a year earlier, the great Portuguese navigator Vasco da Gama had returned to Lisbon from the epic voyage (1497–99) that opened the sea route to India. His success, with its promise of future trading riches, stimulated the Portuguese court to sponsor and organize this new voyage. The commander of the new expedition was Pedro Álvares Cabral, a distinguished nobleman who gave it a social distinction the earlier voyage had lacked.

The stated intent of this expedition was the same as the earlier one: to head for the southern tip of Africa, sail around the Cape of Good Hope, and head north toward India through the Indian Ocean. Almost as soon as the fleet had set out to sea, however, disaster appeared to strike. The lead ship, commanded by Cabral, swung off course into the Atlantic, sailing due west. Cabral and his crew eventually reached the coast of what is now the Brazilian state of Bahia, arriving on April 23, 1500.

They had stumbled on what turned out to be a vast continent. Or was it more than stumbling? There has been considerable speculation over the years that the Portuguese navigators knew exactly what they were doing, that they had in fact planned this "accident" to outflank the Spanish, who had already claimed so much of the new world, and that they were really following the route of previous secret voyages to Brazil. Historians have failed to uncover any evidence in the Portuguese archives or elsewhere to support this version of events. If there were, indeed, previous secret voyages to the new continent, they are still secret. Nor, of course, was the continent new to the several million indigenous Indian people who already lived there.

There is no record of what the Indian residents thought as they were "discovered" by a band of strange sailors with odd clothes and a bad smell, but their reaction can well be imagined. The reaction of Cabral and his men *is* known: They were fascinated by what they saw. Their thoughts were captured in an official account written for King Manuel by Pero Vaz de Caminha, the fleet's scribe. His "Carta" (letter) demonstrated a typical late-Renaissance perception of the new land, naturally emphasizing what was exotic to European eyes. Vaz de Caminha depicted a realm where the resources—human and environmental—were there for the taking. The native women were described as comely, naked, and without shame, and the soil as endlessly fertile. The image of endless fertility was to capture the imagination of the Portuguese and later the Brazilians, a romanticization that has led to a variety of overoptimistic estimates of Brazil's potential. This description of Brazil sounded seductively different from the hardscrabble life facing most Portuguese at home. It was also designed to encourage the monarch to send follow-up expeditions.

Cabral's feat, though dramatic, was in fact part of the continuing success of the Portuguese at overseas exploration. Despite their relatively meager resources (the Portuguese population was about 1 million, compared with England's 3 million, Spain's 7 million, and France's 15 million; Holland was closest with 1.5 million), the Portuguese were, during these years, in the process of creating a trading empire reaching all the way to Asia. Vasco de Gama's arrival in India in 1498 marked the creation of the *Estado de India*, a network of coastal enclaves running along the Indian Ocean, from Mozambique, around the Malabar coast of India, and all the way to Macao on the coast of China. The resulting wealth had made their kingdom a major international power in fifteenth-century Europe.

Such success was made possible by a combination of factors: early consolidation of the monarchy, and a social structure that respected trade, along with leadership in navigational technology, long-standing involvement in oceanic trading networks, an instinct for trade rather than colonization, and a collective thirst for adventure.

Like Spain, Portugal had to fight a long war against the Muslims, who had occupied the Iberian peninsula since the eighth century. But the Portuguese had liberated their kingdom from its Arabic-speaking occupiers by the thirteenth century, two hundred years earlier than the Spanish. In addition, they were able to resist repeated attempts by the kingdom of Castile (the bureaucratic and military core of modern Spain), to manipulate the succession to the Portuguese throne. To strengthen its position against Castile, Portugal forged an alliance with the English crown in 1386. This alliance, which remained the bedrock of Portuguese foreign policy for the following five centuries, was to lay the basis for England's involvement—especially its economic involvement—in modern Brazil. The marriage of Portuguese King João I to the granddaughter of England's Edward III consolidated the Portuguese dynasty (known as the house of Avis, 1385–1578) and created the stable monarchical base that facilitated the country's foray into world exploration and trade.

ENGLISH CONNECTION

In addition to early political stability, Portugal was helped by a social structure in which the merchant class played a major role. Portugal's economy in the fifteenth century combined commercial agriculture, subsistence agriculture, and trade. The merchants were the key to trade and were respected by the crown. Thus, they had the support of their sovereign as they maneuvered on the world stage, pursuing exploration and trade and gaining the cooperation of foreign merchants, especially the Genoese in what is modern-day Italy.

The power of the merchants and the interest of the crown combined to produce the resources necessary to make Portugal a leader in perfecting the technology necessary for traveling long distances by sea. One of her relative advantages in maritime skills was in ship-building, about which the Portuguese had learned much from their Basque neighbors in northern Spain. For example, they produced the *caravel*, the first sailing ship that was reliable on the high seas. Previous European ships were designed for coastal sailing or for use in the relatively calm inland sea of the Mediterranean. When sailed on the open ocean, they were apt to be swamped by ocean waves and often capsized. The Portuguese also excelled at navigation. In particular, they pioneered development of the astrolabe, the first instrument capable of using the sun and stars to determine position at sea. Finally, the Portuguese were skilled at drawing maps, which were based on the increasingly detailed geographical knowledge accumulated on their voyages. Such maps made possible systematic repeat trips. (The astrolabe and the map-making skills give some credence to the speculation that Cabral "discovered" Brazil by design.)

SHIP-BUILDING TECHNOLOGY

NAVIGATION

CARTOGRAPHY

Portugal had yet another asset: a long-standing involvement in the trade routes that linked the Mediterranean and Northern Europe. Over the preceding centuries Lisbon had been a regular stop for Genoese traders traveling from the Mediterranean to European Atlantic ports. By 1450, as a consequence, Portugal was already integrated into the most advanced trading network of the time. Portugal's location on the

TRADE NETWORKS

Atlantic also stimulated a natural focus west, as compared with fleets that had set out from ports inside the Mediterranean.

Portugal was also helped because its small population made it impossible to settle nationals in the colonies on the scale soon to be launched by the English and the Spanish. Rather than subjugate the indigenous population politically, the Portuguese established a network of trading posts—militarily fortified and minimally staffed—in order to exchange goods with the local population. They negotiated in order to obtain the local products (spices, gold, rare textiles, etc.), which would be produced for export by local labor, with minimal Portuguese involvement. Such trading was established in Africa and Asia in the fifteenth and sixteenth centuries to obtain spices (black pepper, ginger, cinnamon, cloves, nutmeg) and other foods. The Portuguese also hoped to find gold or other precious metals.

Between 1450 and 1600, the Portuguese established the most viable network of European trading forts. Greatest competition came from the English, the Dutch, the French, and especially the Spanish—competition that soon made soldiers and naval gunners as vital to the Portuguese kingdom as its navigators and traders.

The catalyst that brought all these factors together was a combination of individual characteristics that led the Portuguese people to excel in exploration and trade. First, they believed in the religious mission to convert the heathen. The sails of their ships bore a cross to announce their commitment to evangelize for the Holy Faith. But their zeal was more pragmatic than that of the Puritans who settled New England. Unlike the Puritans, for example, they did not stress their theological mission in the reports of success they sent back to their homeland. Second, they preferred to solidify trade rather than to impose formal political authority over the indigenous peoples they encountered. This contrasted with the Spanish, whose first order of business in the Valley of Mexico, for example, was to claim legal dominion over the millions of Indian inhabitants of the region. Finally, and perhaps most important, they had a collective thirst to discover the new and the exotic, which drove them to travel the high seas in spite of the obvious and frequently confirmed dangers. Of Cabral's original fleet of thirteen, for example, six went down at sea. This drive to succeed in spite of the odds was captured by the fifteenth century Portuguese poet Camões in his epic poem *The Lusiads*, which remains the literary document of Portugal: "We must sail!" (*Navigar é preciso!*)

SECURING THE FRONTIERS

Running through the story of colonial Brazil is Portugal's continuing struggle to expand its hold on the continent, even as it warded off the efforts by other countries to encroach on the land it had already settled.

The likelihood of competition between the Spanish and the Portuguese in the New World had been foreseen by both sides almost from the beginning. As early as 1493, only a year after Columbus's first voyage and seven years before Cabral had reached Bahia, Pope Alexander VI issued a series of papal bulls dividing up the New World between the two crowns. Everything to the west of the dividing line was to be Spanish, everything to the east was to be Portuguese. The Portuguese resisted the Pope's demarcation (was it because that Pope was Spanish?) and a year later reached an independent agreement with Spain, the Treaty of Tordesilhas. This treaty moved the line of demarcation between what was to be Spanish and what was to be Portuguese 270 leagues to the west—not very much of a difference.

On today's map, that imaginary line goes from the mouth of the Amazon through the coast of the present-day state of Santa Catarina, giving the Portuguese dramatically less territory than is occupied by present-day Brazil. No one could see that, of course, because the area was almost completely unknown. In any event, the Portuguese were to exploit the vagueness over the centuries to come, pushing farther and farther west.

The Treaty of Tordesilhas did not hold. The French, though Catholic, refused to honor the papal bulls or the treaty. They began their own exploration of the Brazilian coast as early as 1504 and continued their incursions throughout the sixteenth century. In the 1550s, led by Nicolas de Villegaignon, a naval officer, they controlled the area of Rio de Janeiro, which was to be the base of what the French saw as "Antarctic France," a future refuge for French Protestants. The French were driven out of Rio by a column of Portuguese and Indian troops in 1565, the year of Rio's official founding by the Portuguese. This did not end the French incursions, however, which continued throughout the sixteenth century. One of the most contested regions was the Amazon Basin. Here the French settled at São Luiz, located on the Atlantic coast. The Portuguese finally drove them out in 1615.

The Spanish also proved a threat to Portuguese America. In the 1520s and 1530s, in spite of the Treaty of 1494, they settled on the coast south of São Paulo. Between 1540 and 1560, they established settlements on the coast of modern Santa Catarina. These settlements did not survive, however. Spanish settlements thereafter were mostly in the Rio de la Plata basin, where the Spanish and Portuguese collided head on. The Portuguese originally claimed sovereignty all the way to the Plata River (including the area of present-day Uruguay, which eventually was ceded to Spanish control). The modern boundaries between Brazil and Spanish America in the south emerged only in 1828, when Britain forced recognition of an independent Uruguay.

Portuguese expansion to the west did not encounter resistance from other colonial powers. Exploration of the interior lay in the hands of armed Portuguese bands, which went west to capture Indians and look for precious metals. These *bandeirantes*, whose expeditions originated primarily in the coastal region of present-day Sao Paulo, were the prime explorers of inland Brazil and became the heroes of much folklore and mythification by the São Paulo elite of the twentieth century.

JESUITS

In all their efforts to secure the frontiers of Brazil, the Portuguese were helped immeasurably by the Portuguese Jesuits. This aggressive religious order established mission networks in many parts of Brazil, particularly in the Amazon valley, harnessing vast supplies of Indian labor to work the Jesuit-run ranches and vineyards. In so doing, they helped "pacify" (read: subjugate) the local Indian peoples and establish the Christian religion. They also played an important role as cultural brokers. Jesuit linguists, for example, were the persons who established a standard form of Tupí, the principal native language. As late as the end of the seventeenth century, this *lingua franca* was more widely spoken than Portuguese, and its standardization eventually facilitated the spread of the Portuguese language.

HOW THE PORTUGUESE ADMINISTERED THE COLONY

In the first three decades after Cabral's voyage, Portugal treated Brazil as merely another set of trading posts, established on the model of the *feitorias* (trading stations) set up earlier in Africa and Asia. Asian exploration and trade was its primary interest, where it had a commanding lead over its European rivals and reaped rich profits. By the early 1530s, however, the incursions by the French and Spanish, and the need for more trade to replace declining activity in the Indian Ocean, forced the Portuguese crown to reconsider its position. Since it lacked the resources to strengthen its foothold in America, it resorted to a semifeudal system of hereditary land grants, or captaincies. These were given to rich nobles, in the hope that they would exploit the Brazil wood and other resources, gaining personal profit while also serving the crown. Fourteen captaincies were granted between 1534 and 1536. (See map: exhibit 1-3.)

LAND GRANTS TO RICH NOBLES

Unfortunately for the crown, the risks were too great and the rewards too uncertain to persuade the grantees to make the required investment. Only two captaincies were successful: São Vicente and Pernambuco. The former was south of the present-day city of São Paulo, and the latter was in the northeast.

In 1550, in a new sign of royal commitment, the Portuguese crown created a governor-generalship. Governor Tomé de Souza arrived in 1549. He founded the city of Salvador, which was to remain the capital of the colony for more than two centuries.

In 1572, the threats of French and Spanish penetration near Rio and the South persuaded the government to divide its administration

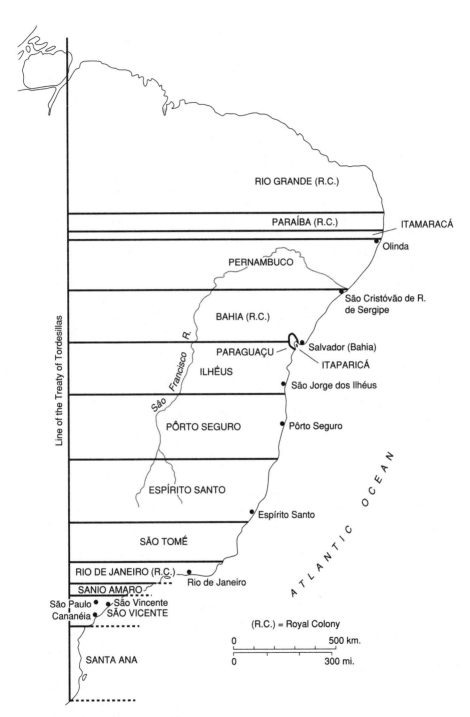

Exhibit 1-3. The captaincies of Brazil in the late sixteenth century. From James Lockhart and Stuart B. Schwartz, *Early Latin America* (Cambridge, 1983), p. 185.

between Salvador and Rio de Janeiro, a dual governorship that was ended in 1578. Two years later, Portugal entered a sixty-year "union" with Spain, as lack of a royal heir in Portugal led to Spain's formal takeover of the Portuguese crown. The Spanish control of Brazil lasted until 1640, when a suitable successor to the Portuguese throne was again found.

Interestingly, the Spanish did not use their formal authority to take over the Portuguese colony in earnest. Their one major activity in Brazil was the constructive one of regularizing administrative and judicial procedures, including development of new civil and penal codes in 1603. Otherwise, Spain's energies were engaged in fighting to retain its possessions elsewhere in the New World.

Brazil was not entirely free of those struggles. The Dutch, in particular, took the occasion to attack this new outpost of "Spanish" imperialism by invading Brazil's northeastern coast in 1624. These Dutch invaders (who were sponsored by the Dutch West India Company) managed to maintain control for thirty years, occupying Recife and taking over the lucrative sugar trade. During the occupation of Recife by the Dutch, under Governor Maurice of Nassau (1637–44), scores of distinguished and mostly Dutch scientists and artists—such as the naturalist Jorge Marcgrave and the painter Frans Post—descended on the area to document its flora and fauna. In 1654, a coalition of Brazilians of all social classes, supported by the local planters' desire to escape their debts to the Dutch, finally drove the Dutch off the coast. Brazilian patriots often point to this resistance campaign as the birth of Brazilian nationalism.

The seventeenth century saw the dramatic expansion of territorial control (north, west, and south) by the Portuguese. The Portuguese administration accommodated this expansion though a codification and extension of the existing authority to newly secured locations, rather than changing the administrative structure. There were two exceptions to this continuity. The first was creation of the position of *juiz de fora*, a regional judgeship, which was intended to reduce the power of the rural landowners. The second was creation in 1620 of a new state, Maranhão, which included the Upper Northeast and the entire Amazon Basin. Maranhão was divided into six hereditary captaincies, following the precedent set in Bahia and Pernambuco. Unlike those other states, however, Maranhão existed as a separate unit until 1774, reporting directly to Lisbon even though the official administrative center of Brazil remained in Salvador. The impetus for the establishment of Maranhão was Portugal's need to consolidate its control of the North after the expulsion of the French. The action was also explicit recognition of the geographical separateness of Maranhão—a consequence of the prevailing southeasterly winds, which often made travel up the coast from Salvador impossible. Land travel was not a realistic alternative, given hostile Indians and jungle terrain. It was common at that time for over-land journeys in Brazil to take months. Rivers were used where possible, but the Amazon flows from west to east, and the most important river in the northeast, the San Francisco, is broken by falls so vast as to be impassable.

The eighteenth century was dominated by the rise and decline of the mining industry, following the discovery of gold in Minas Gerais and Mato Grosso in the early 1690s. (See exhibit 1-4.) The resulting shift in population southward to those regions did have an effect on the administrative structure of the colony. In 1709 the crown created the new

EXHIBIT 1-4

Production of Brazilian Gold in the Eighteenth Century

Years	Total (kg)
1700–1705	1,470
1706–1710	4,410
1711–1715	6,500
1716–1720	6,500
1721–1725	7,600
1726–1729	8,500
1730–1734	9,000
1735–1739	14,137
1740–1744	17,147
1745–1749	14,812
1750–1754	15,760
1755–1759	12,616
1760–1764	10,499
1765–1769	9,759
1770–1774	8,779
1775–1774	8,118
1780–1784	6,284
1785–1789	4,911
1790–1794	4,510
1795–1799	4,399

Source: Leslie Bethell, ed., *The Cambridge History of Latin America,* vol. 2 (Cambridge, 1984), p. 594.

captaincy of São Paulo and Minas de Ouro. Then, in 1721, the separate captaincy of Minas was created and in 1748 separate captaincies were established for Mato Grosso and Goiás. Inevitably, as discussed further in chapter 2, the capital was finally moved from Salvador to Rio de Janeiro in 1763 to keep closer administrative control over the lucrative mining area.

THE PEOPLES OF BRAZIL

One of the best-known facts about Brazil is the multiracial nature of its population—a mixture of indigenous Indian, Portuguese, and African, with the later addition of Japanese, Middle Easterners, and non-Portuguese Europeans. This section gives a brief overview of the Indians and African in colonial Brazil.

When Cabral arrived in 1500, a far-flung and complex network of indigenous peoples was already there. The Indians numbered more than one hundred separate language groups, from the Charrua in the far south to the Macuxi in the far north. These "Indians" (*indios*, the term used by the Portuguese and later the Brazilians) differed significantly from the best-known native peoples of Mesoamerica and the Andes. In both of those regions, at least some of the indigenous civilizations had reached a high level of complexity, as in the ceremonial city-building of the Aztecs (more properly known as the Nahua) in the Valley of Mexico and the Inca in the Peruvian highlands.

The city-building societies were highly disciplined. They mounted armies to resist the Europeans, fighting set battles involving thousands of Indians under strictly organized command. Once defeated, however, as their leaders were disgraced or died, they became leaderless. This dissolution of the Nahua and Inca societies facilitated the Spanish creation of an economy manned by an Indian labor force that was forced to do what it was told.

From the beginning, Portuguese colonists also saw the Indian as an indispensable source of labor. However, the Brazilian indigenous peoples were hunters and gatherers. The Indians inhabiting Brazil did not form set armies and were not inclined to stand and fight. Nor did they have a Nahua- or Inca-style social hierarchy that the Portuguese could take over to enforce work discipline.

Scholars disagree on the number of Native Americans living, when the Portuguese arrived, in the area that is now Brazil. Plausible estimates range anywhere from 500,000 to 2 million, with one going as high as 8 million. However large this population may have been in 1500, it shrank drastically after the Europeans arrived. Epidemic disease was a major cause. The Europeans brought such infectious diseases as smallpox and measles to an American environment lacking any previous exposure—

and therefore immunity—to them. Harsh treatment by the Portuguese, who met native resistance with brute force, further decimated indigenous populations.

Disease and harsh treatment took a heavy toll on the indigenous peoples of Spanish America also, but those who survived were often relatively easy to track down and organize into work crews. The Indians who survived in Brazil retreated into the rain forest or the temperate interior, where the Portuguese had trouble pursuing them. These indigenous peoples were scattered into more than a hundred separate language groups, almost all unintelligible to one another. The language group that proved most important was the Tupí-Guaraní, found especially in coastal Brazil. Theirs was the language standardized by Jesuit missionaries under the label of *Lingua Geral* that became so widely spoken throughout Brazil. But there were other Indian peoples scattered to the west and south who were slowly encountered by the Portuguese in the course of their sixteenth- and seventeenth-century explorations. And there were many language groups in the rain forest of the Amazon Basin whom the Portuguese had no contact with in the colonial era.

The Indians in Brazil were a revelation to the Portuguese. Even before Columbus, Europeans had developed a lively fantasy world to describe the humans, animals, and plants they expected to find beyond the Atlantic horizon. Vaz de Caminha's report reinforced the European prejudice that Portugal had discovered an idyllic world where evil was unknown. As Portuguese King Manuel wrote to his fellow monarch in Spain, "My captain reached a land . . . where he found humans as if in their first innocence, mild and peace-loving." Jean-Jacques Rousseau later based his optimistic theory of human nature at least in part on these early descriptions of the Brazilian Indian.

In his letter describing Cabral's voyage in 1500, Vaz de Caminha described the Indians as "tough, healthy, and innocent." Another alleged Indian trait, bestiality, became the stuff of legend in Europe. A particularly famous example was Hans Staden's 1557 chronicle, *The True History and Description of a Land of Savage, Naked, Fierce, Man-Eating People Found in the New World*. Staden, a German, was shipwrecked on the Brazilian coast and survived imprisonment by Indians. His bloodcurdling narrative described natives who delighted in cooking and devouring their captives in a form of ritual cannibalism. The woodblock illustrations of the book showed human limbs being readied for the boiling pots. The pictures confirmed what Staden's European readers were ready to believe. Throughout the sixteenth and seventeenth centuries, European illustrations of Brazil fixed on cannibalism (about whose extent present-day anthropologists disagree). The existence of this "barbarism" gave the Portuguese further legitimacy for their claim that they were bringing civilization to "savages." It also made easier the theological and legal arguments for subjugating the Indians. As with the Nahuas of Mexico, the image of flesh torn from helpless (especially white) bodies served to justify seizing the land and exploiting native labor, a rationale the Church was eager to support.

The colonists who actually lived in Brazil had a less fanciful and more arrogant attitude towards the Indians, as they coexisted, cohabited, and clashed with them. Their arrogance is epitomized in the words of a chronicler writing in 1570 that the language of all the coastal Indians "lacked the three letters F, L and R, which is startling because it means they have neither *Fé* [faith], nor *Lei* [law], nor *Rei* [king] and live, thus, without justice or order."

The Indians who remained under Portuguese control in the sugar-growing area of the Northeast dwindled as they died from contagious disease and maltreatment, obliging the Portuguese to seize fresh Indians to maintain a labor force. By the end of the eighteenth century, Indians were hardly visible in the Northeastern coastal sugar society. Indians survived in any numbers only in the interior, where they lived relatively free from contact with the Portuguese colonists. This scattering reinforced the fact that, unlike Mexico or Peru, Brazil does not have the glories of an indigenous civilization hovering over its modern existence. There are no massive pyramids such as at Teotiohucán or hidden cities such as Macchu Picchu. This does not mean, however, that the Indian left absolutely no trace on modern Brazil. In language (the place names), diet (the ever-present manioc root), and medicine (innumerable herbal cures), links can still be found.

As the Indian labor force dwindled, the Portuguese turned to Africa. Even before reaching the New World, the Portuguese had used Africans as slaves. As they explored the West African coast in the fifteenth century, they brought back slaves to work on the plantations of the Azores and Madeira islands. By the 1450s, Africans were being brought into Portugal itself at the rate of 700 to 800 a year. It has been argued—most notably by Gilberto Freyre, 1900–87, the Brazilian anthropologist-writer who became the most influential twentieth-century interpreter of Brazilian character and society—that the Portuguese were less prejudiced than other Europeans against Africans, partly because of Portugal's long exposure to the darker skinned Moors, who represented a high culture. But the picture that emerges from the archives does not altogether support Freyre's view. Portuguese writers at times expressed extreme distaste of the physical characteristics of Africans they saw. In 1505, Duarte Pacheco, for example, a Portuguese who traveled extensively, dismissed West Africans as "dog-faced, dog-toothed people, satyrs, wild men and cannibals." In fact, both private and public discourse in Portugal was rife with such concepts as "clean blood," "purity of blood," and "infected races." Yet this trait of prejudice, traceable to such different roots as an aesthetic reaction to Africans and a dogmatic reaction to non-Christians (especially Jews and Muslims), was to play itself out, as we shall see, in unpredictable ways in Brazilian history.

As the Portuguese realized, as early as the 1530s, that the Indians could not provide sufficient labor for the harvesting of Brazil wood and the cultivation of sugar cane, they turned to obtaining slaves from West Africa, where Portuguese slave traders were well established. By 1580, the Portuguese were importing more than 2,000 African slaves a year to work the sugar plantations of Northeastern Brazil. Thus began the slave trade in Brazil, which continued until 1850 at a human cost that was staggering. Shipboard conditions were indescribably bad and disease rampant. More than half the slave cargoes typically died en route. It was a tragic story repeated throughout the Atlantic slave trade. In 1695, the noted Jesuit missionary Padre António Vieira, for example, gave this evaluation of the South Atlantic slave trade: "The kingdom of Angola on the opposite Ethiopian shore, by whose sad blood, and black but fortunate souls, Brazil is nurtured, animated, sustained, served and preserved." Brazil received more African slaves (at least 3.65 million, and some estimates are considerably higher) in total than any other region in the Americas. Present-day Brazil, as a result, has the largest population of African descent of any country outside those of Africa itself.

The Africans who were captured and sent off to colonial Brazil came from several regions of central and southwestern Africa. These regions spanned wide linguistic and cultural differences, bringing many different African traditions. Those differences can still be detected, for example, in the variations of Afro-Brazilian religions practices in present-day Brazil. In the sixteenth century the chief source of slaves was the Senegambia; in the seventeenth century the main source was Angola and the Congo; in the eighteenth century the main source was the Mina Coast and the Bight of Benin.

The Portuguese slave dealers and plantation owners were practiced at evaluating African tribes according to their reputation for work and the likelihood that they would resist. The most "dangerous" groups were divided up and sold off to different regions in order to dilute their effect at any one location. The colonists were also very efficient at mixing Africans of different language groups together, preventing slave solidarity and producing a docile labor force by leaving them little means of communication until they learned Portuguese.

The African slaves and their descendants were soon found throughout Brazil. Such slaves worked in the cattle culture of the far south, the mines of Minas Gerais, and the extractive culture of the Amazon Basin. They also worked in construction and in domestic service. African slave labor and slave-based society typified all of Portuguese America by the early seventeenth century.

What was the nature of slavery in colonial Brazil? Was it significantly different from African slavery in Spanish or English America?

What mark did it leave on the economy and society? Scholars now agree that New World slave labor systems differed little in their basic structure. All denied full legal rights and used coercion, including frequent brutality, to maintain subservience. The Portuguese, Spanish, English, French, and Dutch all used whatever it took to extract labor from those over whom the masters had unlimited de facto power. Within Brazil, as elsewhere, there were obvious differences between field slaves and house slaves on the same plantation, with the latter (on which Gilberto Freyre's famous works focus) having more freedom of movement and greater privileges. But everywhere the work relationship depended on the use or threatened use of violence, by the master and/or by state authorities.

Clerics and crown officials regularly denounced planters who, in the words of one Jesuit, "for trifling offenses threw their slaves alive into the furnace, or killed them in various barbarous and inhumane ways." Even when not subjected to such excesses, slaves in Brazil, as elsewhere, were held to an exhausting schedule, often 'round the clock at harvest time, and subservience and deference were essential for slave survival. The association of a hierarchical structure with black at the bottom was to influence all subsequent race relations in Brazil.

Africans, like the Indians before them, resisted their masters in multiple ways. Among other forms of sabotage, they broke equipment. They also escaped to the interior. Some formed runaway slave communities called *quilombos*, much more possible in the wilds of Brazil than in the United States. The most famous was the fortified settlement at Palmares (in the present-day state of Alagoas), which survived for a century before being wiped out by a large military expedition in 1694. The colonial Governor at the time declared the destruction of Palmares to be no less important than the expulsion of the Dutch. The leader of the Palmares quilombo was the chieftain Zumbi. He escaped when the settlement was destroyed and briefly mounted a new line of resistance to the whites before he was caught and killed in 1695. Zumbi has become a hero to the twentieth-century Afro-Brazilian political movement.

Because in many other regions slaves and free nonwhites often outnumbered the white population, crown authorities worried about the threat of organized revolt. To reduce the danger, the colonists hired hunters to pursue runaway slaves. The returning hunters made a practice of displaying recognizable slave body parts to other potential escapees. But the African-born slaves consistently proved rebellious. The masters ordered public punishment to terrorize the slave population, but the Brazilian colonial elite was always aware of possible death or dismemberment at the hands of its own slaves.

Despite the dangers, neither crown officials nor colonists could conceive of a Brazil without slaves. Although free labor existed and even included numerous free people of color as time passed, slavery was still seen by the economic elite as essential for Brazil's future. Even those few souls who might question slavery on moral grounds believed what they were told—that economic survival demanded slavery.

Did African cultures survive in Brazil? We are handicapped in answering this question for the colonial period, because we have virtually no primary records of African slave culture. Before the nineteenth century our information comes almost entirely from Portuguese documents. Furthermore, the Portuguese made no effort to record or use the languages of their African slaves, which contrasted with their careful attention to indigenous languages. We do know each generation arriving from Africa left more marks than its predecessors. A century and a half after the last African slave arrived in Brazil, African influence in language, cuisine, music, and dance is still clear in Brazil today.

The Colonial Economy and Society

Colonial Brazil's economy began, as already discussed, as a series of crudely constructed trading posts (known as *feitorias*, or factories) scattered along the coast, from Pernambuco in the north to São Vincente (modern-day São Paulo) in the south. Brazil wood was the first main export of the colonists from Brazil, accompanied by more exotic items such as parrots and animal skins. In return, the Portuguese delivered necessities such as clothing and tools. Brazil wood, prized for its dye-making qualities, was a valuable commodity in Europe and the export that eventually gave Brazil its name. (The country's first name, Vera Cruz, or "Land of the True Cross," has mercifully sunk into oblivion.)

When increased Portuguese commitment in the 1530s gave birth to the captaincies, and to smaller land grants (*sesmarias*), the principal crop was cane sugar, grown on enormous plantations to take advantage of economies of scale. Once harvested, the cane was processed and refined in the mills (*engenhos*) belonging to the wealthier plantation owners.

For more than a century Brazil was the world's leading sugar exporter. From 1600 to 1650, sugar accounted for 90 to 95 percent of Brazilian export earnings. Even in the period around 1700, when the sugar sector declined, it continued to represent 15 percent of Brazil's export earnings. Sugar set Brazil on the course of being a single-crop plantation economy for the colonial era and well into the twentieth century.

The typical export-oriented plantation of the colonial era, especially after 1600, was largely self-sufficient, growing much of its own foodstuffs, maintaining its own chapel (often with resident priest), and being marked by an axis of power concentrated in the *casa grande* (big house) of the *fazendeiro* (landowner) and filtering down to the *senzala* (slave quarters). This is the plantation world depicted in Gilberto

Freyre's *The Masters and the Slaves*—the world of the all powerful *fazendeiro* and the closed agrarian horizons that have so deeply influenced modern Brazil.

Cane sugar, the most important export crop after Brazil wood had been pretty much exploited, was grown largely within the humid zone on the Northeastern coast and exported to the Dutch-dominated European trade. But cane cultivation and processing required a labor force far beyond what the colonists could provide. It was a need eventually met, as we have seen, by the import of African slaves. The frailty of the Indian population in a forced-labor environment led to the first major influx of African slaves, brought from Portugal and from the Atlantic islands, such as the Azores and Madeira. Only later did the Brazilian colonists turn to Africa for their major slave supply.

Thus was established the nexus of the Brazilian colonial economy: land-extensive single-crop agriculture based on slave labor, concentrated primarily in the Northeast. This plantation system generated the hierarchical society of the colonial era. It was, in turn, part of the South Atlantic economy, which the Portuguese controlled on both sides of the ocean—one side the source of slaves (West Africa), the other side the location of their work (Brazil). By the seventeenth century, the Brazilian Northeast was one of the richest regions in the Americas, surpassing New England or Virginia. At the same time, however, the intensive cultivation of sugar was to inflict deep ecological damage on the Brazilian Northeast.

Sugar was the foremost but not the only form of rural economy pursued by the colonists. One of the most important additional endeavors, particularly in the Northeastern interior, was the cattle culture, which furnished animal power, meat, natural fertilizer, and leather. In the sixteenth and seventeenth centuries, the cattle culture was an important counterpart to the sugar regions that consumed the cattle products.

But disaster soon appeared to strike. International sugar prices fell in the 1670s and 1680s, as increased production in the Antilles cut into Brazil's world market share. An epidemic of smallpox in Angola and of yellow fever in Bahia and Pernambuco, all in the 1680s, were further blows. As Padre Antonio Vieira (1608–97), the great Jesuit missionary whose sermons became a classic of Portuguese and Brazilian culture, wrote from Bahia in 1684: "We shall shortly relapse into the savage state of the Indians, and become Brazilians instead of Portuguese." This gloomy forecast turned out to be premature, as the Portuguese quest for gold was finally satisfied in the early 1690s. By 1696, the discovery had become official news in Lisbon. The finds (which later included diamonds) were located in the present-day states of Minas Gerais, Mato Grosso, Goiás, and southern Bahia.

The Portuguese had always been interested in precious metals. They wanted above all to find gold, the ultimate currency in Europe's mercantilist trade. And they never lost the hope of equaling the Spanish luck in finding vast supplies of gold and silver. In 1500, Cabral had taken special care to interrogate the natives about the possible presence of gold, "because we wanted to know if there was any in that land." When there were few traces of these metals to be found near the coast, the colonists set out to penetrate the vast interior.

The discovery of gold triggered an immediate gold rush of migrants from all over Brazil, especially the Northeast, as Minas Gerais rapidly became the fastest growing region of eighteenth-century Brazil. It was followed by central Bahia (discoveries in 1718) and Mato Grosso (discoveries in 1725). There was also a sudden increase in new arrivals from Portugal. This drain of Portugal's youth became so large that in 1705 the Crown even attempted (unsuccessfully) to slow the flow.

Within decades, Brazil became the world's greatest gold producer. By the 1720s, Brazil also began producing diamonds. At last, Portugal could enjoy the kind of bonanza Spain had won centuries earlier.

This gold and diamond production had one very positive result. It financed the flowering of a rich culture in South-Central Brazil. The eighteenth-century mining towns in Minas Gerais, for example, saw the building of Christian churches in a unique Brazilian baroque style. Antonio Francisco Lisboa ("Alejadinho"), a mulatto, stood out for the churches he designed in Ouro Preto, Sabará, and São Paulo do Rei, and for his full-size sculptures of the prophets in Congonhas do Campo. He overcame the stigma of his color, not to mention leprosy, to become one of the giants of Brazilian art history.

Gold and diamond mines, like the plantations, depended on African slave labor—necessitating a shift of African slaves from elsewhere in Brazil, as well as new deliveries from the South Atlantic slave trade. What the mining boom did *not* do was change the basic pattern of colonial Brazilian economic development. Like the tropical agricultural products (such as sugar, cotton and tobacco), gold and diamond mining did not stimulate the broad-based economic growth necessary for industrialization.

The mineral riches went to Portugal, where they rescued a kingdom in decline. Portugal was running a steady deficit in its trade with England, and much of the Brazilian gold went to cover Portuguese debts to England. That gold also went to maintain the lifestyle of the royal court and the religious orders.

Portuguese historians have long debated whether the discovery of mineral riches in Brazil was an asset or a liability. As early as 1711, the noted Italian Jesuit chronicler Antonil gave his view that "no prudent person can fail to admit that God permitted the discovery of so much gold in the mines so that he could punish Brazil with it." The gold and diamond windfall undoubtedly helped to finance a standard of living (including lavish church construction) Portugal could not have otherwise enjoyed in the first half of the eighteenth century. Fortified by Brazilian gold, Portugal was able to ignore with impunity, at least for a while, the economic transition toward the modern industrial world that was taking place in West Europe and England.

THE SOCIAL STRUCTURE OF THE PORTUGUESE NEW WORLD

A popular Portuguese saying in the late seventeenth century called Brazil "a hell for blacks, a purgatory for whites, and a paradise for mulattoes." There can be no doubt that the first part was correct.

The social structure established during sixteenth-century Brazil became, with variations, the pattern for the rest of the colonial period. At the top of the hierarchy were white males of Portuguese descent, typically major landholders. Their white wives or daughters were strictly subordinated to the husband or father, who was the patriarch. Such families were described by the historian Capistrano de Abreu as having a "taciturn father, an obedient wife, and cowed children."

GLOOMY, FAMILIES!

In this way, colonial Brazil inherited the Portuguese relegation of women to inferior status, excluding them from any public, state, or ecclesiastical role. One ordinance in particular empowered the husband, on discovery (or suspicion) of adultery, to kill his wife and the adulterer. What is fascinating is the subordinate clause of that ordinance, "unless the husband is a peon [*peão*] and the adulterer a nobleman, a judge [*desembargador*], or someone of high standing." Husbands are documented to have taken repeated advantage of this "right" (thirty cases were reported, for example, in Bahia in 1713), which continues to be honored today by some Brazilian judges.

Unmarried daughters were not much better off. They were often relegated to a convent for life. But at least they did not suffer death "in legitimate defense of honor," as could happen to their mothers. As a consequence, upper class women turned into virtual recluses, seldom venturing out of the house even for mass. The single exception was widows with minor children. They, on their husband's deaths, gained full property rights and assumed the family role of the deceased patriarch. They must account for many of the considerable number of female-headed households that appear in the colonial records.

Marriageable white women were in continuing short supply, which gave white men the excuse to take Indian, African, or mixed-blood women as partners or mistresses, and often to father children by them. The missionaries attacked them for such practices. The correspondence of the Jesuits showed a virtual obsession with the erotic vagaries of the settlers. But most of the priestly clergy, admittedly not often celibate themselves, did not spend much time denouncing the colonists for their infidelity. We shall see below the social implications of this frequent miscegenation.

Beneath the major landholders were ranged the lesser landholders and the small farmers (often of peasant origins in Portugal). The thin urban settlements included landless Portuguese (of Portuguese descent) such as artisans and soldiers. At the bottom of the white hierarchy were the free men (the *degregados*), persons of widely varying social backgrounds whom the crown had banished to exile from Portugal because of various crimes. Some built a constructive new life in Brazil but many failed to rise in the social scale and became troublemakers.

At the very bottom of the hierarchy, both social and legal, were the slaves. Until 1600, these were primarily Indians. By the turn of the century, however, they were increasingly Africans, especially in the Northeast.

One of the crucial characteristics of Brazilian society of that era was disdain for manual labor. In the words of a Portuguese colonist writing in 1690, "it is not the style for the white people of these parts, or of any other of our colonies, to do more than command their slaves to work and tell them what to do." This trait was to persist long after slavery was abolished.

MISCEGENATION: BIOLOGICAL AND CULTURAL

The description so far is of the hierarchy as established in the 1500s, including only Portuguese colonists or those of Portuguese descent and their slaves. The most important change thereafter was the emergence of mixed bloods, predominantly children of unions between the white Portuguese and the indigenous (producing *mamelucos* or *caboclos*) and with the African (producing mulattoes). It should be remembered that bureaucratic barriers meant that few of these unions became formal church marriages. The mixed bloods entered the hierarchy just above the slaves. As time went on, at least some of them rose to higher status. It was especially here where the traditional Portuguese racial prejudice softened in practice. Women of this social segment often became itinerant vendors, specializing in selling every variety of food.

The Portuguese image of Brazil was from the beginning erotic. As the legendary Portuguese phrase had it, "beneath the equator there is no sin." In the words of Amerigo Vespucci, Brazil was "more appropriate for Epicureans than Stoics." Miscegenation between the Indians and the Portuguese produced a category of mixed bloods who often served as intermediaries between the two groups. (Interestingly enough, this extensive miscegenation was not typical of the rest of the Portuguese Empire.) For the first century, mixture with the Indians prevailed, both in the Northeast and in the São Paulo region. By the 1600s, miscegenation with the Africans and their descendants increased. In the South, especially around São Paulo, Indian slavery—and therefore sexual unions with Indians—prevailed until the late 1600s. Such miscegenation has occurred in virtually every slave-holding society—even in the United States, where miscegenation flourished despite legal prohibition of interracial marriage.

The major difference among slave societies is the fate of the mixed-blood offspring. In the colonial United States, the mixed offspring, unless light enough to pass as white, was relegated to the non-white category. The result was the American bipolar system of race relations, which recognized only the categories of black and white—the "one drop" rule, with one drop of non-white blood condemning the child to non-white status. Brazil, like most of Latin America, developed a third category: mulatto or mixed race (*mestiço* in Portuguese, which is roughly equal to *mestizo* in Spanish).

As it happened, a constant shortage of European labor in the higher echelons of the Brazilian labor force left open some job opportunities for free people of color, who were far more numerous in colonial Brazil than in colonial North America. One should not conclude from this that Brazil was a climate without prejudice. On the contrary, colonial legislation discriminated sharply against mulattoes. They were forbidden to carry weapons, wear "costly" clothes, or hold official positions in Church or state. In fact, these rules were frequently breached, as in the case of João Fernandes Vieira, a mulatto sugar planter and leader in the fight to expel the Dutch in the period from 1645 to 1654. He was governor of Angola and Paraíba during that period. Another case was Padre Antonio Vieira, Brazil's most illustrious Jesuit, who had a mulatta grandmother but still entered the highly selective Society of Jesus.

These cases, which are multiplied many times over, illustrate a crucial point about race relations as they developed in the colonial era. Race in colonial Brazil was seen as a spectrum, where individual physical characteristics (quality of hair, shape of nose and lips, skin color) could be interpreted *ad hoc*—i.e., by how people looked rather than who their parents were, and, in special cases, selectively ignoring certain physical features in interpreting where in the race spectrum a particularly favored or unfavored individual was located. This ambiguity in applying racial categories—i.e., blurring the distinction between white and non-white—has continued into the modern era and has made Brazilian race relations especially complex. The nature and effects of miscegenation in colonial Brazil, when it operated both as a means of approximation and of domination, are key to understanding the multiracial Brazilian society of today.

Such miscegenation involves not only physical but also cultural mixture. In Brazil, the combination of European, Indian, and African produced a culture very different from the austere Portuguese original. The African proved to be the most powerful among the non-European influences. African influence can still be seen among the present-day white

Brazilian elite. Afro-Brazilian-influenced religion—such as *umbanda*, for example—attracts followers from every social class in Brazil. And Brazilian music, with its heavy African influence, is the supreme example of Brazil's national popular culture.

THE NATURE OF THE COLONIAL STATE AND CHURCH

All students of modern Brazil agree that the nature of its colonial government has exercised a powerful influence on subsequent political thought and behavior. One scholar has argued that "Brazil had a state before it had a society." It was, in the words of another scholar, the "king's plantation."

The Portuguese colonial state in Brazil closely resembled its counterpart in Spanish America, a resemblance that was strengthened during the sixty years (1580–1640) when Portugal, because of a gap in its royal succession, was formally ruled by Spain. Royal government in colonial Brazil was the opposite of a civil society based on local initiative. It was the tradition, in theory if not always in fact, of the all-directing state to which its subjects looked for direction and material reward.

The Portuguese, like the Spanish, appointed as administrators members of the nobility, who sought through their offices to enrich their personal coffers and their social status. But in general, Portuguese administrative control was looser than was the Spanish—especially in the key Spanish colonies of Mexico and Peru. As the colonial era unfolded, these Portuguese-born administrators faced a growing *crioulo* (more commonly called *mazombo*) elite—whites of Portuguese descent born in Brazil—who began to see their interests differing from the crown's.

For this elite, as for others, family links were crucial in gaining favors from state power. Family clans regularly infiltrated the state structure, turning it to their advantage. In Brazil, the colonists also had to nurture their links with the crown. By doing so successfully, they produced strong clans of long-standing influence. These clans were regional and contributed to the oligarchies that would dominate Brazil after independence.

The crown often saw its orders countermanded or ignored, which was probably inevitable given the colony's size and the meager resources available to the crown. Although sworn to loyalty to the crown, these administrators often used their own authority to enrich themselves and their families. Smuggling was prevalent, for example, especially on the northern and southern borders, losing the crown valuable revenues.

Until the arrival of the first bishop at Bahia in 1552, a few Franciscan friars and a handful of secular priests had cared for the religious needs of the settlers. The scene changed with the arrival of the Jesuits, who soon became the dominant Catholic influence through their control of education (their schools were called *colégios*) and their creation of Indian missions. The model for an aggressive Jesuit missionary style was set by Manuel da Nóbrega (1517–70) and José de Anchieta (1534–97), eloquent defenders of the Indians, whose culture—except for the practices of cannibalism and polygamy—they sought to respect.

The Jesuit monopoly on education and their defense of the Indians made them ready targets for criticism by the colonists, who accused the brothers of stealing their labor supply, often to work at the Jesuit missions. The crown also became suspicious of the Jesuits because of their fierce independence, their secretiveness, and their growing wealth. It should be noted that they were not the only religious order in colonial Brazil. Other orders included the Dominicans, the Augustinians, the Franciscans, the Benedictines, the Oratorians, the Carmelites, the Mercedonians, and the Capuchins. All were dedicated to the implantation of a common scholastic curriculum. But the Jesuits remained the primary target of attack. Caustic comments such as "Everybody has to learn Latin because Latin is the passport to enter the earthly paradise where one eats without working" epitomized colonial resentment against the religious orders in general and the Jesuits in particular. Crown anger in the eighteenth-century flared particularly in the mining areas because the brothers were caught diverting huge sums to finance elaborate church structures. The crown issued a decree banning the construction of any new churches in the mining region. By the mid–eighteenth century, crown officials even saw the clergy, and especially the monastic religious orders, as a threat to the flow of income to Lisbon.

The Beginnings of a Luso-Brazilian Culture

With the powerful help of the Catholic Church and the religious orders, the Portuguese were able to impose their language and culture on a considerable portion of Brazil—possibly as much as one-third of the territory by 1700. After 1750 there was a stepped-up effort to replace Indian languages with Portuguese. The Church and the crown succeeded in this considerable feat by imposing rigid limits on speech and being constantly on the watch against heresy. This task was made easier by the outlawing of the printing press until the arrival of the Portuguese court in 1808 and the systematic suppression of indigenous civilizations wherever they were encountered.

The Church, along with the elite, believed that mass education was neither possible nor desirable. The idea of education as an investment in human capital, which was beginning to take hold in the United States and Western Europe, was totally unknown. As late as 1818, only 2.5 percent of the free male school-age population of São Paulo, was enrolled, for example. Even the elite had no educational opportunities in Brazil beyond a highly rhetorical approach to learning that ended with secondary school. Their only alternative was to leave Brazil for Coimbra University in Portugal, where one hundred of the sons of the colonial Brazilian elite studied law or medicine during the colonial period. Even Coimbra was a very narrow window onto the intellectual revolution that was transforming the rest of Europe. The luckiest of the lucky young colonialists took a diversion to France, which by the early eighteenth century was caught up in the ferment of the Enlightenment.

By the late 1700s, the suffocating Portuguese influence began to lift, as the colonial elite began to produce its own literature, even without a printing press! These early writers, working primarily in the rich mining area of Minas Gerais, drew much of their language and rhetoric from fifteenth century Portugal, above all from the epic poet Camões, author of the line quoted earlier: "We must sail!" It was a language suffused with the imagery of maritime exploration and discovery, recalling the heroic deeds of the early Portuguese sailors. The sea became the primary source of metaphor in Brazilian thought. In the words of one scholar, every Brazilian writer was a "subject of His Majesty Camões."

To this emerging literary tradition was added the beginnings of a popular culture. The first component—religious festivals and folk art and a folklore that revolved around religious holidays—was imported from the Portuguese. A typical example was "Bumba Meu Boi," a fertility rite with costumed cows and costumed attendants. To this was added the Indian and African presence, which furnished the foundation for the rich tradition of popular music and dance in modern Brazil. Colonial Brazil was succeeding, in spite of itself, in absorbing key elements of Indian and African culture. A hybrid society with a hybrid culture, the Brazil of 1750 remained a recognizable product of Portugal.

In part, this evolution came about because Brazil had become richer and more important than the mother country. Portugal's fate was now tied to the wealth of its American colony, rather than the other way around. As will become clear in chapter 2, this realization caused the Brazilian elite to begin to question their subordination to Lisbon.

2 Crisis of the Colonial System and Emergence of an Independent Brazil: 1750–1830

This chapter recounts how the elite of colonial Brazil increasingly came to see their interests (economic and political) as separate from those of the kingdom of Portugal. The story includes some expected subplots—Portugal's need to appropriate the proceeds of Brazil's economic success to shore up the faltering economy at home and conspiracies against the Portuguese authority in the colony—but it also includes some unexpected twists, such as the decision of the Portuguese crown to move its base from Portugal to Brazil and the eventual setting up of a member of the Portuguese royal family as the emperor of an independent Brazil.

Attempts by the settlers to tame and take possession of their new land also continued. The economic importance of Maranhãs increased steadily. In 1774 it was abolished as a state and made subject to Rio de Janeiro, although its direct links to Lisbon continued. In the South, the conflict with the Spanish was largely ended by the Treaty of Madrid (1750), by which Spain agreed to recognize the Portuguese claim to all areas they had effectively occupied. The principle involved was *uti possidetis*, or ownership by possession. This treaty (and its successors in 1777 and 1801) legitimized Portugal's claim to all territories it had occupied west of the imaginary line drawn by the Treaty of Tordesilhas back in 1494. This included the Amazon Basin and parts of Mato Grosso, along with chunks of São Paulo, Paraná, and Santa Catarina, and all of Rio Grande do Sul.

But the colonial government, whatever its intentions, could not be everywhere. Outside the coastal regions and the inland mining districts, the crown had only tenuous control. By 1800, less than 5 percent (about 324,000 square kilometers) had been effectively occupied. In the rest, runaway slaves and "unpacified" Indians were the only occupants.

The Economics and Politics of Post-1750 Brazil

The economics and politics of post-1750 Brazil were played out against the backdrop of an ailing economy in Portugal. In the early years of the eighteenth century (as discussed in chapter 1) the Portuguese economic outlook seemed bright. The Portuguese economy seemed secure in its ability to produce and trade wine and olive oil in return for manufactured items. This trading pattern was in fact formalized back in 1703 in the Methuen Treaty between Portugal and England. Everyone assumed Portugal could count on Brazil, the world's richest source of gold and diamonds, to further increase the standard of living in the home country. Things did not turn out as well as planned, however, in large part because of the Portuguese crown's penchant for ostentatious spending on the maintenance of its court and the inordinately expensive construction of new palaces and churches, which left the economy in continuous deficit. Instead of raising living standards in Portugal, Brazilian gold and diamonds were needed simply to keep the home economy stable.

In 1750, control of all policies of the Portuguese crown went to the Marquis de Pombal, who became de facto prime minister of Portugal (including the colonies) from 1750 to 1777, and whose primary ambition was to bring "enlightened despotism" to Portugal as a means of restoring its economic health. (An enlightened despot is an absolute monarch who uses the power of the crown to impose the most up-to-date administrative mechanisms and technology on the country for the welfare of all.)

Three factors increased the difficulty of the task: the need to rebuild Lisbon after a disastrous earthquake and fire in 1755, the financial drain of massive military expenditures for the wars with Spain in the 1760s and 1770s over the borderlands of southern Brazil, and the gradual exhaustion of Brazilian mines (gold and diamond revenues from Minas Gerais dropped by 50 percent in the two decades after 1750).

Pombal was a mercantilist following the predominant economic theory of the period. As a good mercantilist, he believed that Portugal (the home country) should industrialize, but that the economic function of colonies like Brazil was to continue to produce primary goods for export mainly to the home country.

From Brazil's perspective, Pombal took two major actions. First, he ordered a complete overhaul of the economy's administrative structure. In effect, this meant subjugating all Brazilian law and practice to reinterpretation by jurists sympathetic to the mercantilist view of a colony's economic function. Second, he encouraged creation of three monopoly trading companies between 1755 and 1765. These were to exploit exports from Amazônia, the Pernambuco region, and the coastal whaling industry. Meanwhile, Pombal was promoting the creation of industry in Portugal.

By the mercantilist standards of the day, shared by generations of policymakers in all the major colonizing nations, the economic results of Pombal's efforts were favorable. Sugar production recovered, wheat cultivation was successfully introduced, and rice and indigo exports increased. All of this helped reduce Portugal's trade deficit by about 70 percent between 1751 and 1775. This trend continued after Pombal's fall in 1777. By 1800, the colony's exports were thriving, aided especially by a revolt in Haiti that disrupted the competing Caribbean sugar trade. By 1807, Portugal was showing a healthy surplus in her trade balance and was even solidly in the black with England. Yet this drive to accumulate a trade surplus was, in historical perspective, beside the point. Pombal's aggressive intervention in Luso-Brazilian policy meant that Brazil was losing out on the most important development of the era: the industrial revolution.

Equally significant was the fact that Brazil was furnishing 61 percent of the exports that earned Portugal's trade surplus. This meant that Portugal's major colony had not only far surpassed it in economic importance but that Portugal had become dramatically dependent on Brazil. This reality did not go unnoticed by the Brazilian elite.

TENSIONS IN THE LATE EIGHTEENTH-CENTURY COLONY

By the mid–eighteenth century, Portuguese America, like other European colonies in the Americas, was feeling the influence of Enlightenment ideas. The seventeenth century had seen an intellectual revolution in Europe, especially in France and England, as thinkers such as Descartes and Newton challenged established ideas and authority. Their weapons were reason and measurement, as they preached the virtues of experimentation and observation. Aided by a newly developed type of mathematics, calculus, the Enlightenment scientists were opening a whole new understanding of the physical world.

At first it may seem surprising that the Enlightenment could have reached Brazil. Portuguese America, unlike Spanish and English America, had no printing presses and no universities. How could the new ideas have reached this relatively isolated colony?

The answer, as alluded to briefly in chapter 1, was that young colonists went to Portugal to study. Virtually all went to the University of Coimbra, the most famous and influential in Portugal, where 300 Brazilian-born students enrolled between 1772 and 1785. Once in Portugal, they were exposed directly or indirectly to French influence.

One of the main regions sending students to Coimbra was the mining province of Minas Gerais. These Brazilians were the sons of the wealthiest class, who had benefited from the phenomenal prosperity stimulated by the gold mines, and who, in their youth, had also brought Enlightenment ideas back to Brazil and spread them around. One of their favorite authors was the Frenchman Abbé Raynal, whose four-volume study of European commerce in the Indies criticized the economic policies of both Portugal and England and called for Brazil's ports to be thrown open.

By the 1780s, material issues were combining with Enlightenment ideas to further exacerbate anti-Portuguese feeling, again primarily in Minas Gerais. Since mid-century, the crown had been pressing hard to boost revenues in the face of declining productivity in the now worked-out mines. Efforts to do so included raising taxes on colonial residents ("increase the Brazilian revenues" was the order from Lisbon), which many of the most prominent Brazilian-born figures in Minas had failed to pay. If Brazil could gain independence from Portugal, these local debtors might escape their heavy debt to the Portuguese crown. They could be patriots and good businessmen at the same time.

Enlightenment ideas and material motivations fed the already existing sense among elite Brazilians that they were now economically stronger than Portugal and should be recognized as such. They grew increasingly resentful of the arrogance exhibited by the so-called metropolitans. Open expressions of hostility toward the crown were, of course, dangerous. They could lead to denunciation, arrest, imprisonment, torture, and, in extreme cases, execution. So this resentment simmered beneath the surface, appearing occasionally in satirical verse, such as the *Cartas Chilenas* (circa 1787–1788), by Tomás Antônio Gonzaga, a thinly disguised attack on the governor's rule.

CONSPIRACIES AGAINST THE PORTUGUESE

The first serious anti-Portuguese plot (known as the *Inconfidência* or "Conspiracy") appeared in Minas Gerais. In 1788–89, a group of prominent citizens in Ouro Preto (full name: Vila Rica de Ouro Preto) planned to assassinate the governor and proclaim an independent republic.

One of these conspirators, José Joaquim de Maia (code name "Vendek"), exemplifies the impact of foreign contact. Vendek communicated with Thomas Jefferson in 1786–87, first by letter, then in person (on a visit to Nimes, France) requesting U.S. support for the revolt. Portuguese rule, Vendek wrote to Jefferson, was "rendered each day more insupportable since the epoch of your glorious independence." Jefferson, otherwise noncommittal, noted that a successful revolution in Brazil would "not be uninteresting to the United States . . ." Vendek's correspondence was one of the earliest instances of a long history of Brazilians looking to the United States for political inspiration. The U.S. example was highly relevant for the Brazilians, of course, since Jefferson had apparently seen no inconsistency between writing the Declaration of Independence and owning slaves.

The plotters were, with few exceptions, wealthy men with no wish to upset the socioeconomic order. They made no attempt to recruit slaves or poor freemen to their cause, although their program did call for freeing all native-born slaves. They saw themselves as remaining at the top of a slavocracy of new slaves from Africa, from which they would continue to benefit. To quote historian Kenneth Maxwell, it was "a movement made by oligarchs in the interests of oligarchs, where the name of the people would be evoked merely in justification."

Unfortunately for the would-be rebels, the governor learned of their plot and ordered their movements monitored. The most dedicated conspirator was a jack of all trades named Joaquim José da Silva Xavier. One of his talents was amateur dentistry, a practice that gave him the nickname of Tiradentes ("tooth-puller"). He was also the one non-aristocrat among the leadership. When the crackdown came, his more distinguished coconspirators scrambled to deny or cover up their involvement.

After a show trial, six defendants were sentenced to be hanged. Tiradentes became the fall guy. The other five were granted clemency and banished to prison in Angola, but Tiradentes faced the gallows on April 21, 1792. After being hanged, he was decapitated and his head displayed on a pole in the center of Ouro Preto. To further drive home the crown's message, the remainder of his body was quartered, with pieces displayed around the city; his house was demolished; and his grounds were salted to make sure the land would be barren.

This plot has long been regarded as the precursor of Brazilian independence, and it was indeed significant for several reasons. First, it confirmed that the North American and French Revolutions had influenced the colonial elite, despite the crown's strenuous efforts to insulate its largest colony. Second, it showed the depth of some colonists' resentment against continuing Portuguese control. Third, it highlighted serious economic differences between the colony and Lisbon, especially now that Brazil had surpassed the mother country in total productive capacity. Fourth, it made clear that the crown would bring down the full force of the law on any active enemies, however prominent. Fifth, given the Portuguese crown's official actions to increase tax revenues, it offered circumstances unusually favorable to conspiracy and revolt. Finally, except for Tiradentes, the conspiracy operated entirely within elite society. Since the conspirators had no desire to upset the prevailing social order, they never considered mobilizing nonelite groups.

Six years after Tiradentes was hanged, drawn, and literally quartered, a very different kind of plot was hatched in the port city of Salvador. Later described as Brazil's first "social revolution," it was a conspiracy organized by artisans, soldiers, sharecroppers, and schoolteachers. These plotters were overwhelmingly mulatto, reflecting the predominant racial makeup of such economic groups: not the elite, but certainly not the "have-nots" of colonial Brazil. In August 1798, they posted handwritten manifestos on walls and public places, demanding the end of the "detestable metropolitan yoke of Portugal," the abolition of slavery, and the equality of all citizens, "especially mulattos and blacks." Their government was to be "democratic, free and independent."

The conspiracy also failed. Once again the governor discovered the plot (the handwritten manifestos were an obvious clue) and forty-seven suspects were arrested, nine of them slaves. Three, all free mulattos, got the Tiradentes treatment: beheaded and quartered, and their body pieces displayed publicly. Sixteen prisoners were released. The rest were banished to exile, forced to disembark, and left to fend for themselves on the coast of Africa.

The Bahian conspiracy, although as unsuccessful as its predecessor in Minas, highlights the social and political status of the mulatto in late colonized Brazil. Racial mixing had been occurring at a high rate since the time the Portuguese first arrived. Due to the relative lack of whites, especially for the size of the territory and the scale of African slave imports, there had been increasing "economic space" for those of mixed ancestry, especially mulattoes, to occupy. This mixing into higher levels on the social scale was helped by the Brazilian practice of classifying mixed bloods by their physical appearances—the lighter, the more accepted. At the limit, the lightest-skinned mulattoes were sometimes accepted as whites. We know that this happened from the frequent comments and complaints from whites that survive in the archives.

Such "passing" was inherently unstable, however, creating tension for the apparently successfully mobile mulatto, who never knew whether or when he might lose his privileged status. It also created a folklore about the mulatto as inherently cunning, ambitious, and untrustworthy. Although this phenomenon of blurring the color line was primarily social, it must certainly have given at least some mulattoes reason to resent the reigning political order.

Not least among the factors increasing awareness of the racial dimension in Bahia was news of the Haitian revolt of 1793, which expelled the French and put blacks in power. That scene, described in lurid terms by European visitors, fueled slaveholder nightmares throughout the Americas. Slavery had always been based on intimidation, both physical and moral. What if the slaves lost their fear? Who could guarantee the safety, or even the survival, of the masters and their families?

In fact, neither this conspiracy, nor sporadic slave uprisings (such as in Araçariguama, São Paulo, in 1773–74 and 1779), nor collective slave runaways (such as in Recife in the 1620s), undermined the system as a whole. Any loss of slaves was readily made up from new imports from Africa. And the Haitian revolt (a nightmare for slaveholders everywhere) was not repeated on the South American continent.

But tensions between the leading colonists and the Portuguese crown continued. The 1790s, for example, saw a revival of Portuguese commerce, which strengthened the crown vis-à-vis Brazil. But it also highlighted for Brazilians how much Portugal's improved trade position was due not to her own economic revival, but to her reexporting of Brazil's products.

The Portuguese Court Comes to Brazil

Into these tensions between the Brazilian elite and their masters in Lisbon crashed reverberations of the French Revolution and the Napoleonic era that followed. In 1807, Napoleon's armies invaded the Iberian Peninsula, defeating the Hapsburg and the Bourbon dynasties (who had earlier tried to crush the French Revolution) and replacing them with pro-French puppet regimes.

The British, now locked in a continent-wide battle with Napoleon, sought to save the Portuguese crown, their longtime client. Since they could not stop Napoleon's army, they came up with an alternative: Take the Portuguese court out of Lisbon to Brazil. The idea of moving to Brazil was not, in fact, new to the Portuguese court. It had been discussed on and off for the previous 150 years. The motivation was new, however. The strategy, born of desperation, was to establish a base of power in the New World and, from there, regain sovereignty over Portugal and the whole of its empire.

The move was unprecedented not only in the history of the Americas but in the whole history of colonial exploration. Never before had a European monarch even set foot in a New World colony, much less settled in one as the focus of power.

In November 1807, the entire court and more than ten thousand courtiers and hangers-on set sail in forty-six ships, with four Royal Navy warships to guard the Portuguese entourage during its voyage. The royal party was a strange assemblage. The power of the crown rested with Prince Dom João VI, who had formally assumed the role of regent in 1799, when his mother, Queen Maria I, had been declared mentally incompetent. He was accompanied in the lead ship by his mother and his two sons, Principe Real Dom Pedro (the future Pedro I) and Dom Miguel. Had this ship gone down, the whole Braganza dynasty would have gone down with it.

The voyage began inauspiciously, with the fleet soon running into a fierce storm that drove the ships apart. This storm was survived, but conditions aboard were abominable, with infestations of lice that even attacked the royal family.

The fleet arrived at Salvador on the northeastern coast in January 1808. The Bahian population, largely black and mulatto, greeted the court's arrival with celebrations. The Portuguese royalty were shocked how primitive the city was, in particular the accommodation, and lost no time in commandeering Bahia's best houses. For the residents of

THE
NEW
WORLD

Salvador, the sight must have been bizarre indeed: a mad queen, an obese regent, and thousands of disheveled courtiers aghast at the new world they saw before them after the sumptuous palaces of Portugal.

In February 1808, the royal entourage sailed on to Rio, the real administrative center of the colony where the prince regent was determined to settle. Again there were problems with housing. Prominent Rio residents offered their best mansions, which were quickly accepted. Once more, the royal family found itself in a sea of nonwhite faces. At least two-thirds of the colony's population was now black, mulatto, or of other mixed-blood. The court and its hangers-on settled in for an uncomfortable exile of unknown length.

CREATING A NEW PORTUGUESE AMERICA

ROYAL
REFORM

The prince regent lost no time in consolidating the royal presence. Even while still in Bahia, he opened the colony's ports to ships of all nations, thus ending three centuries of Portuguese monopoly. It was a deliberate jettisoning of the mercantilist philosophy that had dictated Portuguese economic policy since the era of discovery. Once in Rio, the prince founded a bevy of new institutions, including the National Library, the Botanical Garden, the Bank of Brazil, and medical faculties in Bahia and Rio de Janeiro. The crown also set up the first printing press, delivering the colony from its long intellectual isolation.

Although this "Lusitanian invasion," as was inevitable, irritated the local Brazilians—in particular through the assigning of key positions in the expanding state structure to the newly arrived Portuguese—the prince regent himself was popular with his Brazilian compatriots. He rapidly grew fond of his new home city, which, under his auspices, acquired such European-style attractions as an orchestra, a theater, and a lively—though censored—publishing scene. Between 1808 and 1822, as the presence of the court attracted business and in-migrants, Rio's population doubled from 50,000 to 100,000. Meanwhile, back in Portugal, the notables—i.e., the wealthy—were clamoring for the court to return, a clamor that became louder with Napoleon's defeat in 1814. The prince

UNITED
KINGDOM

regent struck a compromise in 1815 by raising the Estado do Brasil to the status of equal partner in a newly created "United Kingdom." With that act, the prince regent legitimized his continued residence outside Portugal while also giving Brazilians new grounds for pride. One year

MAD
MARIA!

later, the "Mad Maria," still formally the monarch, died. Her son became Dom João VI, a monarch in his own right after seventeen years as the prince regent.

As the royal presence was being consolidated in Brazil, the upheaval caused by the French invasion and occupation was turning Portuguese politics upside down. Pre-1807 style loyalty to an absolute monarch was gone. Portuguese liberal revolutionaries, who triumphed by arms in

1820, demanded a more limited monarchy and a liberal constitution, to be drawn up by a *Cortes*, a representative body in Lisbon to which members would be elected by the entire Portuguese Empire (Brazil had been allotted 72 of 181 seats). The revolutionary junta to which the Cortes was responsible called with increasing insistence for Dom João VI's return from Brazil.

Within Brazil, the king's return to Portugal was supported by the higher military and the merchants, who expected to profit from Brazil's renewed subordination to the home country. Opposed to his return were the large landowners, along with the Brazilian-born royal bureaucrats and some Portuguese who had come, either through business or through marriage, to identify with Brazil.

Dom João VI, fearing for the loss of his throne, decided to return. In April 1821 he sailed back across the Atlantic. Four thousand Portuguese, less than half the number who had left Lisbon for Brazil in 1808, accompanied the sovereign on his return. He left behind his son, Pedro, whom he now named the prince regent, to administer Brazil. Dom João VI warned his son that if it ever came to a break between the two kingdoms, he, the prince, should choose Brazil.

The Cortes, now meeting in a truncated session with some Brazilian delegates absent, adopted an aggressive stance toward Brazil, with the intent of restoring it to subservient colonial status. The Cortes proposed to divide the Brazilian realm into separate units, each reporting directly to Portugal. The Brazilian elite reacted as might be expected. They were furious at the suggestion that Brazil's status as a co-kingdom might be revoked—a reaction that did not impress the leaders in the Cortes. In their judgment, the royal family was to be the instrument for regaining Portuguese authority over Brazil, in pursuit of which strategy the *Cortes* now ordered Pedro to return to Portugal. But Pedro refused to cooperate. On September 7, 1822, he followed his father's parting advice, proclaiming—according to legend—*"Fico!"* ("I am staying!"), as he proclaimed Brazil's independence. On December 1, 1822, he was crowned Emperor Pedro I. Thus did Portuguese America assume a unique historical path, declaring independence the following September. No other former colony has ever embraced as its monarch a member of the ruling family of the very country it was rebelling against.

The Portuguese military units that had accompanied the court in 1808 and had not returned with Dom João VI to Portugal did not let Brazil go by default, although the military engagements were nowhere near the epic battles fought over independence in Spanish America. They fought the Brazilian rebels in the far south, (present-day Uruguay), where they were defeated in November 1823, and in Bahia, where they were forced to withdraw in July 1823.

What was the significance of this path to Brazilian independence? First, it meant severing political and administrative ties to Portugal—

ties that went back three centuries. Second, because there was never any question of challenging the socioeconomic order, it meant Brazil would continue to be dominated by the landholding elite, which was strongest in the Northeast, Rio de Janeiro, Minas Gerais, and São Paulo. Third, it meant Brazil would be under the economic influence of England. This had begun when the English sponsored the transfer of the Portuguese court to Brazil and loaned large sums to the Portuguese crown to help consolidate its hold. Brazilians now had to assume the large Portuguese debt with the British (incurred in part to fight *against* Brazilian independence!) and to agree to give British goods favored entry—i.e., lower tariffs.

Important questions also remained unsettled. Most important was slavery. The slave trade was Brazil's all-important source of labor, and the British were threatening to cut if off for Brazil, as they had already done in 1808 for the slave trade to the United States. A second issue was how the monarchy could secure the loyalty of Brazil's scattered provinces, especially where republicanism was particularly strong, such as in Pernambuco and other parts of the Northeast. The final question was the future of this new country's elite. As we have seen, Afro-Brazilians, both slave and free, outnumbered the whites as Brazil became independent. In 1823, one aristocratic observer, discouraged by the wave of liberal revolutions in Spanish America, estimated that within three years the "white race will come to an end at the hands of other races and the province of Bahia will disappear from the civilized world."

SOCIAL HIERARCHIES

As independence came to Brazil, it lacked even the beginnings of a bourgeoisie. The export economy was dominated by agriculture and mining. Local merchants might have formed a bourgeois nucleus, but Brazilians played virtually no role in the overseas marketing of Brazilian exports, which were shipped directly to Portugal. Portuguese merchants were then responsible for the re-exportation to trading centers such as Antwerp. Furthermore, since the crown had prohibited manufacturing in the colony, there was no manufacturing class. However, Brazil had finally established some institutions of higher education, with the creation in 1808 of medical faculties in Bahia and Rio de Janeiro and law faculties in 1827 in São Paulo and Olinda (in the state of Pernambuco). These new faculties now began to produce the core of the future bourgeoisie.

The economic base of the newly independent Brazil was agricultural, now that the mining sector had continued to decline. Sugar, tobacco, cotton, and coffee were the prime commercial crops and earned most of Brazil's foreign exchange. Just as in the era before independence, slaves supplied the labor, so that the most fundamental economic relationship throughout Brazil was that of master and slave.

The Brazilian non-elites in 1822 were the 95 percent of the population who had neither income nor family connections to rise very far above subsistence. Society was a pyramid. At the bottom were the slaves, both native-born and African-born. Slightly above them were the free men, mostly of color, both free-born and emancipated slaves. But these existed in the interstices of the economy, as artisans and tradesmen with little or no leverage in politics (except as cannon-fodder in street fights or regional conflicts). Female street vendors were part of this population. They were of much more concern to the authorities than their numbers would imply, as they were suspected of being smugglers of gold and precious stones out of Minas Gerais. Above them were the subsistence farmers and purveyors of services. Above them was a huge gap between the tiny elite at the top (1 to 2 percent of Brazil's population) and the vast majority below.

Did the huge non-elite pose any real threat to the elite? Not really. Slave uprisings did occur, as in Cachoeira (Bahia) in 1814, when the rebels set fire to the city. But official repression was more than equal to the task. How were the non-elites controlled? The brutality used to maintain slavery was unending, although occasional masters could be exceptions. Whipping and mutilation were commonplace, and execution of slaves was not unknown. Physical punishments were still often administered in the city square to provide maximum impact. Hunters of runaway slaves would also still brandish their captives' ears to prove their prowess. Physical punishments of ordinary criminals were also brutal and dramatic. And the high crime of treason was still rewarded by hanging, decapitation, and the display of the victim's head on a spike.

Incarceration or physical punishment were only the most dramatic forms of control in this society. More insidious was the socialization of the young into an automatic acceptance of the social hierarchy and their place in it. Monarchy combined with slavery created an atmosphere of deference that was powerfully transmitted to the non-elites. The inculcation of this attitude of subservience that must be shown toward any superior was by and large successful in convincing non-elites there was no way to change their world. Religion and folk culture combined to create a vocabulary that articulated deference in a thousand ways. Given the color stratification of the society, the Portuguese attitude of racial superiority reinforced this passive attitude.

THE NEW MONARCHICAL SYSTEM

The elite in the newly independent nation had a clear idea of how to run their economy. The elite's doctrine—a version of the Manchester Liberalism emanating concurrently from England and already seen in action when the prince regent opened Brazil's ports in 1808—held that each country should concentrate on producing what it could produce best and trade with other countries for goods it could buy more cheaply than it could produce them. This doctrine, impeccable in its logic, meant Brazil would continue to export primary products and import most of its finished goods. It was antiprotectionism and, for primary producers such as Brazil, anti-industrialization. Since tariffs, according to this doctrine, should only be levied for revenue, protecting nascent domestic industrialization efforts from foreign competition was out of the question.

The Brazilian elite also absorbed much of the political liberalism of Britain. The constituent assembly drafted a constitution under the direction of José Bonifácio de Andrada e Silva, a prominent landowner and jurist. It largely copied the English parliamentary system, with the objective of creating a government controlled by the elite through a highly restrictive voting eligibility. Emperor Pedro I found it not to his liking. He dissolved the assembly and arbitrarily issued his own constitution. It was an ominous beginning for a colony that had justified its independence by claiming Portuguese authority had been too arbitrary.

The emperor described his Constitution of 1824 as "twice as liberal" as the assembly's version. It created a two-house parliament. The Senate consisted of lifetime members who were chosen by the emperor from a list of three nominated by each province. The Chamber of Deputies was to be elected directly by parliamentary districts. The franchise was limited to wealth holders but the minimum requirement was relatively low. Illiterates who met the property requirement were eligible to vote, although women (whether literate or not) were excluded. Restrictions on the franchise were not unlike those in Britain after the Great Reform Act of 1832 (although a higher percentage of Britons undoubtedly met the property requirement).

The emperor had vast powers under his constitution, should he choose to assert them. He could dissolve the lower house, then call new elections. He also had the power to approve or veto any measure passed by the Chamber or the Senate. This inherent responsibility to act as the final judge and arbiter in vital matters of state was referred to by the Brazilians as the "moderating power" of the crown. This exalted idea of the monarch's role, which was fully shared by the elite, was borrowed in part from the French commentator Benjamin Constant, a favorite author among Brazil's political elite of the era.

The newly independent Brazilian empire was divided into eighteen provinces, each replacing a previous captaincy and each governed by a president appointed by the emperor. The elite's intent was to build a highly centralized structure. Reaction on the provincial level to this centralized design was strongly negative. The new imperial structure represented a far tighter administration than the local landowners had experienced during the colonial era. Some regions, such as Pará and Maranhão in the North, were used to communicating more often with Lisbon than with Bahia or Rio. They now nursed hopes of breaking away from their continental links, as had the viceroyalties and captaincies of Spanish America. In the words of a visiting aristocrat, "Brazil is a country being born, a settlement inhabited by peoples of different colors who have a mutual dislike for each other. . . . The captaincies cannot help each other, as they are separated by enormous expanses so that the country does not yet constitute a single kingdom with unbroken territorial unity."

Revolts occurred not only against the Rio government but also against the monarchical principle itself. One of the most serious broke out in 1824 in Pernambuco, where the local notables were incensed that the monarch had named a new president for the province without consulting them. The rebels were militant republicans who wanted a Brazil free of any royalty. The battle against these and other republican rebels thus elevated the monarchy to the level of defender of Brazil's territorial integrity. The republicans "elected" their own president, whom the imperial authorities unsuccessfully attempted to deport. The rebels then issued a proclamation creating "the Confederation of the Equator." They gained adherents in Paraíba do Norte, Rio Grande do Norte, and southern Ceará. But the imperial forces had superiority at sea, and so conquered the Pernambucan capital of Recife and crushed the rebellion. Just as they would have in colonial times, the crown's representatives executed sixteen rebel leaders, including Frei Caneca, the publisher of the newspaper *Typis Pernambucano*, which had been the ideological voice of the Republicans in the area. The young nation survived this republican revolt, but more uprisings were to come.

The emperor's position was not improved by the outbreak of war in 1825 between his newborn empire and Buenos Aires over the attempt of Brazil's Cisplatine Province (roughly present-day Uruguay) to leave the Brazilian empire and join Argentina. The Brazilian forces (including European mercenaries) were unprepared and unable to win, but English intervention ended the conflict and created the independent nation of Uruguay.

The cost of the war drained the imperial finances, undermined the value of the currency, and raised the cost of imports into Brazil. Since the latter were largely controlled by Portuguese merchants, the locals had yet another reason to feel lusophobic. In 1831, Rio witnessed a five-day "bottle-throwing" riot, in which the pro-Brazilian faction (the *cabras*, or "goats") attacked the houses of the pro-Portuguese (*pés de chumbo*, or "lead feet"). Dom Pedro I was caught in the middle of this rising tension. He may have been the symbol of independence in 1822, but now he was paying for the ambiguity inherent in a member of the Portuguese royal family leading the former colony to independence. He faced pressure from both Brazil and Portugal. In Brazil it was direct pressure from the higher military, who threatened to revolt if he remained in Brazil; in Portugal it was pressure from the monarchists, who wanted him, as the senior Braganza (Dom João VI had died in 1826), back on the Portuguese throne. In 1831, he returned to his homeland, leaving behind his five-year-old son, Pedro II, as the claimant to the Brazilian throne.

In addition to the problem of the succession of power, Brazil had to come to terms with the fact that Great Britain was now the guarantor of Brazil's survival as a new nation. Although U.S. recognition of Brazilian independence came first (1824), Britain was the leading European power of the day, and so its action (1825) was more crucial.

Britain had long been a key actor in the history of Portugal and therefore of Brazil. Portugal's political alliance with Britain went back to the fourteenth century. By the eighteenth century, Britain was Portugal's most important trading partner. And the Royal Navy had saved the Portuguese crown from capture and deposition by Napoleon's armies, thereby guaranteeing new importance for Brazil.

This British support did not come cheap, however. As noted earlier, in 1825 Brazil had agreed to pay the $7,000,000 debt Portugal had incurred with Britain to finance the fight against Brazilian independence. Second, there was another treaty in 1825 continuing to grant British goods preferential tariffs in Brazil at rates lower than charged to the Portuguese. Third, an 1826 treaty forced Brazil to commit itself to ending the African slave trade within a few years. The Brazilian legislation in 1831 reluctantly passed a law banning the trade, but failure to enforce it made the ban ineffectual. Finally, the Brazilians signed a treaty in 1827 giving British subjects the right to be tried by special British courts within Brazil.

All these measures underlined the fact that the British were now the dominant foreign actor in the Brazilian economy, both in trade and in direct investment. They were supreme in banking, shipping, communications, and insurance. Brazil had passed from the Portuguese crown to the British sphere of influence in what historians would later call "informal imperialism."

3 Revolt, Consolidation, and War: 1830-70

The period between the return of Pedro I to Portugal in 1831 and the end of the Paraguayan War in 1870 is fundamentally the story of divisions within the Brazilian elite about the basic principles by which Brazil should be governed. These divisions were first reflected in a series of revolts during the period of the regency. They were then smoothed over but certainly not extinguished in the period following Pedro II's coronation in 1840. In good part because of Pedro II's winning personality and pragmatic approach to governing, this was a period of cooperation between the crown and the coffee-planting oligarchy, whose product stimulated economic growth and gave the crown revenues it badly needed to reduce its debt to the British. This tranquillity was shattered in 1864 by the outbreak of war between Brazil and Paraguay, its immediate neighbor to the southwest—a war that again increased Brazil's debt to the British, reopened divisions within the elite about Brazil's form of government, increased doubts within the country about the durability of slavery, and shook Brazilians' faith more generally in their strength as a nation. The emperor, on the other hand, had seen the war as Brazil's opportunity to prove its mettle on the international scene. He now saw victory in Paraguay as proof that Brazil had finally earned the respect of both the Old World and the New.

[margin handwriting: ⌐. CROWN AND COFFEE]

Uprisings Under the Regency

When Pedro I reluctantly returned to Portugal, leaving his five-year-old son to the mercies of a succession of regents, he also left an elite that was divided about how Brazil should be governed and, indeed, what kind of nation (or nations) Brazil should be.

In the middle were supporters of the Brazilian monarchy and Pedro II. They believed Brazil should continue as a single country, remaining as an empire but totally independent of Portugal. Called by historian Boris Fausto the "moderate liberals," they believed in the defense of individual liberty (for the elite, of course); were drawn primarily from the centrally located provinces of São Paulo, Rio de Janeiro, and Minas Gerais, and controlled the machinery of imperial government in Brazil.

They were helped by the loyalty the hereditary monarchy stimulated among the largely illiterate, socially hierarchical, common population in Brazil. Even to many within the elite, the emperor was revered as the incarnation of absolute power. But the moderate liberals were not unambiguously helped by this reverence for the monarchy, because there were potentially two contenders for the Brazilian throne.

The other contender, of course, was Pedro I, now back on the throne of Portugal. And his existence created the first of two factions opposed to Pedro II and the moderate liberals. This group was called the "absolutists." They, too, believed Brazil should be an empire, but they wanted to bring back Pedro I and restore the united empire of Portugal and Brazil. They also favored a stronger monarchy than the moderate liberals and were more inclined to subordinate liberties to strengthen the crown. The absolutists were supported by the merchants, many of whom had been born in Portugal. Since Brazilian businessmen and planters (many of whom were quite patriotically Brazilian) were typically indebted to these merchants, feelings between the two groups ran high. The absolutists drew their support primarily from coastal cities, including Rio.

The other group opposed to Pedro II and the moderate liberals were the "exaltados." The exaltados wanted greater provincial autonomy than the moderate liberals. Some even favored a republic. They had regional support throughout Brazil, helped by the fact that most Brazilians, including many of the elite, identified with their *patria*—i.e., their regional homeland (*patria paulista* or *patria bahiana*, for example)—before they identified with Brazil. At the extreme, the exaltados believed there should be no united Brazil—that the provinces should become independent states, as had happened in Spanish America.

The first regency to rule in the name of Pedro II was actually a triumvirate, chosen to represent each of three regions where the moderate liberals were strong. This triumvirate lasted from 1831 to 1834 and created many of the legal institutions the Empire needed but still lacked when Pedro I headed back to Portugal. Two initiatives under the triumvirate are worthy of particular note. The first was the application of a Criminal Procedure in 1832 (the criminal code had been passed in 1830), which instituted *habeas corpus*, henceforth the Brazilian citizens' first line of defense against illegal arrest—effective for the elite, virtually a dead letter for the rest of the population. The second, which had almost immediate repercussions, was the Additional Act of 1834. This act, approved by parliament, amended the Constitution of 1824 by giving increased powers to the provinces. Under this act, each province was allowed to create a provincial assembly, which could control taxation and expenditure in that province as well as appoint local officials.

Supporters of the act, which was referred to by many as the regency's "experiment with decentralization," hoped that this deliberate weakening of Rio's imperial government, especially in financial affairs, would create greater unity within Brazil as a whole by recognizing the legitimacy of a Brazilian's first loyalty to his (few worried about political views of women in this era) *patria*.

The result was disastrous from the central government's viewpoint. Brazil erupted in a series of regional revolts. These revolts serve as a reminder that Brazil was subject to the same forces of fragmentation that split Spanish America into several separate countries. Brazil survived as a single nation, however, with central authority successfully defeating every revolt.

The first revolt, the War of the Cabanos in Pernambuco (1832–35), began even before the Additional Act was passed in 1834. The instigators of this uprising were fighting to demand the return of Pedro I and the suppression of the regency. Attracting primarily lower sectors of the population, including Indians and slaves, the movement gained support from the absolutists in Rio, resulting in some street fighting in Rio itself. The revolt was weakened by the death of Pedro I in 1834 and was finally crushed in 1835, by which time the regency triumvirate had been replaced by a single regent, Father Diogo Antonio Feijo. He had been chosen by a narrowly based electoral body that represented the provinces and was authorized to choose a single regent. Father Diogo, in failing health, was himself forced out of the regency in 1837, to be replaced by a fierce defender of central authority, the future Marquês de Olinda.

The first major revolt after passage of the Additional Act was the War of Cabangem (1835–40). It erupted in Belém, the port city for the lower Amazon and the capital of the province of Pará. The initial fighting was between the monarchists (whatever their stripe) and the regionalists, fueled by the strong anti-Portuguese feeling stimulated by the presence of Portuguese-born merchants. It escalated into a social struggle between the elite more generally and a proletariat composed largely of Indians. Atrocities to prisoners were commonplace on both sides, with the Indians withdrawing into the interior and being hunted down by imperial troops. The death toll in Belém was staggering—30,000 in a province whose population before the conflict was estimated at about 150,000. The slaughter during the War of Cabangem stands as further contradiction to the claim of Brazilians and others that Brazil has been blessed with a nonviolent past.

Two other major revolts erupted in the Northeast. Both spread from fighting among the elite to genuine social conflict, with Afro-Brazilians and poor whites capitalizing on the political unrest to attack authority more generally. These social uprisings led to particularly grisly reprisals against the underclasses who lost.

The first (the Sabinada) was a direct challenge to the Empire. It occurred in Bahia (1837–38) and began with a manifesto by the rebels declaring a "free and independent state." What the elite protagonists called "the nonwhite rabble" joined the battle, raising the specter of race war. The rebels attempted to blockade Bahia, but they were easily defeated by the central government, with a death toll of about 1,800.

The second revolt in the Northeast was the Balaida (1838–41) in Maranhão, the second most northern province in Brazil. It was a region where bandits were common. But this fighting also grew into a social rebellion, with a rebel band including a column of 3,000 slaves capturing the major town of Caxias. The imperial army finally recaptured the town, in a shrewd counterinsurgency campaign under the leadership of Brigadier Luis Alves da Lima e Silva. His forces used unconventional movements, including infiltration of rebel lines, to demoralize the enemy. In reward for his exploits, Lima e Silva was made Baron of Caxias, under which name he went on to quell a revolt that was much more dangerous to the Empire. In 1896, he was elevated to Duke of Caxias. The leader of the slave column was hanged in 1842.

The revolt that first earned the Baron of Caxias his place in history was the Guerra dos Farrapos revolt in Rio Grande do Sul, which began in 1835 and dragged on for a decade. The Riograndense rebels declared an independent state in 1838, the "Republic of Piratini," thereby gaining de facto control of the lucrative interregional commerce in leather and meat and posing by far the most difficult political problem for the Empire of any in this decade of revolts. The reason was the revolt's location on the border with Uruguay. At the time of the revolt, Uruguay had only recently been created (1828), largely through the good offices of the British, as a buffer state between Brazil and Argentina. The Empire could not afford to drive the Riograndense rebels into secession from the Empire, which would have created an independent state that might potentially ally with Uruguay and Argentina against Brazil. Nor could the Empire placate the rebels by conceding to them the kind of autonomy that would almost certainly tempt *patrias* in other parts of the country to set up their own "republics."

The man given the task of managing this delicate balancing act was the aforesaid Baron of Caxias. He pursued a twofold strategy that succeeded brilliantly. First, he waged a relentless and winning military campaign to recapture Rio Grande do Sul. Then, to conciliate the losers, whose separatist emotions were still running high, he granted amnesty to all and, in the name of the Empire, assumed all the rebel republic's debt. His approach was to be copied by the central government in dealing with later regional revolts, even in the twentieth century.

Recentralization

The imperial government had had enough of its experiment in decentralization by 1840, a year that saw two major turning points in government. First, the parliament revoked the powers delegated to the provinces in the Additional Act of 1834. Second, the powers behind the throne decided to tap into the latent reverence among many Brazilians for the hereditary monarchy by proclaiming the majority of Pedro II. Given that the new monarch had just turned 14, this was quite a gamble. The hope was that the pomp and circumstance of his installation as sovereign would have a favorable symbolic effect strong enough to spill over into political support for consolidation of the nation. It was a vast country he inherited. Rio was three days from Santos (the principal Paulista port) by ship, another difficult day overland to the city of São Paulo, eight days to Salvador (Bahia), twelve to Recife, and thirty to Belém.

To say that a new fountain of political support for consolidation was not immediately obvious is an understatement. The year 1842 saw three more uprisings in São Paulo and Minas Gerais. These were easily suppressed. Once again the Baron of Caxias was the victorious commander. The end of the decade saw a more serious revolt, the Praieira (1848–50) in Pernambuco.

By this time, there were two rather than three political factions among the elite. The death of Pedro I in 1834 had broken the spirit of those who backed a united empire with Portugal. The pro-Empire forces had become largely one imperial party, the Conservative party. The pro-regionalists had become primarily the Liberal party. In 1848 in Pernambuco, the Conservatives were in power and, as was typical in those days of patronage, had thrown out the Liberal appointees in the police and National Guard and installed their own supporters. The Liberals refused to accept this replacement of *their* appointees and took up arms. The ensuring conflict, as had happened elsewhere, was compounded by an outbreak of rioting among the populace against the Portuguese-born merchants in the port city of Recife, an outbreak that served to support the regionalist interests of the Liberals. The rebels, who had been influenced by the radical ideas that underlay the revolutions of 1848 in Europe, took up the cry of federalism, though stopping short of advocating a republic, and (in a mixture of xenophobia and anti-monarchism) demanded the expulsion of the Portuguese-born and an end to the "moderating power" of the sovereign. The imperial forces crushed the revolt in 1850. It was the last major regionalist challenge to the centralized monarchy. From this point, the nation-state was to hold the upper hand.

THE ROLE OF PEDRO II

The term "moderating power," as noted in an earlier chapter, referred to the monarch's position as the balance wheel of government. It was at his invitation that governments were formed and dissolved. It was he who chose who should be Senator from among three province-chosen nominees. And it was through the crown that national patronage, the politicians' lifeblood, flowed. The success of Pedro II's role would depend on how he used his moderating power and how the elite perceived that use.

Pedro II brought a natural flair to his job. Even at age 14, he was stable, balanced, and discreet. The young Emperor had another asset. As his father had said on the eve of his departure in 1831, "My son has the advantage over me of being Brazilian, and the Brazilians like him. He'll reign without difficulty and the constitution will guarantee his prerogatives." As his reign progressed, he earned a reputation as being fair and objective, projecting the image of an honest and ethical sovereign who would not hesitate to discipline politicians who were caught straying from his strict standards. Here he resembled Queen Victoria, his British contemporary, whose long reign (1837–1901) largely paralleled his own. Pedro II became increasingly a point of political reference for the elite, who used his rectitude and firm hand to distance their own country from the "unstable" Spanish American republics. It was only after 1870 that, visibly aged and exhausted by the Paraguayan War, he became an easy target for politicians who wanted a scapegoat.

Pedro II strengthened his image of civilized urbanity and rectitude by making a habit of presiding over sessions of the Brazilian Historical and Cultural Institute, Brazil's leading learned body of the day. He was especially interested in Brazil's indigenous heritage and took the trouble to learn and speak Guaraní, the most widely spoken Indian language. He also subsidized Brazilian writers and intellectuals to research in European archives the treaties that supposedly defined Brazil's boundaries. Several of these beneficiaries of imperial largesse, such as the poet Antonio Gonçalves Dias, won fame as the leaders of the "Indianist" Romantic movement which dominated Brazilian letters at mid-century. He also maintained personal links with foreign savants, such as Louis Pasteur, the Comte de Gobineau, and Louis Agassiz.

In his public image, the emperor was in tune with his Victorian era. But he was his father's son in at least one respect: Pedro I had been a notorious philanderer, and Pedro II also had an active extramarital life, though his was vastly more discreet than that of his father, who made few concessions to public decorum. Ever mindful of the importance of keeping up appearances, Pedro II required his many mistresses to return his love letters. In a rare act of indiscretion, however, he himself kept them all—to be discovered a century later by an archivist who leaked them to the press. Perhaps that was how he intended things to go—that the world should discover his flesh-and-blood self at some safe interval after his death.

For three decades after Pedro II's succession in 1840, Brazilian politics were dominated by two parties, the Liberals and the Conservatives. This political environment was similar to that of Victorian Britain in the sense that it provided an institutionalized mechanism for alternating power peacefully among the dominant factions of the political elite. But the achievement becomes much more noteworthy when it is remembered that Brazilian parties operated in a country far less advanced, both economically and socially, than Britain. In the nineteenth-century Spanish American republics, for example, contests for power frequently involved civil war and dictatorial rule. And Brazil herself had until very recently been a nation rife with political disagreements at the regional level that often escalated into armed conflict.

Although the two Brazilian parties were accused, at the time and by later commentators, of being indistinguishable versions of a single elite, there were in fact real differences between them. They both supported a unified Brazil under the monarchy. But the Liberals, who had their primary strength in São Paulo, Minas Gerais, and Rio Grande do Sul, supported at least some decentralization. The Conservatives, strongest in Bahia, Pernambuco, and Rio de Janeiro, tended to be strong supporters of a centralized bureaucracy.

It is true that Brazilian electoral politics of the period was often a game in which the stakes were patronage and governmental support for local interests, and the tools were regular doses of bribery, intimidation, and fraud (not unlike British politics only a few decades earlier). But the monarchy was truly consolidated and its authority universally acknowledged, if only implicitly, throughout the country. The Conservative party was dominant between 1850 and 1863, successfully leading to what came to be known as the "conciliation"—a muting of party conflict and an agreement to avoid controversial issues. Politics became routinized. Meanwhile, coffee production was rising and boosting export earnings, allowing the crown to avoid further foreign indebtedness with London between 1840 and 1857.

The Rise of Coffee

The exhaustion of the gold and diamond mines by the second half of the eighteenth century made the Brazilian economy again dependent on agricultural exports, with cotton and rice now complementing long-time exports of tobacco and sugar. By 1830, a new product had appeared: coffee, an export that would fuel Brazil's export economy for the next 140 years. See exhibit 3-1.) Coffee was first successfully commercialized in the late eighteenth century in Brazil in the province of Rio de Janeiro, where the soil was highly adaptable to the coffee bush. In the 1830s and 1840s, that province became the center of coffee cultivation, with the city of Rio as the export center. Rio housed the banks, brokerage houses, and docks that connected Brazil to the world coffee market in Western Europe and North America. Slaves were the main source of the consider-

EXHIBIT 3-1
Principal Exports as a Percent of Brazil's Total Exports, 1650–1950

Years	Sugar	Coffee	Cotton	Other (including minerals & manufactured goods)
1650	95.0	–	–	5.0
1750	47.0	–	–	53.0
1800	31.0	–	6.0	63.0
1841–50	26.7	41.4	7.5	25.4
1891–1900	6.0	64.5	2.7	26.8
1921–30	1.4	69.6	2.4	26.6
1945–49	1.2	41.8	13.3	43.7
1970	4.9	35.8	6.0	53.3

Source: Source: Thomas W. Merrick and Douglas H. Graham, *Population and Economic Development* (Baltimore, 1979), p. 12.

able labor needed to plant the coffee trees, cultivate them, and harvest what would become the coffee beans. Some slaves were acquired from the slave trade, which, though technically illegal since 1826, continued until 1850. Others were purchased from the less profitable sugar plantations, especially in the Northeast.

The soils of Rio de Janeiro province were progressively depleted by the intensive coffee cultivation, as the hilly topography helped to accelerate soil erosion. But Brazil had no shortage of unutilized (or underutilized) land. Although production in Rio remained high, by mid-century the center of coffee cultivation was moving south and west of Rio, spreading into the provinces of São Paulo and Minas Gerais, where the soil proved as productive as Rio soil at its best.

The southward march of coffee and the rapid rise of Brazilian production generated an increased demand for labor. With the end of the slave trade in 1850, the southern provinces were forced to rely on the purchase of slaves from domestic sources, especially in the North and Northeast. This created a demographic shift southward, similar (though on a lesser scale) to the eighteenth-century shift toward Minas Gerais during the mining boom. (See exhibit 3-2.) The Northeastern masters who sold their slaves received payment, but this capital inflow did not stop Northeastern politicians denouncing the "loss" of their labor force as it migrated to the more prosperous South.

The continued shortage of labor in São Paulo led a few planters to import European immigrants to work as sharecroppers on the coffee plantations. The most famous planter who tried this approach was Senator Nicolau Vergueiro, who recruited a group of German and Swiss immigrants in the 1840s. The Brazilian planters paid the passage for these immigrants and promised to provide a job, acceptable working condi-

EXHIBIT 3-2

Percentage Distribution of Slave Population by Regions and Selected Provinces in Brazil, 1823–87

Region	Percent				
	1823	1864	1872	1883	1887
North	4	2	2	2	1
Northeast	53	49	32	28	28
Pernambuco	13	15	6	6	6
Bahia	20	17	11	11	11
Maranhão	8	4	5	4	5
Others	12	13	10	7	6
Southeast	38	44	59	63	67
Espírito Santo	5	1	2	2	2
Minas Gerais	18	15	25	24	26
Rio de Janeiro (province, including city)	13	17	19	21	22
Rio de Janeiro (city)	—	6	3	3	1
São Paulo	2	5	10	13	15
South	2	4	6	6	2
Rio Grande do Sul	—	2	4	5	1
Others	—	2	2	1	1
West	3	1	1	1	1
Total (%)	100	100	100	100	100
Total number	1,163,746	1,715,000	1,510,806	1,240,806	723,419
Rate of Growth (between years)		0.9	−1.1	−2.1	−16.5

Source: Thomas W. Merrick and Douglas H. Graham, *Population and Economic Development* (Baltimore, 1979), p. 66.

tions, and fair earnings in return for labor. The experiment failed, perhaps because of the inherent incompatibility of slave and free labor in a single plantation setting. In any case, many of these immigrants protested to their home governments that they were being treated like slaves—protested so vehemently, in fact, that Prussia responded by prohibiting immigrant recruitment by Brazil. The failure of this and other experiments with European immigrant colonists reinforced the conservative planters' view that there was no alternative to slave labor. The opposite conclusion—that the labor shortage could no longer be met by slaves and that abolition might be an indispensable prerequisite—took longer to sink in.

The system of landownership in colonial Brazil—a succession of royal land grants made personally by the monarch—had led to a pattern of ad hoc land claims that had more to do with actual physical possession (such as squatting) than legal recognition. By 1850, the growth of commercial export agriculture, especially coffee, had dramatically raised the stakes of landownership, and the prospect of increased immigration of free labor from Europe (with the slave trade cut off) raised the urgent question of how the new wage laborers could be made to stay on the plantations instead of settling on the still abundantly available unused land.

In 1850, a land law was passed in Brazil, decreeing that public land could now be obtained only by purchase from the government or by payment of taxes to regularize land agreements already made, making access to land more difficult for small holders. The law's application favored the large holders, especially those involved in export agriculture, and this was exactly its intent. In fact, the chief purpose of the law was to promote the large plantation system. The only way to have lessened the hold of large landowners would have been to impose a stiff tax on uncultivated land. Such a tax was proposed several times after 1850, but was consistently and successfully blocked by large landowner interests.

Twelve years later, the United States, in which small holder access to land had always been easier than in Brazil, took a very different tack. The U.S. government passed the Homestead Act of 1862, encouraging small land holdings by making land grants to small farmers who promised to cultivate the land. The contrary path taken by Brazil has had major implications for economic inequality in modern Brazil, because it institutionalized the concentration of legal land ownership in a country where land was the principal source of wealth.

The Emerging Problems with Slavery as an Institution

In 1830, Brazil was the largest slave economy in the world, with more slaves than free persons. But Brazil's slave population was not replacing itself, requiring Brazil to depend heavily on slave imports. (See exhibit 3-3.) There were three major reasons for this dependence on imports. First, because of its historic reliance on the slave trade, there were far more male than female slaves in Brazil, reducing the birth rate for that reason alone. Second, Brazilian slaves were kept in such grim living conditions that their health was jeopardized, further reducing the child-bearing capacity of the Brazilian female slave population. In the mid–nineteenth century, for example, the life expectancy of a Brazilian slave was only two-thirds that of a Brazilian white man (leaving aside free persons of color), in contrast to the United States in the slave period, where a slave would expect to live almost 90 percent as long as his master. Finally, despite their callousness about slave conditions on the plantations, Brazilian slave masters were much more likely to free the slaves they had than were their U.S. counterparts, perhaps because they were so used to being able to replace lost slaves through the frequent (monthly, according to most estimates) deliveries of new slaves from Africa.

EXHIBIT 3-3
Estimated Slave Imports into the Americas by Region, 1451–1870 (thousands)

Region	1451–1600	1601–1700	%	1701–1810	%	1811–1870	%	Total	%
British North America	—	—	—	348.0	6	51.0	3	399.0	4
Spanish America	75.0	292.5	22	578.6	9	606.0	32	1552.1	16
British Caribbean	—	263.7	19	1401.3	23	—	—	1665.0	17
French Caribbean	—	155.8	11	1348.4	22	96.0	5	1600.2	17
Dutch Caribbean	—	40.0	3	460.0	8	—	—	500.0	5
Danish Caribbean	—	4.0	—	24.0	—	—	—	28.0	—
Brazil	50.0	560.0	41	1891.4	31	1145.4	60	3646.8	38
Old World	149.9	25.1	3	—	—	—	—	175.0	2
TOTAL	274.9	1341.1	100	6051.7	100	1898.4	100	9566.1	100
Annual Average	1.8	13.4		55.0		31.6		22.8	

Source: Philip B. Curtin, *The Atlantic Slave Trade: A Census* (Madison, 1969), p. 88–89.

British pressure to end the slave trade, therefore, threatened the very heart of the Brazilian economy. The British, like the other European settlers of the New World, had, of course, profited from African slavery for centuries through their slaveholding colonies in North America and the Caribbean. They had also profited from investments in the slave trade itself. And it was a rare British politician or cleric who found any convincing moral rationale against enslavement before the eighteenth century. By the late eighteenth century, however, British public opinion in general had moved toward abolition. As enlightenment ideas produced new attitudes toward human relations, the reduction of humans to subhuman status for economic gain began to arouse passionate opposition in Britain as immoral and unchristian.

This moral shift became so powerful that in 1833 the British Parliament prohibited slavery in the British Atlantic colonies. Public opinion was also pressing the British government to suppress the flourishing slave trade from West Africa to the rest of the slaveholding New World. The main motivation for British action was indeed moral and ideological, but an economic dimension also entered the political calculus. The United States had already prohibited the trade in 1807. This left the British Caribbean colonies without a slave trade, putting them at a competitive disadvantage (in labor costs) vis-à-vis slave economies such as Cuba and Brazil. Ending the slave trade throughout the world would have the coincidental advantage of redressing this competitive imbalance.

So the British put growing pressure on Brazil, which was felt in several ways. First, in 1826 Britain pressured Brazil to sign a treaty agreeing to end the slave trade within three years. Although there was no support for this measure among the Brazilian elite, they could hardly explicitly resist the British, to whom they were heavily indebted both politically and financially. Successive Brazilian governments dealt with the problem by simply neglecting to enforce the 1826 treaty, a negligence they applied also to an 1831 law that declared all slaves subsequently entering Brazil as automatically free. Slave ships continued to unload their human cargoes on the Brazilian coast, in open defiance of the legal ban. Britain's Royal Navy, the world's premier naval force, set out to intercept the slave ships and liberate the slave cargoes. Although they had some successes, a massive flow continued to arrive through the 1830s and 1840s. Despite outrage expressed in the English press and parliament, about 712,000 new slaves poured into Brazil during these two decades, averaging as many as 35,000 a year. (Since the trade was technically illegal after 1831, these figures are only estimates.)

Under pressure from the coffee growers and other landowners, who argued that Brazil's economy would collapse if denied a secure supply of slaves, the Brazilian government continued to ignore its diplomatic commitment to Britain until 1850, when the Brazilian parliament finally passed legislation (the Eusebio de Queiroz law) definitively outlawing the slave trade. The reasons were several. Most important was the increased British naval pressure after the Brazilian government refused in 1845 to renew the treaty that had obligated it to suppress the trade. Royal Navy cruisers then cracked down on slave ships headed for Brazil, seizing almost four hundred between 1845 and 1850. This stepped-up intervention, which extended into Brazilian harbors, presented a major threat to Brazilian sovereignty. A second concern motivating the Brazilian elite was a loss of confidence in their ability to control the slaves after they reached Brazil. The successful slave rebellion in Haiti in the 1790s had struck fear into the hearts of slaveowners throughout the Americas. This fear was reinforced in Brazil by the Malé slave revolt in Salvador, Bahia in 1835. From then on, the police and politicians, especially in Rio and Bahia, warned that the newly arriving African slaves had great explosive potential—warnings that were confirmed by a revolt of fugitive slaves in Rio de Janeiro province in 1838 and fugitive slave participation in the Balaiada revolt (1838–40) in Maranhão. Finally, Brazilian authorities were alarmed by the outbreaks of yellow fever and cholera in the 1840s. Medical researchers traced the source of these epidemic diseases to recently arrived African slaves, providing another powerful piece of self-interest for ending the trade.

In 1850, the Brazilian cabinet finally agreed to stop the slave traffic which, even by Brazilian law, had been illegal for almost two decades. The Brazilian government was now truly committed to enforcing the law, and it was estimated that only 6,100 more slaves entered Brazil (clandestinely) from 1850 to 1855. The slave trade continued only to Cuba, where it was finally ended in the 1860s through combined pressure from the British and Spanish governments.

The end of the trade had grave implications for Brazil. As already discussed, continuous imports of slaves were essential to fill the labor needs of the plantations. Although the planters, whose ports were under pressure from the British navy, accepted the final abolition of the trade, they remained pessimistic about its effects on the future of Brazilian agriculture. As the Italian Jesuit Antonil had remarked two centuries earlier, the slaves were "the hands and feet" of Brazil. How could the country survive without its limbs?

The Question of Abolition

When Brazil established its independent empire in 1822, slavery was firmly entrenched. Slavery was central to the economy in every region of the country. The dynamic new coffee sector, for example, depended entirely on slave labor. At the same time, new shipments of slaves were pouring into the country. Slavery had no serious opposition. On the contrary, it was an essential part of Brazil's view of itself.

By 1850, the Brazilians' position on slavery made them increasingly isolated on the world scene. In 1863, U.S. president Lincoln's Emancipation Proclamation freed slaves within the Confederacy and in 1865 the U.S. Congress freed the rest by constitutional amendment. That left Cuba and Brazil as the only major slave states in the Americas. Brazil's isolation was reinforced by increasing pressure from Europe, especially Britain and France. In 1870, for example, a committee of French intellectuals, led by Victor Hugo, wrote Emperor Pedro II, urging him to abolish slavery immediately. In his 1871 speech from the throne, the emperor acknowledged Hugo's letter and promised to work toward abolition. In fact, Pedro II had first become convinced of the need for abolition in 1865, when he visited the Brazilian front during the war against Paraguay. The emperor found that the Paraguayans' citing of Brazilian slavery made effective anti-Brazilian propaganda.

Neither the planters nor the political elite defended slavery with the racist arguments common to their counterparts in the United States. Rather, the position of the Brazilian supporters of slavery was pragmatic. They argued that slave labor was essential to Brazilian agriculture and therefore to the Brazilian economy. But the fate of the slaves was not, in fact, simply about labor supply, important though that issue was. The slavery issue also struck at the heart of the white elite's sense of identity. The issue for them was Brazil's future racial composition and how it would affect the distribution of power.

To understand this (normally) unstated preoccupation of the white elite requires an understanding of Brazil's nineteenth-century racial demography. (As can be seen from exhibit 3-4, the racial balance of the Brazilian population changed significantly in the nineteenth century). In 1798, the Afro-Brazilians, slave and free, were twice as numerous as the white population. But of the almost two million Afro-Brazilians, one-fifth (four hundred thousand) were free. Two decades before independence, in other words, Brazil already had a significant free population of color. Thus, Brazilian society had already had experience in incorporating (with widely varying degrees of economic freedom) manumitted or free-born Afro-Brazilians.

Central to this process was the mulatto. We have seen how the colonial Brazilian economy had created space for mixed bloods, especially mulattos, to rise socially, at least to a limited degree. That trend continued in the early Empire. Before 1850, for example, the *Guarda Nacional*, a kind of militia, allowed its ordinary soldiers to elect their officers. Since the ranks comprised men of color, mulatto officers frequently won the elections. Mulattos nonetheless remained vulnerable in a hierarchical system where the top was always white. Revealing on this score is the case of Antonio Pereira Rebouças, a mulatto and father of the famous abolitionist André Rebouças. In 1824, Antonio, a distinguished lawyer and secretary to the government of the province of Sergipe, was for-

EXHIBIT 3-4
Brazilian Population Growth by Ethnic Origin, 1798–1872

Ethnic Origin	1798	1872	Average Annual Percent Growth, 1798–1872
European	1,010,000	3,787,289 (a)	1.80
African (and Mixed)	1,988,000	5,756,238 (b)	1.44(c)
Free	406,000	4,254,428	
Slave	1,582,000	1,510,810	
Indigenous	252,000	386,955	0.58
TOTAL	3,250,000	9,930,478	1.52

Notes: (a) Includes 383,000 foreign-born reported in 1872 population.
(b) Includes 1,351,600 estimated slave imports.
(c) Freed and slave are combined because it is impossible to separate the effects of natural growth, manumission, and importation in their growth.
Source: Thomas W. Merrick and Douglas H. Graham, *Population and Economic Development* (Baltimore, 1979), p. 29.

mally accused by white landowners of planning a slave uprising and "a general massacre of all whites." Rebouças was cleared in a public hearing, which was a credit to imperial justice. But it was a painful reminder of how any successful mulatto's color could be used against him.

In 1872 (date of the first national census), Afro-Brazilians still outnumbered whites, but by a smaller margin. From two-to-one in 1782 the ratio had dropped to five-to-three. The most dramatic change in the non-white population was the growth of the free Afro-Brazilians, who now outnumbered the whites (4.2 million to 3.8 million). The slave population had remained the same as in 1798 (1.5 million).

What had been true in 1798 was even more true in 1872: Brazil's free society was heavily multiracial. Debate over abolition could not therefore be a debate over how free Brazil might react if it faced, for the first time, a future influx of ex-slaves. For better or for worse, the assimilation process had begun on a large scale long ago.

Nonetheless, the overwhelmingly white Brazilian elite often spoke as if their country had no such racial history. They talked as if they could start *de novo*. Most who addressed the subject believed the country's only hope was to become racially whiter (*branquear*), thus resembling the powerful nations of the North Atlantic. But how would the masses of illiterate, unskilled free Afro-Brazilians, not to speak of the ex-slaves, fit into this picture? The abolition debate involved more than the legal institution of slavery. As the aftermath of Brazil's war with Paraguay made increasingly clear, it involved a reappraisal of Brazilians' view of themselves.

The Paraguayan War

In March 1865, Paraguayan forces trooped across Argentine territory (after being denied permission) to Uruguay, with the intention of countering recent Brazilian intervention there. Brazil claimed it had acted to protect its many citizens living in Uruguay by sending military forces to depose the Uruguayan government and replace it with a pro-Brazilian one. Paraguay's subsequent invasion of the neighboring Brazilian provinces of Mato Grosso was meant to undo the Brazilian intervention, but it ended up triggering a war that pitted Paraguay against the combined forces of Brazil, Argentina, and Uruguay (which had hastily formed a "Triple Alliance") in a conflict that was to last five years. The key to understanding this war and Brazil's involvement in it is the geography of the region.

After the Amazon, the La Plata River system is the largest in South America. It furnishes essential transportation to four countries: Brazil, Argentina, Paraguay, and Uruguay. (See exhibit 3-5.) For the last three of these it is the most important waterborne outlet to the Atlantic ocean and therefore to seaborne contact with Europe and North America. For Brazil at that time, the Paraná River—one of the tributaries of the Plata River, which is technically an estuary—served the important strategic function of connecting Brazil's coast and its far western interior. Since land travel to the Brazilian interior was extremely time-consuming and insecure, the best route from the east coast was to sail down the Atlantic coast to the mouth of the Plata River, up the Plata to the Paraná River, and up the Paraná River. Any interruption to traffic on the Paraná would disrupt this vital military and economic link between the two regions of Brazil.

Brazil's involvement in the Plata region went back to the colonial era. We have seen how Brazil was drawn into war in this area in the 1820s. The result of that clash was an agreement, brokered by the English, to create the nation of Uruguay. By the same agreement, Brazil was guaranteed navigation rights to the Plata and its tributaries. In subsequent decades, Brazil's economic interests in the region grew, especially in Uruguay, where they were directed by Brazil's premier banker and industrialist, Baron Mauá.

The stability of the Plata region had depended on the cooperation of Brazil and Argentina, the two principal regional powers. Paraguay was a most unexpected threat to this stability. A small, poor, Guaraní-speaking country, it had only recently emerged, under a series of military dictators, as an ambitious new nation. In 1865 it was under the con-

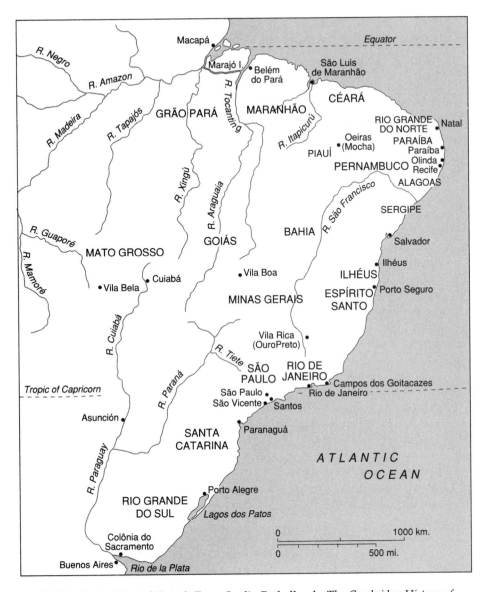

Exhibit 3-5. Colonial Brazil. From Leslie Bethell, ed., *The Cambridge History of Latin America*, vol. 2 (Cambridge, 1984), p. 422.

trol of the latest of these dictators, Francisco Solano López, whose political and personal motivations have long been debated by historians. This colorful dictator's exotic image was enhanced by his Irish-born mistress, whom he had brought back from a trip to Paris and who bore him five sons. A histrionic and flamboyant madame, she attempted, with understandable difficulty, to impose Parisian tastes on bucolic Asunción. She was cordially hated by the ladies of the European colony in the Paraguayan capital and was later to be blamed as the inspiration for López's more savage acts.

International tension in the La Plata area had been rising during the 1860s because of rival efforts by the Brazilians, Paraguayans, and Argentines to manipulate politics in Uruguay, where two factions were struggling for power. One Uruguayan faction, alleging hostile intervention by Argentina and Brazil in 1864, sought help from Paraguay. There followed a chain-reaction of challenge, defiance, and miscalculation, which eventually pitted Paraguay against both Argentina and Brazil. Solano López was so confident of his nation's military prowess that he was little inclined to be intimidated by his larger neighbors. Believing that Paraguay's independence was endangered by Argentine and Brazilian dominance in Uruguay, and nurturing a tragic overconfidence in his nation's strength, he decided to intervene. His first step was to seize a Brazilian steamer on the Paraná River, which was carrying the new Brazilian president-designate of the province of Mato Grosso. The crew and passengers were interned and the ship's flag was made into a rug to bedeck López's office in the presidential palace. Paraguay had brought about the Brazilian nightmare: The fluvial lifeline to its interior had been cut.

Lopez next launched a bold strike into Mato Grosso, where his troops enjoyed a series of rapid victories over the ill-prepared, ill-equipped, and poorly-commanded Brazilians. These reverses sobered the Brazilian officers, who had predicted a quick victory for their troops. In particular, the Paraguayans carried off a valuable cache of captured military stocks, leaving the Brazilian defenders undersupplied and mortified. A second offensive in Rio Grande do Sul ended very differently. A six-thousand-man Paraguayan force fell into a trap at Uruguiana and surrendered without a fight. Pedro II had the pleasure of witnessing this victory.

From this point on (October 1865) combat shifted onto Paraguayan soil. But there were many Brazilian losses yet in store. The logistical challenges alone were staggering. The expedition sent from Rio in 1865, for example, consumed nearly four months in traveling 280 miles. A third of the troops were lost on the way to smallpox, malaria, and desertions. The column finally met the Paraguayans in combat in 1867, suffering a disastrous defeat near Laguna. That Brazilian agony was immortalized by the young writer Alfredo D'Escragnolle Taunay, a member of the expedition, in his 1871 work *The Retreat from Laguna* (first written in French and then translated into Portuguese by the author's son).

The Argentines' contribution proved to be small, leaving the Brazilians to furnish the majority of forces, both army and navy, to fight on. The Brazilian army was led after late 1866 by the same Baron of Caxias who had quelled domestic rebellions earlier in the country. The first few months of the war prompted a wave of volunteers as a burst of patriotism took hold of young Brazilian men. In truth, Brazil did not have a proper national army when the war began. It numbered little more than 18,000 troops, many not available to move south. But once the initial pro-war enthusiasm faded after 1865, the imperial government could not attract enough "volunteers." In 1866 it turned to slaves, who were offered their freedom in return for joining up. This measure aroused the indignation of one Liberal politician, who declared, "To call slaves to defend, alongside free men, the integrity of the Empire and to avenge insults from a small republic is for us to confess before the civilized world . . . that we are incapable, without help from our slaves, of defending ourselves as a nation." Ironically, the author of those works, Viscount Jequitinhonha, was a mulatto who favored gradual abolition. One reason the army was short of soldiers for the Paraguayan campaign was that local commanders in Brazil feared that depleting their ranks might make them unable to deal with slave revolts at home. Paraguayan propaganda cast racist aspersions on the invading Brazilians, dubbing Pedro II "El Macacón" ("the Big Ape").

The Paraguayan army's reputation for being large (said to number 80,000) and well equipped was somewhat overdrawn, but the Paraguayan soldiers proved to be skilled guerrilla fighters, fighting with a ferocity and self-sacrifice the Brazilians could seldom match, and managing to hold off the invaders for two more years. The harsh combat conditions gradually hardened the Brazilian forces, who were finally able to virtually eliminate the Paraguayan army in a series of battles in 1868. Given a population base of perhaps 400,000 in 1864, the 60,000 Paraguayan soldiers who had been killed, captured, or maimed represented an exorbitant loss. By any rational calculation, the war was over. But López assembled another army (of boys, women, and old men), which held out for two more years by fleeing into the hills and forests and launching scattered guerrilla attacks.

The politicians back home in Brazil, who were absorbed in increasingly partisan bickering, began asking why their forces should go on fighting a war that should have been over. There were ugly charges of corruption in procuring supplies. The Liberal party press was especially shrill in its criticisms of the conduct of the war. The Brazilian commanders, in turn, accused the politicians on the home front of back-stabbing the war effort just when they were within reach of victory. And, indeed, the original agreement among Brazil, Uruguay, and Argentina (the Triple Alliance) had committed the combatants to achieving unconditional surrender of the enemy. Pedro II backed up the army by insisting on a fight to the finish. For the emperor, who seemed to have lost his usual pragmatism and good sense, the war had become a personal duel with the Paraguayan dictator. It had also become, in his view, a crucial test of his country's ability to prove itself a "modern" disciplined nation. When the U.S. government was making strenuous efforts to mediate the conflict in 1867, for example, Pedro II told a confidant, "Above all we go on and finish the war with honor. It is a question of honor and I will not compromise." In late 1868, he wrote of "López and his influence," arguing that "it is necessary to destroy completely this influence, whether direct or indirect, by capturing or forcefully expelling López from Paraguayan territory." But the emperor could no longer count on the Liberal cabinet, led by Zacarias de Góis e Vasconcelos, to continue his crusade. He had to turn to the Conservatives to finish the job.

Caxias resigned as commander-in-chief in 1868. Dom Pedro named his own son-in-law as the new commander, the Conde D'Eu, who had the dubious honor of presiding over the mopping-up operation. He also took the opportunity to abolish slavery in Paraguay, a gesture that earned him the enmity of many Brazilian slave owners, who feared the extension of abolition to Brazil.

The end came when Solano López, whose paranoid suspicions had led him to execute many of his own relatives, was hunted down and killed by Brazilian troops in March 1870. The nation of Paraguay had been reduced to rubble, its dead were estimated at 200,000 (no one knew exactly), and its male population had shrunk by as much as three-quarters. The Brazilian military occupation of Paraguay continued for another six years.

Ostensibly, Brazil had achieved its objectives. First, it had defeated Paraguay and eliminated its leader. Second, it had gained some marginal territorial concessions from the Paraguayans. Third, it had asserted itself as a major military power in South America's most volatile geopolitical region. As if to symbolize this triumph, the Brazilian troops carried off the entire Paraguayan archives to be stored in Rio. The Paraguayans had not only lost the war; they had lost the written record of their own history.

Along other dimensions, however, Brazil had not done so well. Emperor Pedro II had optimistically described the war when it began as a "nice electrical shock" to the nation. But looking back from the 1890s, Joaquim Nabuco, the noted legislator-historian-diplomat, found his society had been gripped by a malaise painfully exposed by the army's inept response to Paraguay's invasion of Rio Grande do Sul and Mato Grosso in 1864. There had been a decline in dedication to "public service," Nabuco said, which he attributed to an indolence produced by climate, race, and social habit. "For Brazilians, the old Portuguese discipline was too heavy, too exhausting, like the old clothes and old manners, for a society that just wanted to relax and go to sleep."

To the many observers who shared Nabuco's perception, the five-year war had led Brazil to a variety of uncomfortable confrontations with its own reality. First, the Brazilian army had received very bad press in the United States and Europe for its allegedly brutal tactics against Paraguayan civilians. This reinforced the Brazilian elite's preoccupation with their country's image abroad as uncivilized. Second, Brazil's attitude to slavery was irretrievably changed. The slaves who had been recruited to fill out the ranks of the Brazilian troops in return for their freedom after the war had acquitted themselves well in battle (although they had been ridiculed in the Paraguayan press as "monkeys"). And their performance had given Brazilian officers a new appreciation for the capacity of Afro-Brazilians. This became very important when the Brazilian military was later called upon to pursue runaway slaves. No less important was the realization that Brazil had only been able to win the war by enlisting thousands of slaves. Where was the "whitened" nation the elite yearned to inhabit?

Third, the war had deeply affected the military as an institution. The commanders' successful battle with the politicians over the conduct of the war set a precedent for increasing officer involvement in imperial politics. Officers were now suspicious that the civilians might sacrifice Brazil's military interest for their own purposes. The Paraguayan War therefore set the stage for growing military-civilian tensions during the 1880s.

Fourth, the war had a decisive effect on political party alignments. The forced recruitment of soldiers had especially aroused the opposition. In the war's early years, the Liberal government had been increasingly at odds with the emperor and the Conservative-controlled Senate over government finances, patronage questions, and the management of the war. In 1868, the Baron of Caxias had resigned from his command in Paraguay, ostensibly for health reasons, and had been rewarded by the emperor with the title of duke. In fact, the new Duke of Caxias was in good health. He had resigned in order to use his prestige with the emperor to help his Conservative colleagues in Rio force out the Liberal cabinet. In the ensuing crisis, the incumbent cabinet resigned and the Liberal party split. Although the Liberals retained a majority in the Chamber of Deputies, the emperor invited the Conservatives to form a government, which they did. The emperor's action alienated the Liberals because it was the first time the emperor had ever authorized a party to form a government when it had a majority of votes against it in the Chamber of Deputies. In the process, Pedro II lost the aura of a wise and benign monarch without partisanship and was charged with the abuse of his "moderating power." The war had also taken its toll on him personally. His hair had turned almost white and he now appeared much older than his relatively young age of forty-five. In reaction to the emperor's action, the Liberal party issued a manifesto calling for such measures as decentralization, limited Senate terms, an autonomous judiciary, religious freedom, and gradual abolition. Dissenters in the left branch of the Liberal party issued an even stronger manifesto, followed

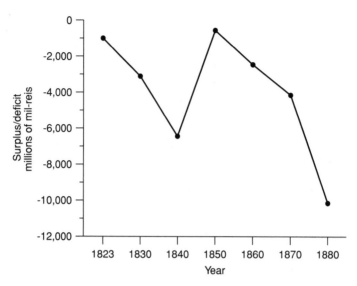

Exhibit 3-6. Federal deficit, 1823–80. From Armin K. Ludwig, *Brazil: A Handbook of Historical Statistics* (Boston, 1985), p. 353.

in 1871 by their decision to split off and form a new Republican party, which called for an end to the Empire.

All in all, the war had a profound psychological effect on the Brazilians' view of themselves. Brazil had entered the conflict with little respect for the Paraguayan troops. Years of heavy combat casualties cured the Brazilians of that arrogance. It had taken largely Afro-Brazilian troops to achieve victory. It had also taken burdensome new loans from England to finance the war. (See exhibit 3-6 for Brazil's federal deficit record between 1823 and 1880.) The Paraguayan War more than eradicated the government's efforts to stabilize the federal budget following the military expenditures necessitated by the revolts of the 1830s and 1840s. Victory over such a small, poor, and desolate country hardly qualified Brazil for the annals of glorious warfare, despite the triumphalist rhetoric of some patriots in Rio. On the contrary, it raised fundamental questions about whether their own ill-integrated society was ready to join the race to modernity.

4 Making Brazil "Modern": 1870–1910

This chapter traces Brazil's evolution in the years after the Paraguayan War. As so often in history, a foreign war had widened fissures in the social fabric that the incumbent political elite had trouble bridging. In addition, Brazil was emerging from relative economic isolation to face a highly competitive North Atlantic world. The tumultuous period between 1870 and 1910 saw the end of slavery, a bloodless military overthrow of the Empire, great efforts by the elite to improve the image of Brazil in both cultural and racial terms, the beginnings of industrialization but difficulties with Brazil's major export earners (coffee and rubber), a breakdown in the machinery of interstate political cooperation, and a revolt among enlisted navy men that further shook the elite's confidence that its efforts to reshape Brazil's image abroad could be successful.

A New Generation and the Military Question

The elite generation reaching maturity around 1870, three generations removed from their forebears who broke with Portugal, were too young to identify automatically with their emperor or their empire. In addition, they were much more uneasy than their fathers about being part of a slavocracy. In addition to the simple passage of time, two doctrines had reached Brazil that helped weaken the hold of earlier commitments and beliefs.

The first was positivism, a doctrine holding that every rationally justifiable assertion can be scientifically verified or is capable of logical or mathematical proof. Auguste Comte, the acknowledged leader of French positivism, had developed a dogma that was particularly admired by the younger army officers of the Rio Military Academy. Comte maintained that the course of history, like the nature of social reality, was subject to scientific law. He thus rejected both theology and metaphysics, arguing instead for a "religion of humanity." Although Comte was a prophet of secularization and one of the spiritual fathers of the modern technocrat, he also advocated strict limits to the role of the state, especially when it came to higher education and religion.

Brazilian positivists, in fact, spanned a wide range of beliefs. On one side of the pure followers of Comte's doctrine were religious positivists so doctrinaire that they founded their own Brazilian Positivist Church in 1881 and demanded doctrinal fidelity from all members. They eventually "excommunicated" the mother Positivist Church in Paris. On the other side were more pragmatic thinkers who agreed with Comte's rejection of Catholicism but did not accept his dogma about historical stages and the circumscribed role of the state. The middle-of-the-road positivists in Brazil were known as "heterodox" positivists. A good example in this group was the São Paulo physician and public health pioneer Luis Pereira Barreto, who published in 1874 the first Brazilian treatise written from a systematic positivist position. Positivism's appeal was strong in late nineteenth-century Brazil because it was the only doctrine offering a strong and coherent structure to pose against a dissolving Catholic ethos. Positivism maintained a strong if diffuse influence in twentieth-century Brazil not for its detailed doctrines but for its intellectual style—above all, the appeal for a scientific approach to understanding society and history. It was similar to the appeal that later made Marxist thought important in Brazil.

The second doctrine influencing the new generation was republicanism. The idea was not new in Brazilian history, having inspired regional revolts in the 1830s and 1840s, but it had faded with the consolidation of the Empire. Now republicanism revived as younger Brazilians questioned whether monarchy, with its accompanying socioeconomic ethos, was the best system for their country. The rapid industrialization of the United States reinforced this doubt in a Brazil that remained overwhelmingly agrarian. Furthermore, Dom Pedro II, once the unifying symbol of the Empire, was now physically and psychologically weaker. His colossal mistake in judgment when he insisted on calling for a Conservative government in 1868, despite the Liberal majority in the Chamber of Deputies, has already been discussed. It was the last straw for the more militant Liberals. Their manifesto, when they left the traditional Liberal party to found the Republican party in 1871, declared that "National sovereignty can only exist, can only be recognized and practiced in a nation whose parliament has the supreme direction and pronounces the final word in public business." The signers left no doubt about their orientation: "We are from America and we want to be Americans."

The younger generation's discontent soon took an extreme form in the army. Pedro II had weathered the political crisis surrounding the Paraguayan War partly because his senior army commanders stood together. By 1880, however, these officers were retired or dead, replaced by a younger generation which noted, among other things, that the overall imperial budget had increased by 70 percent during the period between 1871 and 1880, while the military budget had grown by only 8 percent. They wanted more manpower and new equipment, and they were suspicious that the husband of Princess Isabel, heir to the throne, might have his own reasons to sabotage their budget demands. The implausibility of those suspicions showed how deep the ill will against the prince had gone.

The army commanders also faced a wide class gap between themselves and their troops. The officers, mostly sons of professionals, came from the military academy. The enlisted men were conscripts, usually recruited under duress, illiterate, and serving against their will. The gap was long-standing, but the generation reaching maturity in the last quarter of the nineteenth century was newly sensitive to the danger that troops from the lower social orders might be unable (or unwilling) to maintain social control within the country.

All this was exacerbated by bad feeling between the military elite and the politicians. Open military criticism of cabinet ministers, which had begun during the Paraguayan War, had erupted in increasingly ugly confrontations between 1884 and 1889. Trouble had been brewing since the 1850s, with a faction of officers attacking the empire for its excessive identification with the planters and lawyers and its failure to take the necessary steps—railway construction, promotion of industry, abolition of slavery, and encouragement of immigration—to modernize Brazil. As the ranks of the critics swelled, the growing controversy triggered a constitutional problem. Since military officers were legally subordinate to civilian ministers, when they spoke out against the government (and the topic was often abolition), the civilian Minister of the Army would discipline the offender, typically by placing him under house arrest. The resulting feeling of martyrdom among the officers combined with increasing rigidity and fear among their civilian superiors to become known in the 1880s as the "military question."

This was the environment in which the Brazilians finally abolished slavery.

Abolition and Its Aftermath:
The Brazilian Way

Isolated arguments favoring abolition in Brazil could be found as far back as the era of independence. The preeminent leader of the period, José Bonifácio, was a strong abolitionist, although he believed abolition had to be gradual. In an 1823 draft speech, his attack on slavery was unmistakable: "By what sort of justice does a man steal another man's freedom, and worse yet, the freedom of this man's children, and of his children's children?" Emperor Dom Pedro I published an essay in that same year attacking slavery as "the cancer that is gnawing away at Brazil." The political implications of such a statement from the emperor were so grave that he was forced to use a pseudonym ("the Philanthropist").

Only in the late 1860s and early 1870s, however, did the abolitionist movement begin to gather widespread support, using the same arguments heard earlier in the United States and Britain. The Brazilian counterpart to Harriet Beecher Stowe's *Uncle Tom's Cabin* was the Bahia Romanticist poet Castro Alves's *Navio Negreiro* (*Slave Ship*). Both of these had a strongly Christian and humanist flavor and included the claim that "man is free neither when a slave nor when a master," in the words of Joaquim Nabuco. Nabuco, the scion of a Pernambucan elite family, was to become the best known abolitionist with his publication of *Abolitionism* in 1884. But this white aristocrat was not alone in the leadership. He was joined by effective and eloquent Afro-Brazilian activists (all mulattos) such as José do Patrocínio, André Rebouças, and Luis de Gama, who played key roles in mobilizing public opinion in the 1880s. José de Patrocínio was a mulatto journalist and orator whose paper, *A Cidade de Rio*, was a leading abolitionist voice in the 1880s. André Rebouças was one of the most prominent mulattos of imperial Brazil. Trained as an engineer, he earned a fortune supervising the construction of the docks in Rio and numerous other Atlantic port cities. Of all the abolitionists, as noted, he was the only one to see the need for land reform. Luis de Gama was a talented lawyer and a fiery orator. The presence of these three in the abolitionist leadership was another sign of the mobility of free coloreds.

Foreign pressure also continued to play a part throughout the Brazilian struggle for abolition. Visitors to Brazil from the United States, Britain, and France in the 1870s and 1880s expressed their shock at finding slavery still alive. On the one hand, foreign advice angered Brazilian conservatives such as the Romanticist writer-politician José de Alencar, who played on Brazilian resentment at being subjected to "proclamations of European philanthropy" that prompted "obeisances to foreign opinion." On the other hand, criticism from abroad helped the elite realize that slavery was an obstacle to the country's emergence as a modern nation. In the words of the Anti-Slavery Society (written by Nabuco), "Brazil does not want to be a nation morally isolated, a leper, expelled from the world community. The esteem and respect of foreign nations are as valuable to us as they are to other people."

By the 1880s, although slaveholders in low-productivity areas such as the province of Rio de Janeiro continued to argue that they could not survive without slave labor, the writing was on the wall and everyone knew it. The plain fact was that they could not survive the labor shortage that was inevitable even if abolition was not passed. As already described, the end of the slave trade in 1850 combined with the low birthrate among the Brazilian slave population to guarantee that the slave population would eventually completely die out. Although total slave extinction was not predicted to occur until well into the twentieth century, Brazil's labor shortage was already acute.

Efforts to bring Europeans to Brazil to work in the plantations had largely failed, in good part because it seemed to be impossible to preserve tolerable working conditions for free labor in a slave-holding environment. As already mentioned, many of the earlier immigrants had complained so vociferously about their inhumane treatment that several German states had outlawed all Brazilian recruitment of immigrants in their territory. It was becoming clear to those who gave it any thought that, since slavery and immigrant labor could not work side by side, slavery would have to go.

This conclusion became even more logical as some planters, especially in São Paulo, began to ask whether free labor might not be as effective as and perhaps cheaper than slave labor. Equally important, landowners were discovering, especially in São Paulo, that maintaining control of their labor force did not necessarily depend on its legal status. Neither the economic survival nor the political dominance of the planters was dependent on slavery. In the short run, of course, these planters had no intention of giving up their slaves without compensation. Such a measure, they argued, would destroy Brazilian agriculture, and Brazil's economy along with it. This was a major sticking point for the government, yet how could the government raise the funds to pay for the 1,510,806 human beings (by the 1872 census) still in slavery? One answer, which appealed to the establishment politicians, was to abolish slavery in stages.

In 1871, parliament passed the "Law of the Free Womb," freeing all children henceforth born of slave mothers. But the slaveowners were given a huge concession. The child now born "free" was required to render service to the mother's master until age twenty-one. An alternative provision for the government to buy the freedom of the newborn child was seldom exercised. Although the law was an important precedent, the more militant abolitionists were not satisfied with this long-term solution. They wanted total and immediate abolition.

The militants did not have their way. The anti-abolitionist forces blocked further legislation for more than a decade. Finally, in 1885, the parliament passed the Sexagenarian Law, which freed all slaves over sixty-five years of age. Cynics noted that few slaves ever reached sixty. Statistics from 1872 show that the life expectancy of the Brazilian male slave was only eighteen years. Furthermore, how were the newly freed to survive? There was no organized effort, even among abolitionists, to provide the emancipated with land, education, or housing.

As the political ferment increased, the slaves became important actors in their own drama. By their resistance, often courageous, they gave the lie to the racist stereotype (entertained by whites then and later) of the Afro-Brazilian as inherently passive and unable to defend himself. By 1887, slaves were staging mass escapes from plantations, especially in São Paulo. The escapees formed fugitive communities (called *quilom-*

bos in the colonial era) near Santos and on the Rio beaches. Furthermore, the army officers who had previously followed orders to hunt down runaways began rebelling against such orders.

The struggle ended on May 13, 1888, when the parliament approved total and immediate abolition without compensation (the "Golden Law"). The opposition vote was concentrated among the deputies from the province of Rio de Janeiro (seven of the eight negative votes). Since Pedro II was in Europe, the Golden Law was signed by Princess Isabella, who thereby won the title of the slaves' benefactress. A carnival of celebration erupted in Rio as Brazil joined the company of "civilized" nations.

Unlike abolition in the United States, which was achieved at the cost of a bloody civil war, abolition in Brazil was a gradual, drawn-out affair. How Brazil achieved abolition revealed much about the country's emerging political culture. First, the political elite succeeded in containing the growing social conflict within a strictly legal framework. Second, the landowners deflected any challenge to the structure of landholding—a crucial question for the future of Brazilian agriculture. Only a few abolitionists, such as André Rebouças, saw the need for land reform. Third, the elite had demonstrated its skill at compromising without endangering its own position. In the 1850s, this skill had been called "conciliation," and it would continue to be a key tactic used by the elite in their subsequent dominance in Brazil. Abolition, for example, helped divert attention from Brazil's "social question"—the euphemistic term used in the era to describe government policies on social welfare as well as to control the lower classes. By a simple legal gesture, the elite had "solved" the problem of an obsolete system of forced labor. This fit with the Brazilian elite's tendency to see socioeconomic questions in exclusively legal terms, rather than in structural or social class terms.

Abolition now opened the way for the redefinition of Brazil's system of social stratification. Previously, slaves made up the bottom of the social pyramid. Now that category was removed, yet color would remain a key mark in establishing social status even though everyone of color was now juridically free. In practice, this would not necessarily alter the complex system of race relations, in which the lack of a clear-cut color line made room for limited mobility of mixed bloods. In that system, the top of the pyramid was occupied almost entirely by whites. But there continued to be no absolute color line (like the rest of Latin America and unlike the post-1890s United States), which had made it possible for small numbers of Afro-Brazilians, primarily mulattos, to rise socially, occasionally to the top of the pyramid. Obvious examples were Andre Rebouças, the engineer and prominent abolitionist, and Machado de Assis, Brazil's greatest novelist and founder and long-time president and founder of the Brazilian Academy of Letters.

The coming of abolition also stimulated a dramatic surge of immigration into Brazil that must have surpassed the hopes of its most fervent supporters (see exhibit 4-1), no doubt helped by the Sociedade Promotora da Imigração (Society for Promoting Immigration), organized in 1886 by the planters in the richest coffee state, São Paulo. The number of immigrants entering Brazil jumped from less than 33,000 in 1886 to 132,000 just two years later. As in Argentina and the United States, the large flow of immigrants continued until the First World War.

During the wave of immigration to Brazil that followed abolition, the largest number came from Italy, with the second largest from Portugal, followed by Spain (see exhibit 4-2). These national origins had interesting implications for the future of Brazilian society. First, these immigrants assimilated easily into Brazilian society and culture. Their language, if not Portuguese, was closely related to Portuguese, as were their cultures. On the other hand, they were not the Anglo-Saxon yeomen farmers whom the immigration boosters had often seemed to favor. Rather, the Spanish and Italians came from the same Mediterranean ethos as the Portuguese.

The immigrants went primarily to São Paulo and the South. The largest number entered through the immigrant hostel in Santos (the port for São Paulo) and were then assigned to the coffee fields. A smaller number immigrated to Paraná, Santa Catarina, and Rio Grande do Sul. These were mostly Italians and Germans, with a few East Europeans, who also headed for the countryside. In 1908, the Japanese began immigrating to Brazil, heading primarily to São Paulo and Paraná, where many became highly successful farmers.

The immigrants to Brazil were typically highly versatile, often trying out their work skills in different industries, from agricultural labor to textiles to metallurgy. They were also mobile across national boundaries, moving among Argentina, Brazil, and the United States. They were often capitalistic in their mentality, seeking to maximize the acquisition of new skills and the accumulation of savings.

These immigrants helped create the notion of a Brazilian "melting pot," where ethnic differences would be dissolved in the creation of a single nationality. Missing from this optimistic picture, which the elite liked to promote, was the huge population living in Brazil before the immigrants arrived. Italian immigrants might find assimilation easy, but what about the illiterate, unskilled Brazilians, overwhelmingly of color? For the modern observer an obvious question arises: Why did the planters of the Center-South fail to recruit from the large body of free labor elsewhere in Brazil?

The answer, as historians can best reconstruct it, is several-fold. First, the planters, like the elite in general, had little faith in nonwhites, who were most of the existing Brazilian labor force. The imperial elite considered the Afro-Brazilians, for example, physically inferior and inca-

EXHIBIT 4-1

Immigrants to Brazil, 1872–1910

Years	Number of Immigrants
1872–1879	22,042
1880–1883	26,393
1884	23,574
1895	34,724
1886	32,650
1887	54,932
1888	132,070
1889	65,165
1890	106,819
1891	215,239
1892	85,906
1893	132,589
1894	60,182
1895	164,831
1896	157,423
1897	144,866
1898	76,862
1899	53,610
1900	37,807
1901	83,116
1902	50,472
1903	32,941
1904	44,706
1905	68,488
1906	72,332
1907	57,919
1908	90,536
1909	84,090
1910	86,751

Source: Armin K. Ludwig, *Brazil: A Handbook of Historical Statistics* (Boston, 1985), p. 103.

EXHIBIT 4-2
Immigrants to Brazil, by Nationality, 1872–1909 (Percent)

	1872–79	1880–89	1890–99	1900–09
Italian	25.80	61.80	57.60	35.60
Portuguese	31.2	23.3	18.3	31.4
Spanish	1.9	6.7	13.7	18.2
Germans	8.1	4.2	1.4	2.2
Other	33.0	4.0	8.9	12.4
TOTAL	100	100	100	100

Source: Thomas W. Merrick and Douglas H. Graham, *Population and Economic Development* (Baltimore, 1979), p. 91.

pable of serious work habits. In spite of the grudging admiration felt by the army for the Afro-Brazilian exploits in the Paraguayan War—and the military fear that they were capable of aggressive fighting back if they were hunted down as runaway slaves—a leading military publication made clear in 1882 what it did *not* want as a recruitment source: "the lazy Negro race, whose education and heritage leaves it without energy, and can only be motivated by prodding." Second, they thought European immigrants would bring the qualities the Northeasterners lacked, including needed skills. Third, some planters thought the immigrants would be easier to control than freedmen. Finally, once in Brazil the European immigrants would presumably help improve the ethnic stock. This point is important to a discussion later in the chapter about the elite's preoccupation with Brazil's image abroad.

In preparation for that discussion, the next section recounts the story of the end of the Brazilian Empire, which fell in 1889, fast on the heels of abolition.

The End of the Empire

As the 1880s wore on, Pedro II's health continued to deteriorate. He traveled repeatedly to European spas, seeking a cure for his diabetes, without success. Back in Rio, he was losing the close touch he had always maintained with his ministers. By 1887, he had lost the popular appeal that had once helped bring the country together. The Rio press was openly speculating that he had lost his mind. He even became the butt of popular ridicule, with cartoonists depicting him as "Pedro Banana." The prospect of the succession of his daughter was also very unpopular. Princess Isabel and her consort had failed to win elite support for reasons that did no credit to their detractors. For Isabel, gender was the problem. The elite was by definition male and utterly unaccustomed to seeing a woman in authority. The Brazilians had never had a female monarch and the small insular world of politically powerful men was openly hostile. For her husband, the Conde d'Eu, nationality (he was a French-born nobleman) was the problem. Despite being culturally Francophile, the Brazilian elite was nationalistic when it came to the royal family.

Dom Pedro II had once been a symbol of national unity, presiding skillfully over Latin America's most stable political system. But this meant nothing to the new generation of elite Brazilians. They now had doubts about the monarchy as an institution, doubts that were not at all assuaged by an aging, out-of-touch emperor and a woman as next in line to the throne. The monarchy's most radical critics, the Republicans, were open in saying that the institution was not just an anachronism to be repackaged, but a genuine obstacle to national progress. Brazil, in their view, had outgrown the need for a moderating power.

By late 1889, multiple currents of discontent were swirling, but none seemed truly revolutionary. The Republicans, for example, were concentrated mainly in São Paulo and Minas Gerais. By their numbers (only two members in the Chamber of Deputies from 1884 to 1889) they were no serious threat either to the monarchy or to the two established political parties. Those two parties seemed more concerned with nominations of government officials than with the form of government itself, and were, in any case, even less in touch with popular sentiment than in earlier years because the franchise had become steadily more restrictive during the Empire. For the 1821 elections (for the Constituent Assembly), there had been virtually universal male suffrage. The Constitution of 1824 introduced a property requirement, which was increased in 1846. In 1881, a new electoral law, intended to eliminate fraud, drastically tightened the property requirement and excluded illiterates (thought to be a prime source of fraud), while making the vote optional (it had previously been compulsory). The effect on voter turnout was dramatic. Electoral participation dropped from 1.1 million in 1872 to 117,000 in 1886. That represented a drop from 13 percent of the total populace (excluding slaves) to 0.8 percent. The 1872 percentage was never regained until the election of 1945.

Although the Republicans had converted relatively few of the civilian political elite, they had made serious inroads among the discontented military, especially the positivists among them. On November 15, 1889, a group of junior officers, determined to intervene despite a lack of broad civilian support, convinced Marshall Deodoro da Fonseca, their commander, to rise from his sickbed and lead a coup against the emperor.

Deodoro was also motivated by fear that the emperor might invite one of the marshall's political enemies to form a new government.

Like most major political transitions in Brazil, the fall of the Empire was virtually bloodless. The emperor simply accepted the military ultimatum. He and his family grabbed a few belongings and made their way, under military escort, to the Rio docks. There they boarded an ocean steamer to exile in Portugal. The Brazilian Braganzas were now back in the land of their ancestors. Brazil's imperial experiment, unique for its length and viability in the New World, was over.

The Brazilian empire had been overthrown by a military coup, not a social revolution, and the Republic began as a military government. A military junta assumed power while much of the imperial elite withdrew from politics, some even choosing exile. The military lost no time in collecting their payoff from the coup. Military salaries were immediately increased 50 percent, a new law was passed regulating the retirement or immediate promotion of almost all higher officers (the army officer corps was notoriously top-heavy), and the army was authorized to expand from 13,000 to 25,000 troops.

The Republicans, previously a minority, took charge of shaping the new institutions. From 1890 to 1891 a newly elected constituent assembly wrote Brazil's second Constitution. The key author was Rui Barbosa, a Bahian deputy and noted legal scholar, who was to be finance minister in the new government. The 1891 Constitution's most important feature was radical decentralization. Brazil was now to become a federation, a goal long urged by provincial rebels. Each state (formerly province) would now directly elect its own governor and legislature, and would have extensive powers, such as the authority to contract foreign loans, to levy interstate tariffs, and to maintain militia. The Constitution of 1891 thus gave carte blanche for the economically most dynamic states—such as São Paulo—to direct their own development. The new Constitution also replaced the monarchy with a directly elected president, who was to be Brazil's symbolic and functional head of government. Clearly, power would now rest with the Republican oligarchies of the leading states. The property requirement for voting was abolished but illiterates (and women) were still excluded.

The Republicans also created new symbols to celebrate Brazil's entrance into the world without monarchs. The new flag bore the slogan "Order and Progress" (a positivist phrase) and Republican-commissioned paintings and graphics featured a half-clad female figure modeled on the comparable "Marianne" heroine of the French Revolution. The Roman Catholic Church was disestablished. At the same time, the Republicans set out to extinguish all evidence of the Empire. As the new finance minister, Rui Barbosa ordered the burning of the slave trade records so as to destroy all trace of what Rui considered a shameful chapter in Brazilian history. (This step also had the great advantage of making impossible any attempt to compensate the slaveholders.) The highly prestigious Colegio Pedro II was renamed the Ginásio Nacional (until 1911, when it regained its old name) and the heraldry of the royal family was banned. No more aristocratic titles could be created.

But Brazil had to do more than adopt a new flag, disestablish the Church, and eliminate titles if it wanted to join the outside world as an equal economic partner. Brazil had to change the image it presented to the world in order to compete with its neighbors in the dynamic North Atlantic world. Among the other South American states, Argentina, in particular, was already showing spectacular success in attracting both immigrants and investment.

SELLING BRAZIL

With the Paraguayan War over and slavery abolished, Brazil had eliminated two obstacles in the way of achieving respectability in the wider world. Now it set to work with a vengeance to improve its image still further. One tack was to produce glossy volumes showing how modern Brazil was in its transportation, education, and communication systems. These were gross exaggerations, of course, but they and exhibits with a similar purpose were shown off proudly by Brazilians at international events such as the Paris Exposition of 1889 and the Chicago Colombian Exposition of 1893.

More fundamental efforts were made in Europeanizing the physical appearance of its cities—in particular its capital city, Rio—and in "whitening" its population.

As Brazil entered the twentieth century, its cities retained many of the sights, sounds, and smells of their colonial past. In Rio de Janeiro, it was an ambiance that repelled many foreign visitors. Rio had a reputation for disease, especially yellow fever. Italian shipping lines even advertised their voyages to Argentina as making "no stops in Brazil." Save for minor changes made in the mid-1870s by Viscount Rio Branco's government, the layout of Rio's streets had changed little since the eighteenth century. They were narrow, crowded, unhygienic, and difficult to navigate. Sanitation was primitive and the water supply suspect. In short, Rio was a poor advertisement for a country hoping to join the North Atlantic march to modernity.

The Brazilian elite looked longingly at Paris, which Baron Hausmann had transformed with his grand boulevards. They knew there was a desperate need to bring Brazilian municipal services up to standard. It would not be easy, however, because wealthy interests, especially the many Portuguese building owners, had much to lose from the demolition involved in any major rebuilding of Rio.

The 1902 election of President Rodrigues Alves, a Paulista, set the scene for a major campaign to attack this problem. The Rio mayor, Fran-

cisco Pereira Passos—also a Paulista—presided over a massive rebuilding of downtown Rio, including the construction of two wide boulevards branching out from the docks. To create the needed right of way,
590 buildings had to be demolished. Many of these structures (known
as *cortiços*, or tenements) had housed working-class families who were
now forced to find new housing, often much further from their work.
Whether intending to or not, the political elite was turning downtown
Rio into a "rabble free" zone that would impress the foreigner and keep
the "dangerous classes" at a distance.

There was now room to construct stately new public buildings, such
as the Biblioteca Nacional and the Teatro Municipal (modeled on the
Paris Opera). In their "European" style, they resembled new public structures recently erected in Buenos Aires and Mexico City. The Rio elite described this ambitious rebuilding program as "Rio civilizing itself." Yet
the rebuilding touched only the traditional downtown, doing nothing
for those in the *favelas* (shanty towns) already covering the hills in Rio.

The renovation of downtown Rio was accompanied by a major public health campaign, supervised by the noted medical administrator Oswaldo Cruz. The campaign's principal goal was eradication of the *Aedes
aegypti* mosquito, the carrier of yellow fever. (President Rodrigues Alves
had lost a child to the disease.) This required eliminating or treating all
standing water where mosquitoes could breed. The campaign aroused
impassioned opposition as the health officials (dubbed *mata mosquitos*,
or "mosquito killers") went from door to door. A simultaneous campaign
to require vaccination against smallpox provoked even stronger opposition, which managed to delay the campaign's start for five years. The
positivists were the most militant opponents, especially of compulsory
vaccination, which contradicted their concept of personal freedom. They
were joined by community organizers, who were reacting to the frequent
government invasions of their neighborhoods. Finally, the health campaign was seen by many Afro-Brazilians as aimed at liquidating their
African culture (traditional cures, etc.). In 1909, Oswaldo Cruz declared
Rio to be free from yellow fever and all other major epidemics. But subsequent statistics show that this did not apply to the poorer sections of
the city.

The public health crusaders hoped to extend their work into the interior, where disease and malnutrition were more serious than in the
major cities. Most of the resources, however, went to the coastal cities.
These contained the loudest political voices and were the best venue to
impress the foreigners.

"WHITENING" BRAZIL

In the effort to improve Brazil's image abroad, the elite were particularly concerned about race. Although the percentage of the population

classified as white in the Brazilian Census had increased between 1872 and 1890, the increase was modest and large proportions of Brazilians were still classified as black or mulatto in 1890. (See exhibit 4-3.) It was in the area of race that Brazilians felt especially disadvantaged vis-à-vis largely white Argentina, their prime South American rival.

In contemplating their position, the post-1870 Brazilian elite soon fell under the influence of European and North American doctrines of scientific racism, which pointed to biological and historical "evidence" to justify their claims of white superiority. These claims, in turn, underlay a new phase of European and United States territorial expansionism, as imperialism and racism went hand in hand. In the aftermath of its Civil War, the United States had even adopted a legal system ("Jim Crow") to keep the races physically separate in public places.

But Brazil could hardly hope to copy the United States in race relations, however much its elite might yearn to. Brazil was in a more vulnerable position (from the white viewpoint) because its nonwhite population far exceeded that of the United States as a proportion of the total population. How then could Brazil whiten itself? The elite believed the answer was through miscegenation, combined with high (natural) Afro-Brazilian mortality. In other words, the white Brazilians were betting primarily on race mixture, a process that horrified white North Americans, to gradually turn themselves into the equivalent of the superior race. In the words of João Batista de Lacerda, a leading doctor and anthropologist, "in the course of another century the mixed bloods will have disappeared from Brazil. This will coincide with the extinction of the black race in our midst." Lacerda's confident words were spoken at the "First Universal Race Congress" in London in 1911.

As the elite began accepting the theory of scientific racism, social reality took an ominous turn. The end of both slavery and the Empire had

EXHIBIT 4-3
Racial Composition of Brazil's Population, 1872 and 1890*

| | 1872 | | 1890 | |
	Number	*%*	*Number*	*%*
White	3,783,512	38.1	6,306,923	44.0
Mulatto	4,190,662	42.2	5,934,241	41.4
Black	1,956,304	19.7	2,092,752	14.6
TOTAL	9,930,478	100	14,333,915	100

*Excludes the indigenous population.
Source: Brazilian Censuses, 1872 and 1890.

cast race relations into a new light in the eyes of the victorious Republicans. Rio now loomed as a "black city" with a raucous culture that did not fit the ideas of the Europeanizing elite. Although little is known about this as yet, it appears that Brazilian society became institutionally more race conscious, in favor of whites, after the birth of the Republic, as mobility for non-white Brazilians apparently began to decline. The barriers were never legal, and therefore never comparable to Jim Crow in the United States. But unwritten color bars were observed, for example, in the Ministry of Foreign Affairs, the officer corps of the navy (the army was slightly better), and the higher levels of the Catholic church.

THE REALITY BEHIND THE FACADE

In the early 1900s, the vast majority of Brazilians (almost 84 percent in 1900) lived in the two main coastal areas—the Southeast and the Northeast—as they had throughout Brazil's history. Perceptive Brazilians could identify at least two Brazils: the coast and the interior. This historic pattern of settlement, once described as "crabs clinging to the coast," broke down only slowly, with the Southeast and the Northeast still accounting for over 70 percent of the population in 1991. (See exhibit 4-4.) Although there had long been important exceptions, such as the inland state of Minas Gerais, the vast majority of states bordered on the sea and most had as their capital city a coastal port. It was not that the elite lived exclusively in the coastal cities. Virtually all had family

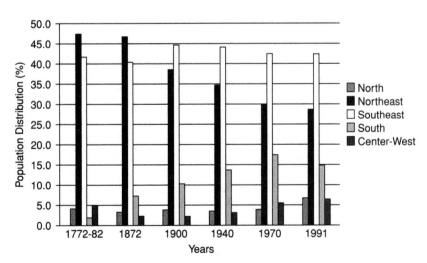

Exhibit 4-4. Distribution of Brazilian population by major regions, 1772–1991. From [1872–1970] Thomas W. Merrick and Douglas H. Graham, *Population and Economic Development* (Baltimore, 1979), p. 119, and [1991] Instituto Brasileiro de Geografia e Estatística, Diretoria de Pesquisas, Population Census.

connections with landowners and visited their farms and ranches in the agriculturally developed zones. But traveling to the distant and less settled interior was far less frequent.

The most dramatic illustration of this geographical divide between coast and interior was the military siege of Canudos in the 1890s. This interior town, several hundred miles from the state capital of Bahia, housed a religious community headed by a lay clergyman, popularly known as Antonio Conselheiro ("Anthony the Counselor"). In 1895, the community ran afoul of local authorities in a dispute over a failed delivery of wood. The townsmen killed several police in the resulting clash, and the Bahian state authorities called for federal help. Rio responded by ordering the federal army to end the trouble.

Although we do not know the exact nature of the community's religious orientation, they were self-proclaimed monarchists and were clearly prepared to defend their homes. They had good reason, since the authorities had virtually declared war on Canudos. The conflict escalated in stages. First, the state government of Bahia tried to subdue the community. When that failed, Bahian authorities enlisted the federal government, which was then being pressured by fanatical Jacobins (the label for extreme Republicans) in Rio who wanted to extinguish all traces of monarchism. The news that the Canudos resisters were monarchists only increased Jacobin demands that the national army intervene.

The federal army's initial attacks failed, as the Canudenses fought with unexpected ferocity. The army commanders had underestimated their enemy (who used guerrilla tactics) and overestimated themselves. Frustrated and humiliated, they redoubled their efforts, having to mount three expeditions before they could declare victory. In the end, it took Krupp canons to demolish the defenses. When the dust cleared, not a single male defender of Canudos had survived. The terrified women and children were herded together and shipped elsewhere. The human cost to the army was also heavy. Of the 12,000 soldiers who fought in the siege, 5,000 had been wounded or killed.

The three-year war of extermination at Canudos might have gone unnoticed by the rest of Brazil had it not been for Euclides da Cunha, the journalist- intellectual who immortalized it in his 1902 book *Rebellion in the Backlands* (*Os Sertões*). Euclides, a former army officer, was astounded by what he saw when he arrived from São Paulo to cover the unfolding story for *O Estado de S. Paulo*, the city's leading daily. He admired the defenders' military skills and their raw courage. At the same time, he was uneasy because, by the racist doctrines of the day, he had to regard the locals as half-breeds whose "unstable" nature boded ill for Brazil's future.

But Euclides's main message was about the gap between the politicians and bishops on the coast, who had an army to enforce their will, and the neglected masses of the interior. Euclides's book made a major impact on the small reading public, despite his dense prose. Any reader of *Os Sertões* could understand the desperation that had driven the Canudenses to revere their preacher and defend their homes. Antonio Conselheiro was, after all, a lay preacher filling the void created by the failure of the church to staff its parishes in the interior. And many who never read it knew its story, especially since army officials loudly attacked the author for highlighting their incompetence.

The existence, let alone the fate, of Brazil's indigenous people, like most people of the distant interior, was virtually ignored by coast-dwelling Brazilians at the turn of the century. A pioneering Brazilian ethnographer wrote in 1913 that "even now . . . the census takers do not reach the savages of the wild interior, and quite recently Colonel Rondon discovered in the state of Mato Grosso a numerous tribe of which only the name, and that vaguely, had been known." The intermittent European-Indian coexistence of the early colonial days was long past. The Indians had been assimilated, annihilated, or pushed beyond the margins of Portuguese (and later, Brazilian) settlement. As a result, the Indian was as exotic a figure for most Brazilians as he was for the schoolchildren of Europe and North America. In the words of John Hemming, an English expert on the history of the Brazilian indigenous, "Indians were becoming curiosities rather than a serious threat."

The Indian reappeared in Brazilian official thought in the early twentieth century through the efforts of dedicated public officials such as Cândido Rondon, an army officer and a positivist. Rondon first encountered Indian settlements in his role as an army officer on assignment to build telegraph lines through the interior. He decided to devote himself to the protection of the remaining "unassimilated" Indians. In 1910, he became the first director of the Service for the Protection of the Indians (SPI) and laid down strict guidelines for its operation. The SPI's mission was the difficult one of bringing basic services (health care, education) to the Indians without destroying their culture or social structure. This noble ambition was bound to collide with other Brazilians' determination to destroy any Indian who blocked their way to the land, minerals, or animals they wanted. It was an unequal contest, and the Indian population continued to decline.

The drama of opening up the vast interior attracted attention abroad. The early decades of the twentieth century brought to Brazil a wave of foreign explorers drawn by the stories of the country's natural and material riches. In 1913, former U.S. president Theodore Roosevelt arrived for an epic trip down the Dúvida (now Roosevelt) River, accompanied by Rondon. Roosevelt, ever the adept of challenging physical feats, plunged into his jungle adventure, ending up with a broken leg and a near fatal fever. On his return to the United States he sang the praises of Rondon and wrote a stirring account (*Through the Brazilian Wilderness*, 1914) of his perilous journey. His enthusiastic description of Brazil's resources was a reaction typical of the many Americans and Europeans who were now discovering the country's economic potential. Meanwhile, Rondon continued his exploration of the interior, surveying vast stretches of the Brazilian frontier.

Brazil now saw a succession of scientists who attempted to take an inventory of the inland expanse and its social problems. "Brazil is a vast hospital," was the gloomy diagnosis from one. Perhaps the most famous was Carlos Chagas, a brilliant medical researcher who helped eradicate malaria in several regions. He is best known for conquering in 1909 a deadly disease that bears his name (Chagas Disease), and had been killing and blinding its victims in the interior. He identified the carrier (a beetle that lives in walls and ceilings of mud dwellings) and spent a great deal of effort educating public authorities about how to fight the carrier and the disease.

Pioneers such as Rondon and Chagas led a growing attempt to educate the public to understand that so many Brazilians were so unproductive because of disease caused by unmet medical and sanitary needs. And the efforts of these pioneers would lead to major health campaigns in the 1910s and 1920s, campaigns that helped thoughtful Brazilians challenge the determinist racial and climatic theories that had so often dominated the elite's discussions of Brazil's place in the world.

Coffee Fluctuations, Emerging Industry, and Urban Labor

The explosion in coffee production that had caused the Brazilian economy to boom in the mid to late nineteenth century turned into a liability in the early twentieth century, when the world coffee market ran a surplus, primarily because of Brazilian overproduction. Export earnings declined with drops in coffee prices abroad, a decline that was exacerbated by an increase since 1898 in the exchange value of the Brazilian currency (due to an increase in foreign capital inflow). Since Brazil was by far the world's largest coffee producer (75 percent of world production in 1900–01), the temptation was natural for the Brazilians to use their market power to try to manipulate the price. (The Brazilian term for this was "valorization.") With that goal in mind, the governors of its three leading coffee-producing states—São Paulo, Rio de Janeiro, and Minas Gerais—signed a valorization agreement in 1906 known as the Treaty of Taubaté, which aimed to limit production and exports in the hope of raising international coffee prices to pre-1900 levels by withholding Brazilian coffee (production had doubled in 1906) from the market. The large expense of storage was partially covered by foreign loans, which the federal government began to guarantee in 1907. This agreement did not raise prices but it could have been a factor in preventing them from declining more. (See exhibit 4-5 for fluctuations in the quantity and international value of coffee exports between 1870 and 1910.) It was also a sign that Brazilian politicians and planters were willing to use government power to interfere with the operations of the market, both world and domestic, more than their laissez- faire rhetoric would suggest. Other examples abound. In the years between 1889 and 1930, the federal government ended up acquiring—primarily as rescue operations—and operating such important enterprises as the Banco do Brasil, Lloyd Brasileiro (shipping), and a number of railways.

Most underdeveloped economies have either continued to depend largely on primary products for their export earnings or have failed in their efforts to industrialize. This was not the fate of Brazil.

EXHIBIT 4-5
Brazilian Coffee Exports

	Quantity (per thousand 60kg. sacks)	International Value per Thousand Sacks (thousand lbs. gold)
1870–71	3.8	7.8
1880–81	3.7	11.6
1890	5.1	17.9
1895	6.7	22.4
1900	9.2	18.9
1901	14.8	24.0
1902	13.2	20.3
1903	12.9	19.1
1904	10.0	20.0
1905	10.8	21.4
1906	14.0	27.6
1907	15.7	28.6
1908	12.7	23.0
1909	16.9	33.5
1910	9.7	26.7

Source: IBGE, *Estatísticas Históricas do Brasil*, 2nd ed. (Rio de Janeiro, 1990), p. 350.

THE ROOTS OF INDUSTRIALIZATION

Brazil had been creating industry, on a small scale, since the early nineteenth century. Its tactic was to manufacture for domestic consumption those products for which costs were lower than the competing imports. By and large these were products whose value was low in proportion to their weight—making their price as imports particularly exorbitant relative to their true value. Soap, construction materials, and beverages were prime examples. Textiles were another area for early industrialization, since their needed capital equipment was relatively inexpensive to import. Most capital goods and technology-intensive products—such as railroad rails, locomotives, turbines, and field artillery—continued to be imported for many years to come, paid for by export earnings primarily from coffee and natural rubber. Foreign firms often supplied the necessary electric power for the industrializing sector. For example, Light and Power, a Canadian firm, supplied electricity in Rio and São Paulo.

Industrialization occurred largely without government support until about 1930, most of the political elite believed that industrialization was against Brazil's long-run economic interests. Here they were repeating the doctrines of their creditors in Europe and North America, who were still schooled in the doctrines of Manchester liberalism—i.e., a belief in free market economics, with minimal government intervention and a reliance on free trade. Brazilian tariffs, for example, were intended primarily to produce revenues, not to protect domestic industry (approximately 70 percent of federal revenues came from import duties between 1890 and 1910). Furthermore, there was no strong industrial bourgeoisie to press its claims with the politicians. Even when presidents such as Floriano Peixoto in the 1890s or Afonso Pena in the early 1900s engaged in pro-industry rhetoric, they were far from ready to take the comprehensive steps (monetary policy, allocation of foreign exchange) required to give their words substance.

In spite of doctrinal beliefs, however, industrialization proceeded, albeit modestly, largely as an unintended consequence of other government policies (especially on exchange rates), which, though usually designed to protect the primary goods export sector, helped the domestic industrialists. It is true that an ostensibly high tariff was instituted in 1895, followed by a more modest tariff in 1900, which remained in force until 1930. But tariffs were never intended to jeopardize Brazil's "agricultural vocation," as the coffee growers and their apologists liked to describe it.

An ambitious industrialization policy would have required much more than higher tariffs. It would have required ample credit, an efficient financial system, incentives for capital goods imports, and increased investment in human capital (especially education) and infrastructure. Such a comprehensive policy, which Germany and Japan were then pursuing, was never even a question for the overwhelming majority of the Brazilian elite. Nonetheless, by 1910, São Paulo, for example, was on the path that would make it by the 1960s the largest industrial park in the developing world. As the leader in modernization, São Paulo was also in the vanguard as measured by such modernization criteria as public education, sanitary facilities, and transportation. This gave Paulistas a sense of superiority with respect to the rest of Brazil. In fact, though, other parts of Brazil were making slow progress on the industrialization front, primarily the Center-South states of Rio de Janeiro and Minas Gerais and a few regions outside that area, notably Bahia in the Northeast.

Industrialists, a high proportion of whom were of Italian or Lebanese descent, were often overshadowed politically by the export-import merchants who operated through powerful commercial associations. Not infrequently, however, merchant and industrialist overlapped, as in the case of Francisco Matarazzo (1854–1937), an Italian immigrant who was involved in both importing and manufacturing. After arriving in São Paulo in 1881, he first established a foodstuff-importing firm and then began to manufacture containers for distribution of his food imports within Brazil. There were not only links between industrialists and export-import merchants but also between those two groups and the bankers. And merchants and bankers were also linked to the coffee growers. The resulting web of contacts was extremely important in facilitating the transfer of a capital surplus from agriculture to the emerging industrial sector, just as the infant industry theory of development would have prescribed.

Brazilian factory owners, like their capitalist counterparts everywhere, faced the need to enforce worker discipline. Brazilian workers, many of whom came from the countryside, had to be taught to adapt to the process of mass production, which meant the tyranny of the clock. Employers often preferred immigrant workers, who were sometimes better trained in the rhythms of urban work. In fact, however, most of the industrial workplaces were relatively small. Metalworking, for example, was dominated by shops of less than ten employees. In these cases, the ambiance was not one of mass employment but something closer to the intimacy of small agricultural units. Large-scale factories were restricted to a few industries, especially textiles.

A further problem was illiteracy. Since most native-born Brazilians, especially of rural background, lacked basic schooling, they could not follow written instructions. This deficiency favored immigrants, who were more likely to be at least minimally literate.

The working conditions and pay in Brazilian factories left much to be desired by modern standards. The textile industry, for example, which employed mostly women, made its employees work long hours in poorly ventilated plants. It is worth remembering, however, that in this era working conditions in Europe and North America were also, by today's criteria, grossly substandard. Laws to protect workers were passed in Britain only around the First World War and even later in the United States. It is also far from clear that urban working conditions were worse than those facing agricultural workers. Brazilian factory workers in major cities such as São Paulo and Rio enjoyed one advantage over all other workers in Brazil. They had better access to government services and better prospects for their children's mobility (even if still pretty limited).

Most urban workers were not, however, employed in industry. Even in the major urban centers of São Paulo and Rio de Janeiro, most worked in the service sector or the informal sector. Service workers, who included shop clerks, trolley drivers, household domestics, and building custodians, often faced a work routine as unrelenting as that of the factory. Service workers in small family-owned businesses worked at the pleasure of their employer and had little recourse in case of arbitrary treatment by employers.

The informal sector included street peddlers, washerwomen, messenger boys, prostitutes, petty thieves, and vagrant handymen. Many came directly from the countryside and returned there when times got bad in the city. They escaped enumeration in the census unless they turned up on the police blotter, and lived outside the realm of formal regulations and structures. Workers in the informal sector aroused particular anxiety among the elite. Politicians and journalists frequently attacked them as "the dangerous classes," always ready to revolt. They were the target of regular police repression and received little mercy from the court system.

WORKER ORGANIZATION AND EMPLOYERS' STRATEGY

Brazil's first labor unions appeared in the 1880s, among the dock workers and the railway workers. Not coincidentally, they emerged at the same time as the arrival of immigrant workers who had union experience in Spain and Italy. These unions, relatively and not surprisingly weak, were led primary by anarcho-syndicalists who hoped to end all formal organization of the workplace in the long run and believed a utopia would arrive when the workers had gained full control. In the meantime, the anarcho-syndicalists fought for better working conditions, higher pay, and worker organization as the key to radical democracy. Their chief rivals were the socialists, who thought only an eventual socialist government would solve the workers' problems, but fought, meanwhile, for short-term concessions. Local political differences influenced the fortunes of the two groups, with the anarcho-syndicalists dominating in São Paulo and the socialists dominating in Rio.

Any labor union organizers of this era faced serious obstacles. First, they were constantly repressed by the government and the police, who consistently supported the employers whatever the particular issue of the moment. More important was the enormous vulnerability of the workers themselves, who knew there were masses of other applicants (the immigrants from the countryside) for their jobs. Industrial workers who challenged their employers could be, and were, summarily fired and replaced by new hires. The mere threat of such action was often enough to maintain discipline. Given such a labor surplus, especially the potential in-migrants from the countryside, this was no idle threat. The work of union organizers was also made more difficult by the overwhelmingly rural background of Brazilian workers. The rural sector had a strong tradition of deference to elites. The concept of collective action, such as striking, was not easy to sell to these workers, especially if it meant lost wages. Finally, fear of retaliation was rife. Employers routinely blacklisted labor organizers and circulated their names to other employers. Furthermore, police tactics against strikers were extremely harsh. When, for example, São Paulo railway workers struck to protest a 10 percent wage cut in 1906, they were met with mass arrests and military intervention on the trains. Given the prospect of permanent loss of income, workers hesitated to follow their union leaders. Given these obstacles, it is hardly surprising that organized labor was a minor force at best in the Brazil of 1910, although it had the potential for growth and increased power in the future.

Brazilian urban employers followed the same management logic as their counterparts in the North Atlantic economies. They wanted to keep wages as low as possible, in which they were aided by the fact that virtually no benefits (health, pensions, etc.) were routinely provided. The concept that employees were also consumers, vital to the growth of the economy—as capitalists were beginning to understand in the United States and Western Europe—had not yet penetrated South America. Consumption above the minimum remained the privilege of a small stratum. There were, as elsewhere, rare "enlightened" employers—Jorge Street, a São Paulo factory owner, was one of these, but his paternalistic policies (such as employer-furnished housing) were rarely duplicated. Employers typically harbored racist attitudes and doubted their workers could ever rise above menial tasks. Conspicuously missing was an appropriate recognition of the value of skilled labor, not only for industry but also for the multiple tasks of a modern economy. While the industrialized countries (and Argentina) were pouring money into public education at the turn of the century, Brazil continued to neglect this basic form of resource development. In 1900, only about one-quarter of the population was classified as literate. In 1920, the proportion was essentially the same. The result was a shortage of skilled labor, which reinforced the lack of capital needed for the operation of a more advanced industrial society. In a crisis such as a strike, employers relied upon the power of the police bludgeon to maintain worker discipline. The coercive world of the plantation big house had given way to the almost equally coercive urban workplace.

EVAPORATION OF THE OLIGARCHICAL CONSENSUS

The Republican political system had operated smoothly since the emperor's bloodless overthrow in 1889 because of the cooperation of the principal state governors. The dominant political machines in each state were led by the Republican parties, which included some former Liberal and Conservative party members who chose to support the Republic. As long as there was agreement among these state machines, they could deliver the popular vote necessary to win a national presidential election for the official candidate.

But trouble began when the officially designated candidate for the 1910 presidential election, Governor João Pinheiro of Minas Gerais, died in 1908. The Republican party bosses of the leading states could not agree upon a new candidate, leading to the first seriously contested presidential election of the Republic. The official nomination went to a general, Marshall Hermes da Fonseca. He ran as a civilian (having retired from the army) but was soon accused of heading a military conspiracy to subvert civilian rule. He did not help his cause by his stubborn refusal to quit wearing his uniform. His prime accuser—and campaign opponent—was Senator Rui Barbosa, chief author of the 1891 Constitution and the country's leading orator and legal mind.

Rui was a throwback to the liberal political tradition of the Empire. As a prime representative of the legalistic culture that had long produced utopian interpretations of Brazilian reality, he saw Brazil as a liberal democracy where human rights and the rule of law should and could prevail. Rui's Brazil, of course, was not the Brazil of Canudos or of the São Paulo factories. His accusation that the official candidate was a military threat infuriated many army officers, who felt their professional honor had been impugned. By framing the choice as between military and civilian government, Rui had raised a red herring. There was in fact no danger of a military takeover at the federal level. The real danger of political instability was at the state level.

Irresponsible though it may have been, Rui's campaign tactic successfully cast him as a courageous lawyer defending constitutionalism against would-be tyrants. Although Rui lost the election, he reinforced the appeal of the kind of abstract legalism so evident among the abolitionists. In fact, Rui spoke eloquently also of the "social question," but that was lost amid his charges of militarism, which cast him as the ultimate *bacharel*, the erudite lawyer armed with endless legal formulae and a precarious hold on political reality.

A MESSAGE FROM BELOW

In 1910, the elite view of a harmonious Brazil was again shaken from another quarter: The navy enlisted men revolted. The navy was one of the most racially segregated institutions in early twentieth-century Brazil. The officer corps was entirely white and the enlisted ranks virtually all black or mulatto—segregation that resulted not from any legal provision (as in the United States) but from custom.

Whipping was commonly used to discipline enlisted men—a brutal practice that continued even though it had been outlawed briefly by federal decree in 1889. The mutiny began as a protest against whipping but soon grew into a full-scale revolt. The black sailors overpowered their white officers and seized control of two dreadnoughts (the *Minas Gerais* and the *São Paulo*) that were anchored in the Rio harbor. Taking command, the sailors maneuvered the ships around the bay, threatening to shell the city if their demands were not met. Unfortunately for Foreign Minister Baron Rio Branco, the mutiny coincided with the presence of distinguished foreign visitors, including Lord Bryce, the noted English constitutional scholar. Bryce later wrote, "we were lunching at the Ministry of Foreign Affairs . . . when suddenly the heavy boom of the guns was heard, and continued at intervals all through the repast." Rio Branco's attempts to sell his visitors on Brazilian progress had suffered an embarrassing setback.

The Rio elite, aghast at the menacing sight of the dreadnoughts and their guns, were both stunned and impressed by the mutiny. On the one hand, they were ashamed to have such a "barbaric" eruption occurring in their supposedly Europeanized city—a threat, moreover, that came from Afro- Brazilians, whom the elite wanted to eliminate through whitening. On the other hand, they were amazed at the navigational skills of the black sailors. Where had they learned to command these ships? How could supposed illiterates direct such complex vessels?

Naval officers negotiated a truce with the rebels, guaranteeing them fair treatment—a promise that was not kept. Instead, the rebels were herded off to an isolated island (appropriately named Snake Island) to face torture and lengthy imprisonment. The navy had answered the black sailors' protest with repression, the response perfected so well over the centuries of slavery. Rui Barbosa attacked the unconstitutionality and immorality of the government's behavior in a blistering speech in the Senate in May 1911, thereby deepening the growing rift between civilian and military.

ECONOMIC STRAINS

As the nineteenth century turned into the twentieth, Brazil ran into problems with its primary export earners, coffee and natural rubber. Coffee earnings had become unreliable, as we have seen, when coffee devel-

EXHIBIT 4-6
Quantity and Value of Natural Rubber Exports, 1900–1920

Year	Quantity (tons)	Percent Growth in Quantity	Percent Growth in Value
1900	24,302	16.9	6.1
1901	30,241	24.4	32.7
1902	28,632	−5.3	−15.5
1903	31,717	10.8	33.5
1904	31,866	0.5	15.3
1905	35,393	11.1	28.5
1906	34,960	−1.2	−2.5
1907	36,490	4.4	−2.6
1908	38,206	4.7	−13.9
1909	39,027	2.1	60.6
1910	38,547	−1.2	30.2
1911	36,547	−5.2	−38.9
1912	42,286	15.7	6.9
1913	36,232	−14.3	−35.5
1914	33,531	−7.5	−31.9
1915	35,165	4.9	−0.3
1916	31,495	−10.4	6.5
1917	33,998	7.9	−0.2
1918	22,662	−33.3	−46.6
1919	33,252	46.7	42.2
1920	23,586	−29.1	−51.8

Source: IBGE, *Estatísticas Históricas do Brasil*, 2nd ed. (Rio de Janeiro, 1990), p. 347.

oped a surplus on the world market. Brazil's response—to hold part of its production off the market—was only partly successful. Although the strategy made sense in theory, it had two defects. First, by maintaining high prices it attracted other coffee producers, especially Central and South American, into the market. Second, the profits were diverted, much going to coffee brokers based outside of Brazil, and some to the bankers and the federal government.

Brazilian problems with its rubber monopoly were of a different sort. Rubber was a product unique to the huge trees of the Amazon forest, and was now in heavy demand to make tires for the rapidly growing number of internal combustion engine vehicles in Europe and the United States. Between 1900 and 1910, Brazil was the world's only natural rubber exporter, but it lost its monopoly on this export when the British and Dutch planted their own rubber trees in the East Indies. (See exhibit 4-6 for the trend in Brazil's rubber exports between 1900 and 1920.) A publicity-seeking English adventurer, Henry Wickham, later claimed to have smuggled out a shipment of Brazilian rubber tree seeds and delivered them to the hands of British growers. In any case, the Brazilians' hold on the world rubber market was broken.

These difficulties by no means neutralized Brazil's long-term growth. Indeed, Brazil's economic growth between 1850 and 1913 was relatively high by international standards, averaging 2.4 percent (constant prices) a year. (The average annual growth for Western Europe and North America from 1870 to 1913 was 2.7 percent). The difficulty was that Brazil's population, thanks partly to immigration, was growing almost as rapidly, averaging 2.2 percent a year. Thus, Brazil's per capita growth—the crucial measure of the economy's capacity to raise the standard of living—was significantly lower than the overall growth rate of the economy. In fact, the gross domestic product per capita (measured in constant terms) in 1913 was actually slightly less than it had been in 1870. (See exhibit 4-7.)

None of the possible options for increasing Brazil's economic growth seemed open to Brazilian policy makers around the turn of the century.

EXHIBIT 4-7
Population and Gross Domestic Product (GDP), 1850–1913

	1880 (base year) = 100				Annual Percentage Rate of Growth			
	1850	1870	1889	1913	1851–1870	1871–1889	1890–1913	1851–1913
Population	61	82	119	214	1.5	2.0	2.5	2.2
GDP (@ current prices)	24	78	119	442	6.1	2.1	5.9	4.7
Total GDP (@ constant prices)	49	85	108	220	2.8	1.3	3.0	2.4
GDP per capita (@ constant prices)	80	104	91	103	1.3	−0.7	0.5	0.4

Source: Raymond W. Goldsmith, *Brasil 1850–1984: Desenvolvimento Fincanceiro sob um Século de Inflação* (São Paulo, 1986), p. 134.

The first option would have been to slow down population growth by reducing immigration or by encouraging smaller families, but this option was unthinkable in the Brazil of 1900. The elite fervently believed in increasing their country's population as fast as possible. Brazil's problem, they argued, was a *falta de braços* ("lack of arms"). Restricting population growth was precisely the opposite of what policy makers thought Brazil needed.

Another option would have been to accelerate growth, so as to overcome the drag of a rapidly growing population. Here Brazil faced a clear limit. Brazil's capacity to increase its exports, and therefore its domestic growth rate, was limited by its foreign markets. As was becoming clear by 1910, growth in those markets was not rapid enough to sustain the growth in exports Brazil needed to increase significantly its per capita growth rate. The gamble on export-led growth was not meeting expectations.

A third approach to higher growth would have been to concentrate on the domestic market by channeling investment into sectors that produced for domestic consumption, but such a strategy would have run into two difficulties immediately. Firstly, Brazil lacked the technology and the capital goods needed for massive industrialization (as opposed to the moderate level achieved). In addition, the prevailing economic ideology of Manchester-style liberalism, widely endorsed by the Brazilian elite, strongly condemned attempted industrialization in "peripheral" countries such as Brazil. Further, there was powerful opposition to industrialization from the urban merchants, who had an obvious stake in maintaining Brazil's dependence on imported finished goods.

Even if Brazil had chosen to concentrate on its domestic markets, it would have needed to make massive investment. Since exports would almost certainly not have generated the surplus capital needed to finance that investment, the capital would have had to come from within Brazil. But that would have required extraordinary high domestic savings rates. Such savings would have required sharply reduced consumption, something few democracies, either then or since, have ever achieved.

All of this is not to say that these options were inherently impossible in the decades after the Republic's creation in 1889. Rather, it is to say that the historic odds were heavily against adoption of policies that could have increased economic growth per capita fast enough to close the gap in living standards between Brazil and the North Atlantic industrial economies.

5 World War I, the Great Depression, and Dictatorship: 1910–45

The Brazilian elite had always admired and imitated Europe, so the outbreak of World War I came as a shock. It also provided a catalyst to the efforts of the nascent nationalist movement in Brazil to spread the doctrine that Brazil could only survive and prosper by recognizing and playing on the separateness of its identity.

Partly as a result of this nationalist pressure, Brazil followed the United States in a tardy entry into the war on the side of the Allies. Brazil's hopes that such an act would increase its influence on the world stage were dashed, but the postwar economic surge did help Brazil industrialize, albeit unevenly. The economic bubble burst, as it did everywhere else, with the crash of 1929, although Brazil recovered faster than most countries in the wake of the Great Depression.

Along with increased industrialization came increased discontent with domestic politics. This expressed itself as a growing repudiation of the liberal belief that democracy was the best protector of individual liberties and the economic interests of all. And indeed, democracy in Brazil in the early twentieth century was fraught with the suspicion, and the reality, of voter fraud.

In 1930, the military, playing on these critiques of democracy, took power in a coup that was as bloodless as most Brazilian military takeovers and installed Getúlio Vargas as dictator. A consummate political strategist, Vargas kept popularity as well as power through the 1930s and World War II, in which Brazil again intervened on the side of the Allies. During much of this period, he built a corporatist state (one based on a hierarchical, organic view of society)—in particular, a corporatist labor movement, with symmetrical associations of employees and workers and the state as arbiter between them—that provided an important part of the built-in support he needed to remain in power.

Victory over Hitler and Mussolini, however, exposed the inherent contradiction between fighting authoritarianism abroad while practicing it at home. The army persuaded Vargas to leave power (again without bloodshed) in 1945.

The Shock of World War I

The Brazilian elite had believed in Europe as a cosmopolitan, politically stable, mature model for Latin America. They had imbibed its philosophies, embraced its literature, and celebrated its great men. Despite copying the U.S. constitutional structure, Brazil's soul was still European. Suddenly, the peace of a century was shattered. (The last continental conflict in Europe had been the Napoleonic Wars that ended in 1815.) The European powers slid into a horrifying war of attrition as millions of conscripted soldiers died or were mutilated in battles over seemingly meaningless meters of mud.

For the first three years of the war, Brazil remained neutral. Most Brazilians favored the Allied side, not surprising given the elite's strong identification with France. One other Brazilian faction, a distinct minority, favored Germany. This movement, with strong links to the German colony in the South of Brazil, argued for Brazilian neutrality. In addition, although the army as a whole did not have a position, certain senior military officers favored Germany. This position sprang partly from the pragmatic judgment that the German military was the best in Europe—an impression strengthened by the experience of thirty-two Brazilian officers who had trained with the German army between 1906 and 1912. Whether favoring or not favoring Germany, the military as a whole were happy to participate in, and even stimulate, discussion of Brazil's possible mobilization, believing that it could only help them in their battles for increased budgets.

Also fanning the flames of the debate over Brazil's intervention were two recently formed civic associations which argued that Brazil must make its own way in the world—contradicting the elite cosmopolitanism typical of the Republic. The first of these was the Liga da Defesa Nacional, with the prominent poet Olavo Bilac as patron. Founded in 1912, it had close links to the army and was dedicated to creating civilian support for the military, especially on such issues as compulsory military service and increased appropriations. The second was the Liga Nacionalista, which was founded in July 1917, was centered in São Paulo, and was focused less narrowly on the interests of the military.

Brazil, like the United States, was jolted out of its passivity by the German high command's 1917 decision to launch unrestricted submarine warfare in the Atlantic. The Brazilian Congress finally chose to join the Allies, making Brazil the only Latin American belligerent in the Great War.

As the European war dragged on and German submarines closed the Atlantic sealanes, Brazil, like the rest of Latin America, was cut off from its principal trading partners. Before the war, Brazil had had little incentive to pursue trade relations with other Latin American countries, since all produced primary products and all needed to import finished goods from the North Atlantic industrial economies. Now the war had deprived Brazil, along with its neighbors, of its regular supply of industrial goods. (See exhibit 5-1.) Furthermore, its exports were blocked by German submarines, reducing its ability to earn the foreign exchange needed to pay for imports.

Historians have long argued that the restriction of trade caused by World War I stimulated Brazilian industrialization. Recent research has shown, however, that the supply of imported capital goods, such as machine tools, was not and could not have been replaced by domestic production. Thus, the drop in sophisticated capital imports brought on by the war actually delayed further industrialization. Yet there was a positive aspect: The foreign exchange accumulated during the war later helped finance the surge of capital goods purchases after 1918.

The war in Europe also raised questions for the elite about the future political reliability of the Brazilian labor force. The collapse of Czarist Russia had opened the way to power for the Bolsheviks in that vast country. Their Communist comrades also took power briefly in Munich, southern Germany's major city. Marxist intellectuals in Europe were using this evidence to declare that the war had brought the beginning of the end of capitalism in Europe. Could Brazil remain immune to this radical message?

EXHIBIT 5-1
Brazilian Imports of Industrial Equipment, 1870–1925

Years	Pounds Sterling*
1890	819,011
1895	985,722
1900	535,963
1905	891,185
1910	1,733,234
1912	2,693,600
1914	1,157,885
1916	375,121
1918	424,971
1920	1,271,030
1925	2,609,991

*At 1913 prices.

Source: IBGE, Estatísticas Históricas do Brasil, 2nd ed. (Rio de Janeiro, 1990), p. 385.

The Brazilian elite hoped their entry into the war would bring their country world status. Argentina, Brazil's big rival on the international stage, had remained neutral, partly out of a desire to avoid joining any alliance with England and the United States. Brazil's material commitment was admittedly minimal, limited to a hospital unit sent to France, along with a few officers who saw combat with the French army. Even so, Brazilian politicians and intellectuals thought that their action, contrasting so sharply with Argentina's, would increase their influence among the North Atlantic democracies.

Brazilian diplomats and politicians alike were convinced that the next step would be a seat on the Permanent Council of the newly founded League of Nations. (Gaining that seat was a "question of national dignity," in the words of Brazilian president Artur Bernardes.) The Brazilians launched a vigorous campaign but ultimately failed to win the seat, partly because of opposition (expressed through ugly infighting) from the other Latin American delegations. Frustrated in its campaign to win a permanent seat, Brazil withdrew from the League in 1926 in protest. It would take more than a tardy entry into a distant war to make Brazil a major power.

The Economy After the War

The First World War dramatized a change in the pattern of world trade that had begun before 1914. Most important was the relative decline in Britain's world economic position vis-à-vis Germany and the United States. Britain had to spend much of its overseas investment to finance the war effort. Furthermore, British technology, industrial skills, and productivity were all lagging behind the United States and Germany. The momentum sustaining Britain's rise to world economic predominance in the nineteenth century had irretrievably slowed. It was still Brazil's primary foreign investor, but it was losing ground, especially in industry. During the course of the 1920s, U.S. and German investment in Brazilian industry rose significantly, with the United States going from $50 million in 1914 to $557 million in 1930. This represented a more than eightfold increase in the U.S. share of total foreign investment in Brazil. Brazil's fortunes in the competition for foreign investment would from now on depend increasingly on the United States and Germany.

Although the Brazilian economy came out of the war years with high inflation, the economy proved remarkably resilient in the 1920s. Brazil was still heavily dependent on coffee exports, just as it had been before the First World War. Fortunately, world prices for Brazil's exports started to climb in 1923 and had more than doubled by 1925, a level maintained with only a slight decline until the crash of 1929. These high prices enabled Brazil to increase its imports by 150 percent between 1922 and 1929. In the same period, Brazilian industry was able to double its imports of capital goods (the essential element for further industrialization). What these data tell us is that Brazil was using much of its export earnings to finance the imports needed for industrialization. In other words, Brazil was diversifying its economy away from dependence on agriculture.

The rapid growth of industry in the 1920s created the opportunity for more effective organization of the urban labor unions. In fact, however, unions continued to be weak for reasons discussed earlier—the small scale of most workplaces, the surplus supply of workers, and, most notably, the unending repression of union activity by employers, police, and government.

One of the most significant developments within labor and the left was the founding of the Brazilian Communist Party (PCB) in 1922. The PCB subsequently succeeded in recruiting many of the former anarcho-syndicalists, who had dominated urban labor organization before the war. By 1930, the PCB was to become the best-organized force on the left.

The economic bubble burst when the world capitalist economy collapsed in 1929. The price of coffee, which still earned 70 percent of Brazil's foreign exchange, began to fall even before the Wall Street crash of October 1929, declining 50 percent between September 1929 and January 1930. Brazil lost all its foreign exchange reserves in a few months as traders cashed in their Brazilian currency for gold, dollars, or sterling. The government's commitment to orthodox economics had led it to guarantee conversion of Brazilian currency at a fixed rate, virtually ensuring the exhaustion of the country's foreign exchange reserves in such an unstable financial climate.

Brazil, along with the rest of Latin America, now faced bleak prospects. The collapse of capitalism at its center in Europe and the United States had left the peripheral economies, such as Brazil, with no formula for recovery. Brazilian policymakers, like their counterparts elsewhere in Latin America, entered a policy vacuum, as experts from London and New York advised them to apply new and stronger doses of economic orthodoxy—a major ingredient of which was to cut government spending and balance the budget.

More through inadvertence than design, the Brazilian government failed to follow the prescribed treatment. Federal expenditures continued to increase and budget deficits were as ubiquitous in the 1930s in Brazil as they were during World War II. (See exhibit 5-2.) One particularly large expenditure was for buying excess coffee stocks that had resulted from overplanting in the 1920s (coffee plants take seven years to mature, making predictions of future demand virtually impossible) and the drop in world demand with the world crash in 1929. The government's intent was to pacify the angry planters at home while boosting

EXHIBIT 5-2
Receipts and Expenditures of the Brazilian Federal Government, 1910–45

Fiscal Year	Receipts mil-reis	Expenditures mil-reis	Surplus/Deficit mil-reis
1927	2,039,506	2,025,959	13,547
1928	2,216,513	2,350,107	−133,594
1929	2,201,246	2,422,393	−221,147
1930	1,677,952	2,510,544	−832,592
1931	1,752,665	2,046,620	−293,955
1932	1,750,790	2,859,668	−1,108,878
1933	2,078,476	2,391,813	−313,337
1934	2,519,530	3,050,188	−530,658
1935	2,722,693	2,872,001	−149,308
1936	3,127,460	3,226,081	−98,621
1937	3,462,476	4,143,959	−681,483
1938	3,879,768	4,735,434	−855,666
1939	4,352,809	4,850,338	−497,529
1940	4,644,813	5,188,986	−544,173
1941	4,765,084	5,438,389	−673,305
1942	4,987,728	6,343,206	−1,355,478
1943	6,010,972	6,512,235	−501,263
1944	8,311,049	8,399,164	−88,115
1945	9,845,154	10,839,323	−994,169

Source: Armin K. Ludwig, *Brazil: A Handbook of Historical Statistics* (Boston, 1985), p. 353.

coffee prices abroad. The result, as a product of monetary expansion, was to stimulate overall demand in the Brazilian economy and thus spark an early recovery in Brazil—a recovery that was quicker and stronger than that in the United States. It also brought a new stimulus to Brazilian industrialization. It is tempting to credit the emerging Keynesian doctrines with this result, but John Maynard Keynes had yet to publish his *General Theory* and he was unknown in Brazil. With foreign exchange scarce enough to make imports prohibitively expensive, Brazilian industrialists were presented with a protected national market. Their domestic supply of capital goods was also larger than during the First

World War, thus giving an alternative source for many of the industrial goods that had previously been imported.

BRAZIL'S UNEVEN DEVELOPMENT

The economic diversification following World War I had extremely uneven effects. Industrialization was concentrated in the south and southeast, especially in the triangle formed by the states of Minas Gerais, Rio de Janeiro, and São Paulo. When the First World War began, Rio still had more industry than São Paulo, but in the 1920s São Paulo overtook it once and for all, increasing that state's share of Brazilian industry from 15.9 percent in 1907 to 45.4 percent in 1937.

Between 1900 and 1940, Brazil continued to see a significantly regional shift in its population. Most striking was the decline in the Northeast's relative share (from 38.7 percent to 35 percent) and the increased share of the South (from 10.3 percent to 13.9 percent). Although the Southeastern share was virtually constant (going from 44.9 percent to 44.5 percent), that population's education and skills had improved disproportionally.

While the Southeast and South were making economic progress, the Northeast and the North (especially the Amazon Basin) suffered a decline in the 1920s and 1930s. Sugar, which had been the economic basis of the Northeast, proved less and less competitive on the international market, and no other crop appeared to replace it in sufficient quantity. Although the Northeast's share of the population decreased (from 38.7 percent in 1900 to 35 percent in 1940), its absolute population remained large and highly fertile. This meant a widening gap between the resource base and the population in that area.

The Amazon Basin was another area on the margin of development. It had earlier enjoyed a boom based on natural rubber, but that bubble burst in 1912 when competing sources of natural rubber came onto the world market. The region then returned to a low-productivity gathering economy, carried out by a widely dispersed ($\frac{1}{2}$ person per square mile before 1960) and malnourished population. The area attracted little attention from national politicians or the elite, although it was a never-ending source of fascination to North Americans and Europeans, both scientists and laymen.

In spite of diversification and major economic growth in the urban regions of the South and Southeast, Brazil remained predominantly rural. As late as the 1940 census, for example, less than a third (31.2 percent) of Brazil was urban. Transportation was difficult and slow, with less than 1,800 miles of paved highway in the entire country. Rapid communication had to be by telegraph or radio, which since the 1920s had become the principal form of mass communication. The print press existed only for the wealthier literate Brazilians in the larger cities.

New Currents in the 1920s

The 1920s saw increasing discontent with the liberalism that had been the underlying influence of the Brazilian Republic since its creation in 1889. The military were active participants in this restive discussion, but they were certainly not the only participants. The cultural community and the intellectuals also took part.

The First World War gave the Brazilian army a welcome opportunity to lobby for its long-standing needs. The army had had no foreign combat experience since the Paraguayan War forty years earlier. The army commanders knew their equipment was obsolete. They also were extremely aware that their training methods were inadequate. Even though their fighting skills had only been tested at home, those tests had had pretty disastrous results. Their record during the revolt at Canudos has already been described in chapter 3. The war of the Contestado in Santa Catarina (1912–16) was another case in which committed civil resisters, headed by a charismatic leader protesting the building of a railroad across their land, held the federal army at bay far longer than it had expected and inflicted considerable loss of life through selective guerrilla-type raids. Protest as they might, however, Brazil's entry into the European war did not help the military significantly in their struggle to modernize equipment or training, leaving them at the end of the war feeling inadequate and ill done by. In the words of one military historian, "the cavalry had no horses, the artillery had no artillery pieces and the infantry had no rifles."

The end of the war also stimulated new questions, particularly among the junior officers, about Brazil's failure to catch up with the economic growth rates of Argentina and the United States. Unlike the military's intellectual discontents in the late Empire, when they were influenced by the then-new doctrines of republicanism and positivism, there was no clear ideological rationale for the military discontent of the early 1920s. It most commonly took the form of attacking liberalism as an ill-considered aping of a foreign formula—a formula that could not help. In this, the younger military were mirroring the views of dissenters among the civilian society more generally, as discussed further below.

A particularly active group in raising these unsettling questions about Brazil's development were the junior officers who had been sent for training with the German army. They had returned from Germany in 1912, had founded a journal, *A Defesa Nacional,* and had organized a lobbying group to promote new ideas within the army officer corps. They became known as the "Young Turks," because they admired Mustafa Kemal (later Atatürk), who had transformed the Ottoman Empire by relying on the military.

As in the presidency of Marshal Hermes da Fonseca (1910–14), these young military malcontents started intervening in state party politics.

The Republican parties in several states had splintered into warring factions, whose contenders frequently tried to enlist the local military on their side. But when the military did intervene, of course, they were seen as destroying the supposed political neutrality of the army and giving credence to the image of militarism painted by Rui Barbosa in his unsuccessful presidential campaign of 1910.

The young officers' anger eventually burst forth in a typically Latin American form: barracks revolts. The young officers (whose ideas will be discussed below), participating in these revolts were called collectively the *tenentes* (literally meaning "lieutenants"). The first revolt occurred in 1922 at the army fort at the tip of Copacabana Beach in Rio de Janeiro. Eighteen of the Copacabana rebels fled the bombarded fort and marched down the beach. It was to have been part of a series of coordinated revolts, but the would-be rebels in the other locales lost their courage. The revolt was quickly contained, with all the rebels either killed, captured, or forced into hiding. Another important but also unsuccessful rebellion erupted in São Paulo in 1924. The military revolt destined to become the most famous of this series was the last. Launched in 1924 in Rio Grande do Sul, it was led by Captain Luiz Carlos Prestes, who proved to be the most charismatic of the rebels. Failing to achieve his objective of seizing a local military base, Prestes led a band of rebel soldiers, joined by a contingent of surviving *tenentes* from the São Paulo revolt, on a 24,000 kilometer, three-year march through the interior of southern and western Brazil. The "Prestes Column," as it became known, managed to elude state and federal forces for that entire time and thereby demonstrate the weakness (often the nonexistence) of government authority in large parts of the country. Prestes's rebels became national heroes. But exhaustion and dwindling supplies finally overtook them in 1927, when they dissolved the column and crossed into exile in Bolivia.

These revolts, particularly the success of the Prestes Column, left a significant mark on Brazilian politics. First, they demonstrated a profound lack of discipline in the army, with the higher commands never certain of being obeyed. Second, the rebels' ability to survive showed the ineffectiveness of the federal army and its lack of coordination with the state and local authorities. Third, the revolts showed that some of the younger generation were ready to take up arms against the national politicians in power. Fourth, the successful resistance of the Prestes Column dramatized the weakness of the civilian political elite. As had happened with their military counterparts during the late empire, neither the presidents nor the governors were able to impose authority over rebellious officers. As for the ideas of the rebels (the movement was called *tenentismo*), they were expressed in varying and seldom precise forms. During the late Empire, the junior military had been influenced by the new doctrines of republicanism and positivism. In the 1920s, the junior military showed a similar but less focused intellectual influence. They were infected by the growing wave of disillusionment with the Republic. But there was no clear ideological rationale for this discontent. Behind it all lay the general realization that Brazil had fallen behind in the struggle for modernity. They wanted a strong central government that would unify Brazil and put an end to "professional politicians becoming rich at public expense." They also wanted progressive social legislation such as a minimum wage and child labor legislation.

MODERNISM, BRAZILIAN STYLE

Until World War I, Brazil had been living its own version of the "Belle Époque." Its French-oriented literary and artistic world largely copied European styles, with little room for artistic originality. When the war ended, Brazil faced new and more varied European influences, as the traditional artistic canons of the Old World came under attack from radical innovators such as the futurists and the surrealists. Adventurous Brazilian writers and artists from Pernambuco, Minas Gerais, Rio de Janeiro, Rio Grande do Sul and, of course, São Paulo, headed for Europe soon after 1918 and absorbed these new ideas, which soon began to surface in Brazilian poetry, sculpture, and painting.

The benchmark year dating Brazil's entry into what came to be called "modernism" (not to be confused with the very different Spanish-American modernism) was 1922. In February of that year, a "Modern Art Week" festival was held in the city of São Paulo. It was no accident that the new movement would first appear in the Brazilian city whose material progress best entitled it to claim the title "modern." The Modern Art Week was a series of expositions, plays, concerts, and poetry readings. It was financed largely by Paulo Prado, scion of a wealthy São Paulo family (their wealth had come from cattle and coffee) and led by Mário de Andrade, a multitalented mulatto (worth noting, since mulattos were not common in high artistic circles) artist, playwright, and musician, also from São Paulo.

This artistic revolt was fed also by a new postwar attitude toward the Afro-Brazilian. The early Republic had been dominated by the dogma of "whitening"—an elite belief that accepted the "scientific" superiority of the white (as preached in the learned quarters of the United States and West Europe) but went on to assume that Brazil would, over the next century at most, virtually "bleach out" the non-white element. Along with this went a view that the African *per se* (as in Afro-Brazilian art and religion) was primitive and barbaric.

Frontal challenges to this racist attitude were few and far between before 1918. Among the outspoken opponents of scientific racism in that era were the jurist-politician Albert Torres and the educator-writer Manuel Bomfim. Their most distinguished predecessor was the literary critic Silvio Romero, who extolled the African and Indian contribution to Brazilian culture in his 1883 (first edition) history of Brazilian literature. Nonetheless, Romero, although an inspiration to later champions of Afro-Brazilian culture, could never bring himself to completely disown scientific racism.

Romero, Torres, and Bomfim all served as anti-racist mentors for the new generation of Brazilian thinkers that emerged after World War I. Its most influential spokesman was Gilberto Freyre, the Pernambucan writer-sociologist who began publishing in the early 1920s his pioneering analysis of Brazilian social history. Freyre's writing (of which the high point was *The Masters and the Slaves*, first published in 1933), combined with that of like- minded writers, artists, and scientists, resulted in a radical reorientation of elite thought about race in Brazil. The nonwhite element—especially the African element—was now seen as a positive factor in Brazilian social formation. Racist conceptions, among at least a significant part of the elite, were increasingly replaced with emphasis on the roles of health and education in countering the apparent backwardness of non-whites. The result of this intellectual *bouleversement* was to reinforce the transformation of Brazilian culture associated with the modernist movement. This artistic and literary transformation added another force undermining the Old Republic. The cultural upheaval helped deepen the generation gap and raise questions about the value system that had surrounded the Republic's creation. Fascism had already appeared in Italy and was showing strength in Spain and Portugal. Was Brazilian electoral democracy just another fragile ornament borrowed from a European civilization that was now discarding it?

RISE OF ANTI-LIBERAL THOUGHT

Post–World War I attacks on liberalism were not unique to Brazil. European thinkers such as Oswald Spengler were producing grand theories to explain the decline of western civilization. Sigmund Freud's theories, spreading rapidly among the intellectuals, threatened traditional religion and morals. Conflict over values shook the United States, as epitomized by the prohibition experiment. What was unique to Brazil was a focus primarily on the alleged defects of the political system rather than on philosophical issues.

One such defect was the repeated breakdown of the political system itself, into widespread fraud and voter manipulation on both state and federal levels. A second was disappointment at the failure of the economy to grow more rapidly, attributed by many to the faults of the political system. By 1920, Brazil's inability to match United States and Argentine development was evident to all. The ambitious republican promises of the late 1880s had not been fulfilled. Although having industrialized to a certain degree, Brazil remained dependent for export earnings primarily on a single product: coffee. The country had failed to win a seat on the Permanent Council of the League of Nations in 1926. Disease and illiteracy were rife. And the elite was beginning to take real notice of the huge gap between urban and rural Brazil.

When Brazilian critics looked to Europe, they found liberal electoral democracy challenged by bolshevism in Russia, by fascism in Italy and Germany, and by anarchism and corporatism in Spain and Portugal. All called into question the assumptions on which Brazil's Republic had been founded, suggesting that capitalism had to be eliminated or deeply transformed to enable industrial society to survive in the twentieth century.

The early 1920s brought to center stage a chorus of intellectual critics in Brazil. Most considered themselves disciples of the jurist-politician Alberto Torres, an anti-racist thinker before his time. He condemned racist doctrines as instruments used by foreign countries in their attempt to dominate Brazil's economy. A "historic" republican in the late Empire, Torres had been minister of justice (1896–97), and governor of the state of Rio de Janeiro (1898–1900), and later served on the Brazilian Supreme Court (1901–1909). In 1909, however, he had become disillusioned with the entire constitutional system and resigned from the bench in order to publicize his criticisms. Writing mainly in the form of newspaper articles (his books consist primarily of collections of these), Torres's principal message was that Brazilians must study their own problems and devise their own solutions—that mindlessly applying foreign formulae was doomed to failure.

He was a highly idiosyncratic thinker in many respects. He vigorously condemned urbanization, for example, branding cities as pernicious and detrimental to Brazilian development, which he thought had to remain agrarian. His disciples, which included army officers writing in *A Defesa Nacional*, concentrated on the arguments that fitted their purposes—in particular, his critique of the republican political structure and the need to find Brazilian solutions for Brazilian problems (which became a virtual mantra for this generation).

Most prominent among the Torres disciples was Oliveira Vianna, a lawyer from the state of Rio de Janeiro, who expounded his views in a two-volume history of southern Brazil and numerous other writings. In it he charged that the Republic had been founded on idealistic formulae totally inappropriate for Brazil. And he argued that Brazil had lacked any tradition of grassroots democracy (such as in the colonial United States and early modern England), which he thought essential for a liberal democracy. For Vianna, therefore, the systemic breakdown now evident on the state and federal level was inevitable. Representative democracy in Brazil was a sham. Real power lay in the hands of the bosses or "colonels." Vianna also extolled the "aryan" as Brazil's most creative actor. But here again, judging from the reviews, his readers neglected his racist arguments in favor of his political conclusions.

Vianna was joined in his political critique by lesser known but equally vociferous critics such as Gilberto Amado, Carneiro Leão, Pontes de Mirada, and Vicente Licínio Cardoso. They all argued that the evolution of the republic had gone fundamentally wrong.

By the end of the 1920s, the republican system had more critics than defenders among intellectuals. The legitimacy of electoral democracy as practiced was in doubt, although its critics, including the *tenentes*, were notably vague about preferred alternatives. They drifted into talk of "national solutions for national problems," better representation of the entire populace, and the need for greater discipline. But there was little debate over the specific institutions needed to bring about such change.

THE DISINTEGRATION OF THE OLD POLITICS

One innovation of the Republic had increasingly dramatic implications for politics as usual as the twentieth century wore on: The decentralization stimulated by the new Constitution had resulted in greatly fragmented federal authority, just as capitalism was facing increasingly severe tests of its viability. (See exhibit 5-3.)

Ever since the Constitution of 1891, states could levy tariffs on goods crossing their borders and also could contract loans abroad. They also had authority over such key areas as coffee exports and railway construction. These powers had facilitated industrial development in regions such as São Paulo but had left poorer regions—such as the Northeast—for example, to languish economically. Brazil's vast regions were drifting farther from one another economically, a trend that was partic-

EXHIBIT 5-3
Distribution of Government Revenues by Levels of Government

	Total Government Percentage of GDP	Percentage Participation by Branch of Government		
		Federal	Provincial or State	Municipal
1856	9.9	81.5*	15.5	3.0
1885–6	10.2	76.3	18.5	5.2
1907	16.4	65.8	25.4	8.8
1929	12.5	54.2	35.4	10.4
1945	13.2	55.7	36.1	8.2

*Average of fiscal years 1855–86 and 1856–57.

Source: Raymond W. Goldsmith, *Brasil 1850–1984: Desenvolvimento Fincarceiro sob um Século de Inflação* (São Paulo, 1986), p. 71.

ularly alarming to many army officers, who feared that Brazil was coming apart.

This fear was exacerbated by another development. The continuing weakness of the national army had stimulated the major states to build up their own military forces. São Paulo hired a French military mission from 1906 to 1924 to train its state military, or Força Publica (which even included a cavalry brigade and the beginnings of an air force in the late 1920s). Rio Grande do Sul's state military had combat experience in the Plata region. Added together, the troops of the state militaries totaled more than the federal army. In São Paulo state between 1894 and 1930, the Força Publica routinely outnumbered federal troops stationed there by ten to one. Although many of these state militaries acted more like police than soldiers, they were forces to be reckoned with, calling the ultimate test of any central government (i.e., its monopoly of force) into question.

Most important, elections had lost their perceived legitimacy as a means of allocating political power in republican Brazil. However manipulated they may have been (such as in the exclusion of monarchist candidates in the 1890s), they had generally been tolerated by the elite (with the possible exception of 1910) in earlier decades. By the 1920s, this was no longer true. First, exercise of the franchise was increasingly clouded by allegations of fraud as state elections turned ever more frequently into electoral farces. It was impossible to settle such conflicts impartially because the incumbent state governments controlled vote-counting (elections and electoral law were strictly a state matter) and certified the winners. Claims of vote fraud usually centered on the countryside, where landowner-hired agents could readily manipulate semi-literate voters.

The presidential elections of 1918 and 1922 furnished ample ammunition for the system's critics. In 1918, the state party leaders could not agree on a new face to nominate for president and turned to Rodrigues Alves, the Paulista politician who had been president from 1902 to 1906 and who had presided over Rio's rebuilding, but who was by now old and politically very weak. Alves was duly elected but died before inauguration day. A substitute, Epitácio Pessôa, a distinguished jurist from Pernambuco, was found, elected, and inaugurated. But he lacked consensus support in the major states and was soon the target of internecine political battles that continued throughout his presidency.

The succeeding president, Artur Bernardes (1922–26), an autocratic ex-governor of Minas Gerais, proved even more divisive. He was a stern, often vindictive figure (the perception of his sternness accentuated by his pince-nez glasses) who showed little inclination to conciliate. His election campaign began on an ugly note when pro-military sources leaked alleged Bernardes letters (later proved to be forgeries) mocking the army. And the barracks revolts (such as at Fort Copacabana in 1922) early in his presidency forced him to rule by state of siege (complete with Amazonian internment camps), a poor omen for the system's future. By 1926, when the Paulista Washington Luiz was elected president, the divisions among the state political machines went very deep. The politicians had done as much as the military, the artists, and the intellectuals to undermine the political system they had all inherited.

The Revolution of 1930

Preparations for the presidential campaign of 1929 occurred amid even more than usual suspicion and manipulation. The nominee of the majority of state machines was Júlio Prestes, the governor of São Paulo, the same state as that of the incumbent president, Washington Luiz. This was significant because state rivalries were running strong, pitting São Paulo against the major states of Minas Gerais and Rio Grande do Sul and the minor state of Paraíba. The opposition to the official ticket formed a liberal alliance that nominated for president Getúlio Vargas, a former federal finance minister and currently governor of Rio Grande do Sul. His running mate was João Pessôa, a politician from Paraíba. During the campaign, the opposition, distrustful of the eventual vote count, had considered organizing a coup if Júlio Prestes was declared the winner, which he was. Many in the opposition cried fraud at the result, but Vargas decided they lacked the power to contest the election successfully. His changed his mind when João Pessoa, Vargas's running mate, was assassinated. Even though his death was due to a romantic involvement enmeshed in local politics, it was the shock needed to mobilize the opposition to take up arms.

Vargas and his coconspirators now set about organizing an attack on the incumbent federal government. As a first step, the governors of Rio Grande do Sul, Minas Gerais, and the rebel states of the Northeast used their state military to secure their states. They then convinced the part of the federal army stationed in Rio Grande do Sul to join them and were able to add a series of rebel columns from other regions. The collection of armed conspirators converged on Rio from the north, south, and west.

In Rio, President Washington Luiz was determined to remain in office long enough to hand power over to his fellow Paulista. But the military commanders in Rio decided that continued support for the incumbent president would needlessly prolong what looked like an impending civil war. When they suggested to Washington Luiz that he resign, he refused. Cardinal Dom Sebastiã o Leme, the archbishop of Brazil, agreed with the Rio military and convinced the president that his time was up, and Washington Luiz went off into exile.

At this point, the rebel columns had not yet reached Rio. The army and navy commanders of the Rio garrison declared themselves a ruling junta and began issuing their own decrees, even though the territory they in fact controlled was restricted to Rio. They even considered remaining in power. After a few days, however, Getúlio Vargas himself reached Rio with his comrades, who—in a gesture of gaucho machismo—hitched their horses to the obelisk at the foot of Avenida Rio Branco, a famous landmark in downtown Rio. The junta reconsidered and handed power to Vargas as provisional president.

Vargas's victory had been the work of a complex coalition, of which the political leaders of Minas Gerais and Rio Grande do Sul, resentful of São Paulo's dominance of national politics, were only one element. Second was the recently founded (1926) Partido Democrático of São Paulo, the sworn opponent of the state's ruling official Republican party. Third were the *tenentes*, who had rebelled against both military and civilian authority. Fourth were the coffee growers (many but not all of them in the Partido Democrático), who were angered by the federal government's failure to compensate them for the plunge in coffee prices. Such a heterogeneous coalition was obviously unstable, with potential strains that were bound to appear as soon as the provisional government started to make decisions.

The losers in 1930 were also numerous. First were the São Paulo Republican party bosses, who had supported Júlio Prestes. Second were the top army commanders, most of whom found themselves summarily retired. Third were the bankers, who had insisted Brazil cling to the gold standard and who now found their financial links abroad badly frayed by the abrupt change in government.

But most Brazilians hardly noticed the break in the legal succession in 1930. Their lives had been far more affected by the great crash, which had cost jobs and income. Real GDP per capita fell 4 percent in 1930 and another 5 percent in 1931. Nor had the revolution of 1930 brought any major change in property relations or working conditions, despite the creation of a federal Ministry of Labor, Industry and Commerce in 1930. Brazil was still a country where landowners, merchants, industrialists, and bankers controlled power. The source of most wealth was still rural and there was still no talk of serious land reform.

SWING TOWARD CENTRALIZATION

The world financial crash of 1929 had created a powerful economic rationale for strengthening central government in Brazil. Vargas seized the moment, dissolved congress, instituted an emergency regime (legitimized by decree on November 11, 1930), and assumed full policy-making authority via federal decree power. He was strongly supported by the newly ascendant army generals—led by the ambitious military politician General Goes Monteiro—as he named "interventors" to administer the states, whose governors (technically known as "presidents") had almost universally been deposed by the new provisional federal government. Only in Minas Gerais was the governor, Benedito Valladares, allowed to remain and act as the interventor.

This assertion of federal authority was bound to threaten the state political elites, and it did. The implications for tax collection and budget allocation were obvious. Equally important was the threat of federal intervention in state politics. Although São Paulo, whose internal political divisions had helped bring Vargas to power, had the most to lose, other state leaders, such as those of Minas Gerais and Rio Grande do Sul, also saw dangers ahead.

The confrontation between the Vargas government and São Paulo was not long in coming. The Paulista elite, among whose ranks were some who had favored Vargas, quickly recovered their solidarity. Paulista opponents had always suspected his intentions toward their state and his former Paulista supporters soon concluded that he would never keep his promise to hold elections. The Paulista *amour propre* was especially offended when Vargas appointed a non-Paulista, João Alberto Lins de Barros, as the interventor in the state. Since the interventor was the federal authority there to monitor the state government, this was an unmistakable sign that recentralization was underway. Despite his best efforts, João Alberto could not placate the Paulista politicians and press, which successfully turned him into a target of local ridicule and hostility.

As the Paulista political elite resolved to fight the new powers in Rio, they thought they had recruited the leadership of Minas Gerais and Rio Grande do Sul to join them. Unfortunately for them, their would-be allies chose to sit on the sidelines. In July 1932, the Paulistas launched their revolt, led primarily by army officers who had refused to join the Vargas-led conspiracy of 1930 and who, as a consequence, had been cashiered. The Paulista rebels were left to fight the federal army alone. The Paulistas mobilized their wealthy matriarchs to turn in their gold and silver jewelry to help finance the war. The city's metalworking shops produced homemade tanks, and a minor armament industry blossomed. The Constitutionalist Revolution, as the Paulistas called their revolt, lasted only three months (July 9 to October 2, 1932). Vargas and his army commanders did not invade the city of São Paulo, where the revolt centered. Nor did they bomb it, as the government had done during the 1924 revolt in São Paulo. Instead, they merely surrounded it. Actual fighting was confined to the city outskirts. By October, the Paulistas surrendered, lowering their flag of secession. Vargas again reacted with restraint. He imposed relatively soft peace terms and even ordered the federal government to assume half the debt incurred by the rebels. The federal military were rewarded for their victory with a budget increase of 159 percent. Political power was clearly flowing back to the center.

The unsuccessful revolt had discredited the Paulista political elite in the country at large. It seemed a reprise of the Paulista threat to secede in the late empire, and confirmed fears in other regions that Brazil's most powerful state would always put its own interests ahead of the nation. São Paulo's "disloyalty" in 1932 gravely weakened its ability to act in national politics. It would be almost three decades before a Paulista occupied the presidency again. One consolation for the Paulistas was creation of the University of São Paulo in the mid-1930s. Intended to be the state's assertion of power on the intellectual level (and to compensate for its political loss in 1932), it was to become Latin America's premier university.

Vargas kept his promise (made before the São Paulo revolt) to hold national elections for a Constituent Assembly, which occurred in May 1933. These elections brought an important innovation: For the first time in Brazilian history, a Vargas-sponsored 1932 law gave responsibility for guaranteeing an honest vote throughout the country. As noted, the voting had previously been supervised by *município* and state authorities, with much leeway for fraud and manipulation. Now a federal authority, known as Justiça Eleitoral (Electoral Justice), was in place to protect the secret vote.

The Constituent Assembly met in 1933–34 and produced a new Constitution (the Constitution of 1934, Brazil's third), which was a mixture of political liberalism and socioeconomic reformism. There were now guarantees for an impartial judiciary, along with an assertion of new government responsibility for economic development and social welfare. Elections were held for president (Getúlio was elected to a four-year term by the Assembly, which had become the Chamber of Deputies) and for the state legislature. It looked as if Brazil was finally going to be allowed an experiment in modern democracy. Such, as we shall see, did not prove to be the case.

IDEOLOGICAL POLARIZATION

The 1930s brought the ideological radicalization Brazil had lacked during its upheaval of the 1920s. Anchoring the left was the Brazilian Communist Party (Partido Comunista Brasileiro, or PCB). Founded in 1922, it was under the supervision of the Comintern in Moscow, though its subservience was concealed under an elaborate clandestine apparatus. Many of its members were ex-anarchists or anarcho-syndicalists, whose former organizations the PCB was gradually defeating within the power struggles of the left. The PCB was essentially limited to a few major cities (Recife, Rio, Pôrto Alegre, and São Paulo) and some mining areas in Minas Gerais. In the early 1930s, the party followed the Comintern line of all-out struggle against the forces of "fascism." This strategy led to the creation in 1935 of a leftist front called the Aliança Nacional Libertadora

(ANL). Its titular head was Luiz Carlos Prestes, the hero who had refused Vargas's offer to take military command of the 1930 rebellion and who was continuing to pursue politics while in exile. Prestes had begun his career as an army officer in Rio Grande do Sul, and had achieved legendary status in public opinion as the "Cavalier of Hope," which referred to his leadership of a rebel column through the Brazilian backlands from 1924 to 1927. (The rebels were survivors of the 1924 military revolts in São Paulo and Rio Grande do Sul.) The Brazilian public considered him an ethically outstanding figure with no political commitments other than the good of Brazil. Unknown to the public, however, he had in fact joined the Communist Party and was now under direction from Moscow. The ANL included other parties, such as the Socialists, but control remained with the Communists.

In carrying out the Comintern strategy, the Brazilian Communists were faced with the same difficulty as their comrades in most Third World countries. Communist Party doctrine focused entirely on urban workers, the assumption being that working class consciousness could best be cultivated among urban workers, while rural workers offered little or no revolutionary potential. Yet Brazil was still primarily an agrarian society. There was the further difficulty that even industrial workers in Brazil worked primarily in small establishments, where organizing was especially difficult. Furthermore, the city workers came mostly from rural backgrounds and did not take easily to appeals for short-run sacrifice—e.g., the loss of wages while striking. The task of organizing such workers therefore ran into employee resistance as well as police repression. But whatever its difficulties with the workers, the Communist-dominated left had aroused the fears of the elite, both civilian and military. The politicians and the generals had long been suspicious of worker organization (the "dangerous classes," as they were known), and the Moscow- based Communist ideology gave the elite new reason to impose repressive laws.

There were also new groups on the right of the political spectrum. In the 1920s, for example, the Brazilian Roman Catholic Church underwent a revival as both laymen and clergy struggled to breathe new life into a weak institution. By the early 1930s, the revived Church was exerting new political force on the right. An even more important force was the Ação Integralista Brasileira (AIB). Its members wore green uniforms, had a quasi-military hierarchy, and engaged in paramilitary parades and exercises. They also relished street confrontations with their enemies on the left. Although it bore an obvious superficial resemblance to European fascism, in fact, the AIB lacked the racist (with the exception of a few spokesmen, such as Gustavo Barroso), expansionist, fully militaristic qualities typical of European—especially German—fascism. The Integralista vision was of a Christian Brazil based on a disciplined society, with little tolerance for revolutionary action on the left.

The Integralists attracted a wide following among the middle and upper classes, especially among naval officers and the clergy. They even attracted some following among urban workers in Rio Grande do Sul and were well represented in Ceará. Their most visible leader was Plínio Salgado, a Paulista writer who had been involved in the modernist movement in São Paulo. Gaining confidence from their swelling numbers, the Integralists sought national influence. Like the Communists, they were prepared to seek it through direct action rather than through the ballot box. Some foreign countries thought them to be a major political actor on the Brazilian scene—Benito Mussolini's government, for example, gave them direct financial help—and their possible link to European fascism began to alarm the British and American governments, which already saw Germany as a geopolitical threat in Latin America.

The Communists and the Integralists saw themselves as natural antagonists. They staged marches, counter-marches, and street fights paralleling what was happening in Central Europe. This ideological radicalization helped contribute to the public's growing doubts about the effectiveness of electoral politics.

That point was dramatized in November 1935 when a faction of Communist officers and enlisted men attempted a coup within the Brazilian army. The PCB and Comintern were gambling on a military coup to overthrow the Brazilian government. This strategy would weaken the U.S. and British governments and strengthen the Soviet Union's international position. It involved little organizing of workers and little attention to the industrial heartland of São Paulo. It would be a proletarian revolution without a proletariat.

Detailed instructions for carrying out the revolt were given to Luiz Carlos Prestes in Moscow, where he had been since 1931. He then reentered Brazil in mid-1935 with a precise timetable from the Comintern, whose non-Brazilian agents were laying the groundwork in Brazil. The revolt broke out in a series of uprisings in November 1935 at three military bases in Natal, Recife, and Rio. The Comintern leaders were convinced that the Communist Party had sufficiently infiltrated the army to be able to seize power. But after brief fighting, with some casualties among officers and enlisted men, the pro- government army commanders crushed the revolts at all three bases, with the Natal rebels holding out longest. The Comintern and the PCB, who were apparently unaware that they were already under surveillance by the Brazilian police, had unwittingly played into Vargas's hands. They had given him the ideal evidence of the "Bolshevik threat."

The Vargas government had a propaganda field day after it crushed the revolt, circulating wildly exaggerated stories (later discredited by military records) about loyalist officers shot unarmed in their beds. Vargas immediately convinced Congress to declare a state of emergency, allowing police to suspend civil rights in their hunt for suspects. Vargas now had the atmosphere he needed to intimidate opponents of whatever ideological stripe. It was a perfect backdrop for increased presidential power and the further centralization such an increase in power implied.

Getúlio Vargas as Dictator

For the next two years, Vargas convinced Congress to keep renewing the 90- day state of siege. Throughout these years his government enjoyed extraordinary police powers, stultifying political life and stimulating growing suspicions that Vargas was preparing his own coup. This fear was reinforced by the pro-authoritarian views of his two top generals, Pedro Goes Monteiro and Eurico Dutra, whose views assumed particular importance because, in the radicalized political climate, Vargas was becoming increasingly dependent on military support. Both admired German military skills and both doubted the capacities of the Anglo-Saxon democracies (if they remained immobilized) to resist German power. This was a view shared in many circles—even some in the United States—and with some justification. The U.S. army in 1938, for example, was no larger than that of Greece or Bulgaria. As late as 1940, U.S. troops lacked rifles to use on maneuvers and had to be content with wooden cutouts.

Political attention in Brazil now focused on the upcoming presidential election of 1938. Vargas had been elected by the Constituent Assembly of 1933–34, which had provided for a direct election (Vargas was constitutionally ineligible to run for another term immediately, although he could after a four-year interval) to follow in 1938. Vargas's opposition coalesced behind Armando Salles de Oliveira, a leading member of the Paulista elite, who were now trying to gain through the vote what they had failed to gain by arms in 1932. The government-supported candidate was José Américo de Almeida, a writer and minor politician from the Northeast. The Paulistas believed that their time had come as they solicited support among the anti-Vargas forces.

Vargas was indeed conspiring with his generals to stage a coup and thereby preempt the election. On November 10, 1937, congressmen arrived in Rio to find the Congress building surrounded by troops refusing them access. That night, Vargas announced over the radio to the Brazilian people that they had a new Constitution for what he termed the Estado Nôvo (New State). Brazil had become a full-fledged dictatorship. The new Constitution provided for a plebiscite to approve the new document, but it was never held. As in 1932, the military was rewarded with an increased budget, up by 49 percent in 1937 over 1936.

The Paulista elite, which had feared just such a move, had lost again. Vargas's most prominent opponents, such as ex-candidate Salles de

Oliveira, fled into exile. The public fell silent as censorship settled over the media and the police were given a free hand.

The Integralistas were initially pleased by the coup, believing they would benefit from this swing to the right. Their leaders expected fellow Integralista Plínio Salgado to be offered a cabinet post. But the Vargas government did the opposite, imposing new restrictions on Integralista activities. In response, a band of armed Integralists tried their own coup in March 1938, attacking the presidential palace where Vargas was sleeping. In the middle of the night, the armed Integralists, aided by disloyal palace guards, penetrated the grounds of the palace and began firing at the main building. What followed was more comedy than combat. Vargas and his then 23-year-old daughter, Alzira, appeared at the windows and returned fire. The Integralists hesitated and settled into a multi-hour siege. It took until dawn for government reinforcements to arrive, as Alzira kept making increasingly frantic phone calls to the military commanders. The surviving attackers (at least four were killed) were rounded up and ushered off to prison. Vargas now had the perfect excuse to repress the Integralistas, in addition to the Communists. Salgado sought exile in Portugal, and Brazil was left with no organized alternative to the new dictatorship.

If Vargas's coup simplified politics at home, it created problems abroad. The White House demanded an immediate explanation from Brazil's ambassador, Oswaldo Aranha. The U.S. government was preoccupied with the geopolitical implications of Brazilian events for any future war with Germany (Brazil's position on the Atlantic coast meant that it could play a vital role in controlling transatlantic air and sea traffic) and the U.S. military feared that the coup would move Brazil closer to Nazi Germany. They were well aware of Dutra's and Goes Monteiro's sentiments and had been struggling to woo them away from German influence. The presence of a large German-speaking colony in southern Brazil reinforced American worries about the future direction of the Vargas dictatorship. At the very least, the coup meant Brazil had deserted the ideological ranks of the democracies.

THE VARGAS STYLE

Getúlio Vargas was about as uncharismatic a dictator as the world is likely to see. He lacked the electric charm of his Argentine counterpart Juan Perón and never cultivated the melodramatic personal appearance of a Hitler or a Mussolini. Unprepossessing physically, his chief physical features were his paunch and a habitual ironic smile. But he used his unimpressive persona to huge advantage because he combined it with an uncanny ability to size up his fellow humans and induce his enemies to underestimate him. He was a superb listener and had the ability to convince most of his interlocutors, whatever their position, that he genuinely understood them, if not agreed with them. Although capable of appalling cruelty (he allowed the extradition of Luis Carlos Prestes's German-born Jewish wife to Nazi Germany, where she died in a death camp), he preferred to turn enemies into collaborators. There is no evidence that he amassed inappropriate wealth while in office, although he did not hesitate to enjoy the full powers of the presidency.

Vargas was probably the opposite of a visionary, but he had firm ideas about where Brazil should be headed. Judging from his speeches and government initiatives in the years following 1937, he wanted, first and foremost, to build a strong central government—a goal enthusiastically shared by the higher military. This would require increased investment in education, economic development (to support industrialization at least in the military- related sectors), and increased integration of the lands to the west. Second, he wanted to project Brazilian power abroad, which would require a stronger position in international trade. Third, he wanted to improve social welfare for urban workers. Here he had a non-economic goal in mind: A satisfied set of government-controlled unions would then furnish Vargas with a political base.

Vargas's strategy during the Estado Nôvo (1937–45) was to rely on the military for political stability and on his technocrats for administration. Here, Vargas was borrowing from both European fascism (discarding electoral democracy) and the American New Deal (relying on modernizing technocrats). Fundamentally, he and his intellectual apologists, such as Azevedo Amaral and Oliveira Vianna, justified the Vargas dictatorship on the grounds that Brazil could ill afford the "petty politics" of an open society, given the dangers from its enemies, internal and external.

This rationale led directly to the repressive apparatus that accompanied the Estado Novo. Most visible were the police, who in Rio were commanded by the notorious sadist Filinto Muller. His staff even had a secret working agreement with the Gestapo. Torture of political suspects was frequent and there was no reliable recourse to the courts, given the government's constant invocation of the National Security Law. There were also detention camps at such distant sites as the island of Fernando de Noronha, off the northeastern coast. One survivor of a camp in Alagoas, Graciliano Ramos, wrote a searing memoir of his suffering in *Memórias do Cárcere* (only published in 1955), which became a classic of Brazilian literature and later a highly successful film. And there was the omnipotent censorship, carried out by the Departamento da Imprensa e Propaganda (DIP).

CORPORATIST INROADS

In 1937, the Southeast triangle formed by Minas Gerais, Rio de Janeiro, and São Paulo, along with a few urban centers elsewhere on the coast, was approaching a modern capitalist economy. As early as 1900, part of its urban work force (a very small fraction of the Brazilian total) had become organized in unions, as we have seen. In some industries, such as the railways and the docks, they had won benefits, including pensions and holidays—something unheard of elsewhere in Brazil. Most workers, however, even in the cities, were neither unionized nor covered for benefits.

Brazil's industrial unions had begun to show strength in the 1920s and particularly the 1930s, when political turmoil had brought the question of workers' social welfare to the forefront. In the contemporary industrialized world, the least interventionist model was the United States. England, in contrast, had instituted government-sponsored social insurance even before the First World War. Germany had acted even earlier, under Bismarck in the 1880s. Spain, Portugal, and Italy were now experimenting with the new form of social organization known as *corporatism*. Vargas and his technocrats chose the corporatist route.

The intent of corporatism was to facilitate the adoption of modern capitalism while avoiding the extremes of laissez-faire permissiveness on the one hand and total state direction on the other. The idea was to establish separate corporate entities (syndicates), each representing specific economic sectors. Employers and employees in each sector had their own syndicates, for example. The coordination of relations between these corporate entities was the national government's responsibility, eliminating conflict between competing syndicates and leaving the last word (on wages, benefits, and working conditions) to the central government.

Vargas's first corporatist target was labor. Since fear of labor and the left had in part prompted the repressive policies followed after 1935, Vargas was now concerned to turn the other cheek while at the same time protecting himself against the potential threat of labor unrest. Much inspiration for the new legislation (especially the labor law of 1939) came from the Carta di Lavoro of the Italian fascist state.

Over the course of the 1930s, government technocrats, led by the lawyer and political philosopher Oliveira Vianna, used their arbitrary powers to shape a network of officially established labor unions (organized by trade) at the local level. Each *município*-based union was barred from direct relations with other *município*-based unions within the state, even of the same trade. State federations and national confederations were permitted, but these were also barred from having direct links with local-level organizations. The Ministry of Labor collected and channeled all union dues (equal to one day's pay a year automatically deducted from the worker's paycheck), and exercised veto power over all union elections. Strikes were illegal between 1937 and 1946 and no direct bargaining existed between unions and employers. All workplace-level grievances had to be directed to government-appointed labor courts within the Labor Justice System (Justiça do Trabalho), which until 1946 were subordinated to the minister of labor.

It is important to note that Vargas and his technocrats made no effort to extend this system to the rural sector, although legislation provided for future coverage. The rural sector got less attention because it represented less danger of worker mobilization—not only because rural workers were harder to organize but also because repression by management (the landowners and their hired gunmen) was easier in the countryside. Political power in the Brazilian rural sector—whether by the ballot or otherwise—was effectively controlled by landowners, who did not look kindly on any kind of worker organizations. In this respect, Brazil was much easier to handle within a corporatist system than Mexico, where rebel movements regularly stimulated rural worker uprisings.

With respect to employers, Vargas applied the corporatist model to the existing trade associations, which were already organized by industry. Each trade association, such as textile manufacturing in the city of São Paulo, was organized into a syndicate. Each syndicate was in turn a member of a new statewide federation, such as the Federation of Industries of the State of São Paulo (FIESP). In 1943, the state federations were brought together in a National Confederation of Industry. This corporatist structure gave the federal government a convenient channel not only for regulating industry but also for co-opting industrialists in the process. The corporatist structures for labor and industry effectively took both sectors out of the active political process.

A NEW SEARCH FOR NATIONAL IDENTITY

The advent of the Estado Nôvo was a decisive victory against the liberalism of the Old Republic, with many anti-liberal critics now joining the dictatorship. A leading example was Francisco Campos, a Mineiro intellectual who had directed educational reform in his state. He wrote the authoritarian Constitution of 1937 and went on to serve as Vargas's justice minister. Azevedo Amaral, another leading anti-liberal, edited an official magazine, *A Nôva Política*, which published authors supportive of the Estado Novo. Finally, as noted, Oliveira Vianna, one of the most famous enemies of liberalism, helped draft and administer the corporatist labor laws.

The Vargas dictatorship had a keen sense of the political importance of popular culture as a way of cementing government support by making Brazil look good in the international context. One example was soccer, where Brazil excelled in international competition.

Soccer had been introduced into Brazil and much of South America in the late nineteenth century by British businessmen and sailors. The game (called *futebol*) quickly caught on, with private clubs and factories sponsoring white, upper-class amateur teams. By the 1920s, a democratization had begun, with Afro-Brazilians beginning to appear on teams. By the 1938 World Cup, even Brazil's national team was no longer all white. Meanwhile, the Vargas government in 1941 created a National Sport Council, which formed an organizing umbrella for the extensive national network of private soccer clubs. Vargas's lieutenants channeled government money to fund the national team. Subsequent success was impressive. Brazil is the only country in the world to have qualified for every World Cup between 1930 and 1998, and the only country to have won the cup four times. There are few accomplishments that mean as much to Brazilian national identity as their supremacy in soccer, and Vargas was one of the first politicians to appreciate the political payoff from supporting it.

A second example of promoting popular culture was the Rio Carnival. As in the case of soccer, there had been a spontaneous growth of private groups dedicated to a popular pastime. In this case it was samba, a unique Brazilian music and dance form born among the shacks of poor Afro-Brazilians in the late nineteenth century. By the 1920s, the "schools" of samba singers and dancers had become the centerpiece of the annual pre-Lenten Carnival.

Vargas's was the first federal government to promote the samba schools and the Rio parades (previous support had come from the municipal government), which became an internationally recognized symbol of Brazilian culture. This policy, which was clearest after the coup of 1937, had not only an economic rationale (to attract tourism) but also sought to play a role in strengthening the nation's new sense of its own identity as at least partly Afro-Brazilian through such powerful instruments as music and dance. Finally, the government launched an extensive program of restoration of historic (especially religious) architecture, sculpture, and painting through a new institute dedicated to the national artistic and historic patrimony. Restoration of the Imperial Palace in Petrópolis was a good example. Another was inviting the famous French architect Le Corbusier (aided by a Brazilian team of architects) to design the much-celebrated Ministry of Education and Culture building in Rio in 1936 (construction finished in 1943). All of these programs were designed to help soften the dictatorship's image of repression and censorship and present it as the promoter of national culture and, therefore, national unity. It was no accident, of course, that DIP, the agency in charge of all censorship, also handled public relations for the government, including the sponsorship of cultural events (as well as political rallies). Each samba school, for example, had to clear with DIP its plans for its annual Carnival appearance.

There was also a darker side to the Vargas-sponsored preoccupation with national identity. This was the attempt to "protect" the country from those defined as "un-Brazilian," such as those of Japanese or Jewish descent. They were subject to discrimination, both official and unofficial, although it never approached the comprehensive and systematic level of Nazi Germany. Such measures were largely restricted to closing newspapers, schools, and organizations deemed "foreign."

JUGGLING THE INTERNATIONAL OPTIONS

By 1934, the pattern of European geopolitical confrontation had already become clear. Nazi Germany had its eyes not only on its European neighbors, but also on increased influence in the Western Hemisphere. It had identified Brazil as a prime trading partner and proceeded to exercise leverage over this bilateral relationship. The mechanism was a special German currency used to pay for Brazilian exports, which could only be redeemed by buying German exports, making it a form of tied trade. From 1933 to 1938, German-Brazilian trade rose sharply—primarily Brazilian cotton in return for German industrial goods—with Britain the principal loser.

The Germans were interested in more than trade, however. They also wanted to draw Brazil into the German politico-military sphere. They systematically cultivated Brazilian army officers known to be admirers of German military prowess. They also offered Brazil arms and technical training. Just as in the pre–World War I period, the U.S. government worried about this German strategy. The State Department denounced German trade policy as discriminatory and the U.S. military tried to counter the German offer of arms and training. In this effort they failed. Vargas had tried to get U.S. military equipment first, but the U.S. Congress, a very isolationist body during the 1930s, outlawed foreign arms sales by the United States.

Throughout the period, Vargas's police and intelligence forces often relied on British agents for information about other foreign penetration of the country. The army's rapid response to the 1935 Communist revolt probably owed much to British intelligence in identifying the Comintern agents. The British joined the Americans in watching nervously as Nazi and Italian agents operated both openly and clandestinely in Brazil. For example, Germany's official airline, Condor, was a known conduit for German intelligence (as was Pan American for the United States).

Brazilian public opinion was the target in a battle over which side to support in the coming European war. Elite sentiment still heavily favored the Allies for cultural reasons, and until their suppression in 1935, the Communists had also been effective in promoting anti-Nazi opinion. But some Brazilians, as in 1914, favored Germany, regardless of the historical ties of culture.

Vargas had shown an inclination to look to the United States for military links. As noted, he had tried to buy arms from the United States before turning to Germany. In 1937, he had also offered President Roosevelt the use of Brazilian coastal bases. This offer had been refused, presumably because Roosevelt could not afford to alienate the isolationist Congress by looking as if he were preparing for war. And a Brazilian bid to buy surplus U.S. destroyers fell through when U.S. authorities caved in to Argentine protests against the planned sale. When war finally broke out in 1939, Vargas and his generals remembered these rebuffs and chose to remain neutral until the United States was prepared to pay a fair price for Brazil's support. Furthermore, the Brazilians continued to cultivate relations with the Axis powers as part of the game of playing them off against the United States.

Brazil did not declare war until mid-1942. By then, even the fence-sitters could see that the military odds had tipped in favor of the Allies. The 1941 invasion of Russia had caught the Wehrmacht in a ferocious Russian winter, and the German U-boats were taking heavy losses in the Battle of the Atlantic. Brazil could not wait much longer if it hoped to extract an attractive compensation for entering the war.

Brazil had at least two assets the allies needed. One was raw materials, including natural rubber, quartz (essential for radio communications), and other minerals. The other was its coastline, which offered air and sea bases at strategic points on the Atlantic Ocean. Vargas won an attractive deal. Brazil agreed to supply the raw materials and furnish the bases, but only in return for U.S. military equipment, technical assistance, and financing for a Brazilian steel mill (located at Volta Redonda). This alliance made Brazil the United States's most conspicuous Latin American partner in the war. Furthermore, it set the precedent for American government support of basic industrialization in a Third World country.

In 1941, Vargas began the move toward the Allies by approving a Pan American Airways project (under U.S. Army contract) to modernize airports in the North and Northeast. In January 1942, at the Rio de Janeiro conference where Latin American support for entering the war now prevailed thanks to the Japanese attack on Pearl Harbor, Brazil broke openly with the Axis. Brazil's entry into the war had an important implication for politics at home. The decision to join the democracies was a blow to the authoritarians who had argued that democracy had no place in Brazil and had assumed Vargas agreed with them. Vargas and his generals, by calling that assumption into question, were setting the stage for a debate that would eventually end Vargas's dictatorship.

WORLD WAR II AND THE RISE OF U.S. INFLUENCE

As Brazil entered the war, a wave of American officials, both military and civilian, came to Brazil. Brazilian officers now cooperated closely with the U.S. Navy and Air Force in waging anti-submarine warfare, a process that included supplying the Brazilians with American planes and ships, as well as land weapons. In turn, that meant the need for U.S. military maintenance personnel in Brazil itself. By 1943, the Brazilians and Americans had built a network of modern military air and sea bases down the coast of Northeast Brazil.

Along with the U.S. military offensive in Brazil came a cultural offensive. President Roosevelt appointed the multimillionaire Nelson Rockefeller to direct a new office to promote improved cultural relations with Latin America, with Brazil a prime target. Rockefeller's office recruited talent such as Orson Welles and Walt Disney to make films aimed at strengthening pro-U.S. opinion. Especially memorable was the cartoon ("Saludos Amigos") that sent Donald Duck to Latin America to meet his Spanish- and Portuguese-speaking cronies. The Brazilian was a parrot ("Zé Carioca") who delighted Brazilian audiences. Rockefeller's offensive also included visits by American writers and artists, who reinforced the U.S. cultural impact in Brazil.

Behind these activities lay longer-run U.S. objectives: One was increased U.S. economic penetration of Brazil. Although American investment in Brazil already exceeded British investment there, U.S. investors were anxious to make further inroads. In the area of mass culture, U.S. penetration had been steadily increasing since the First World War. Between 1928 and 1937, for example, 85 percent of the films shown in Brazil came from Hollywood. In advertising, U.S. firms were becoming dominant by the 1930s and the entire field was "Americanized." Wartime collaboration offered an excellent basis for the later U.S. economic offensive. U.S. aircraft came to dominate not only military but also civilian use. American industrial specifications and commercial measurements became more frequently used in Brazil. American brand names were becoming better known. And English was now the third most frequently spoken foreign language (after French and Italian).

Vargas's desire to identify Brazil with the Allied cause led him to offer three Brazilian army divisions to fight the Germans in the Mediterranean theater. Brazilian officers were enthusiastic about the idea. Vargas had two major purposes in insisting on a Brazilian military role. One was to dramatize Brazil's role as the only Latin American country to commit land forces under its own flag in the war (a Mexican air force unit fought in the Pacific and many Mexicans volunteered for service in the U.S. Army). The second was to touch Brazilian pride and give the public a patriotic reason to rally behind the government.

To emphasize that this was a national effort, Vargas wanted the troops recruited countrywide. He insisted that every state be represented, whatever the quality of the local recruits. The resulting force was highly heterogeneous, lacking common training and completely devoid of combat experience. The U.S. military command had also worried about the physical condition of these troops—doubts that proved justified when the Brazilians were able to furnish only one healthy division. Furthermore, preparations in Brazil misfired even for the healthy troops. The commanders expected to be fighting in North Africa, so the troops were provided with summer uniforms. The Brazilian expeditionary force (Força Expeditionária Brasileira, or FEB) was assigned to operate with the U.S. Fifth Army, however, which was driving against stubborn German defense in mountainous terrain north of Rome, just as a harsh winter was setting in. The Brazilians were thrown into battle to scale a precipice on which the Germans had commanding gun positions. Caught in murderous fire, they suffered heavy casualties and withdrew in disorder.

Though hardly surprising, given their troops' lack of combat experience and insufficient clothing, failure in their first combat engagement was extremely upsetting to the Brazilian commanders, who turned to the Americans for help and advice. The Brazilian troops went through rapid retraining and soon reentered battle, where they performed significantly better, helping to capture Monte Casino, the historic monastery that marked a principal German position. The Brazilian combat record in Italy subsequently became a subject of bitter controversy. The official accounts stressed the very real Brazilian heroism after retraining, but the critics (including some Brazilian officers) stressed the early combat failure, which they unfairly blamed on incompetent commanders.

Brazil's combat involvement left a significant legacy. First, it furnished a basis for the country's claim to a major postwar role—a sentiment that resembled Brazil's similar hope upon emerging from World War I. This time, however, Brazil's military participation had been much greater and hopes were high that the political rewards would be commensurate. Second, sending the expeditionary force greatly increased the Brazilian army's prestige. As the only Latin Americans to fight in Europe, Brazilians could hold their head up among the Allies. Third, joint combat in Italy strengthened the ties between the U.S. and Brazilian militaries, even though Brazil remained very much the junior partner.

Brazil's economy had emerged from the Depression sooner than that of either the United States or England, a recovery that, after slight setbacks in 1940 and 1942, was sustained by the Second World War. (See exhibit 5-4.) As production rose, Brazil benefited from receiving war-related American technology and equipment. Brazil also received such items as railway rolling stock and trucks. Meanwhile, the disrupted shipping lanes had cut Brazilian consumers off from imports, forcing them to turn to Brazilian producers. A domestic paper industry was one of the beneficial results.

The war also greatly accelerated governmental centralization. The need to ration essentials, such as petroleum, put new power in the hands

EXHIBIT 5-4
Gross Domestic Product (Indexed to 1949 = 100.00)

| Year | Aggregate GDP | | 1929 Prices | Percent Growth (from previous year) |
	Current Prices	Percent Growth (from previous year)		
1925	87.9	18.6	76.2	0.0
1926	76.2	−13.3	80.1	5.1
1927	83.2	9.2	88.8	10.9
1928	102.3	23.0	98.9	11.4
1929	**100.0**	−2.2	**100.0**	1.1
1930	83.6	−16.4	97.9	−2.1
1931	74.3	−11.1	94.7	−3.3
1932	78.3	5.4	98.8	4.3
1933	88.8	13.4	107.6	8.9
1934	88.9	0.1	117.5	9.2
1935	105.0	18.1	120.9	2.9
1936	119.3	13.6	135.5	12.1
1937	136.4	14.3	141.7	4.6
1938	147.2	7.9	148.1	4.5
1939	154.3	4.8	151.8	2.5
1940	163.8	6.2	150.2	−1.1
1941	188.8	15.3	157.7	5.0
1942	211.8	12.2	153.4	−2.7
1943	266.5	25.8	166.5	8.5
1944	345.9	29.8	179.1	7.6
1945	411.1	18.8	184.8	3.2

Source: Raymond W. Goldsmith, *Brasil 1850–1984: Desenvolvimento Fincarceiro sob um Século de Inflação* (São Paulo, 1986), p. 147.

of the Vargas government. Allocation of most resources had to go through a national mobilization board, thereby bringing São Paulo industry under increased direction by the federal government.

A final economic effect of the war was a surge in inflationary demand as the general mobilization led to an overheated economy. This pent-up demand could not be met without imports. In Rio, the cost of living between 1939 and 1945 almost doubled, and in São Paulo it almost tripled, creating a significant problem for postwar economic policy.

COLLAPSE OF THE DICTATORSHIP AT HOME

When Vargas canceled the presidential election scheduled for 1938 and assumed dictatorial powers in 1937, he promised to hold presidential elections in 1943. It was his acknowledgment of Brazil's tradition of electoral democracy, even as he was snuffing it out. As the date neared, few expected Vargas to keep his promise. In 1943, Vargas announced that the wartime emergency would not permit the uncertainty of a presidential election and postponed the resumption of electoral politics "until after the war."

The anti-Vargistas, who doubted he ever intended to surrender power, grew increasingly preoccupied as the war neared its end. Every politically conscious Brazilian could see the contradiction: Brazil was fighting dictatorships yet itself had a dictatorial regime. In early 1945, all eyes centered on Vargas. Would he allow a free election and thereby put at risk his fifteen-year rule? In late February, his government issued a lengthy "constitutional law" that called for the popular election of a new president. The only eligibility requirement was to be a native-born Brazilian at least thirty-five years old. Vargas qualified on both counts.

Already a domestic opposition had appeared with the 1943 Manifesto of Mineiro leaders, and Vargas's exiled opponents began returning and in mid-1945 helped organize, along with Brazil-based Vargas opponents, a new party, the União Democratica Nacional (UDN). The UDN was dominated by the liberal constitutionalists who had fought Vargas since 1931. Their strongest support came from the middle and upper civilian classes and army officers. Interestingly enough, the UDN initially included leaders of the (still illegal) Communist Party, now enjoying prestige by its association with the hero Luis Carlos Prestes and with the victorious Soviet Red Army. The Communists withdrew from the coalition in June 1945, although numerous Socialists stayed in. The UDN, suspicious of Vargas's motives, demanded that he resign. They were supported by state politicians who were maneuvering for position in a post-Vargas era.

Vargas maintained an ambiguous stand up to the last minute. He scheduled an election for October, but declined to define his own role. As campaign preparations began, Vargas and his aides encouraged the creation of two more new parties. The first was the Partido Social Democrático (PSD) led by the Vargas-appointed political bosses of the leading states. It was preeminently a party of the "ins." The second was the Partido Trabalhista Brasileiro (PTB), intended as the political arm of the newly organized urban workers. Suddenly, another group materialized to further alarm Vargas's opponents: A movement called the "Queremistas" emerged with the slogan "Queremos Getúlio" ("We Want Getúlio"). They appeared to have support from the presidential palace as well as from labor union and Communist Party leaders. Again Vargas remained enigmatic, refusing to endorse or denounce the Queremistas. Such a refusal was tantamount, in the view of his opponents, to proof of his worst intentions.

The army generals in the Rio area—led by General Goes Monteiro, who was influenced by the UDN—shared the worry of the opposition. So too did the U.S. ambassador, Adolph Berle, who suggested publicly (by praising "the solemn promise of free elections") that Vargas resign. U.S. secretary of state, Edward Stetinius, also visited Brazil to plead for redemocratization. The suspicions of all parties were confirmed: President Vargas tried to instigate a nationalist reaction to Berle's intervention, but it was too late. The army command served Vargas with an ultimatum: Unless he resigned immediately, the army would besiege the palace, cutting off all water, power, and other supplies. Vargas decided he had no choice but to accept and cooperate in a bloodless coup. He resigned and returned to his ranch in Rio Grande do Sul.

Once again the generals had presided over a fundamental change in the constitutional structure of Brazil. It was a script familiar from 1930, 1935, and 1937. They had been motivated in part by wishing to head off a Perón-type regime in Brazil. Only weeks earlier, Argentina's General Juan Perón had been freed from military-imposed house arrest and restored to power as the urban workers cheered. Perón's worker mobilization was a clear threat to the Argentine army and to the established social order. The Brazilian generals wanted to foreclose any such threat in their country.

6 Democracy Under Vargas, Halcyon Days with Kubitschek, and a Military Coup: 1945–64

The year 1945 promised to bring epic changes around the world. The defeat of Germany and Japan had left major power vacuums in Europe and Asia. National boundaries were suddenly in question. Millions of displaced persons were seeking refuge. Property destruction was massive, even in such victorious countries as Britain and the Soviet Union. This specter led some commentators to predict the permanent demise of Europe.

Latin America had remained far from the combat. Like the United States, it had escaped the impact of saturation bombing and the punishment of marauding armies. An interesting question now arose: Had fate selected Latin America to benefit from this tragedy by opening up new markets, creating new immigrants, and putting a new premium on its immense natural resources? More specifically, had the future finally arrived for Brazil, the largest, most populous, and best-endowed country of Latin America? It was in this optimistic climate that the Brazilian political elite confronted the postwar world.

The two decades following World War II saw a flood of political changes in Brazil. Democracy and free elections returned in 1945. Vargas, the former dictator, was able to use democracy to his advantage and returned to power as a democratically elected president in 1951.

One of Vargas's fundamental goals as an elected leader was to develop and carry out an ambitious economic program, a major part of which called for state control of the petroleum industry. This caused a major political fight at the same time Brazil was forced to introduce an economic stabilization program that dashed Vargas's hopes for growth. The weakness of the economy played into the hands of Vargas's enemies, leading to a political crisis and Vargas's suicide.

A brilliant and ebullient politician from Vargas's own camp succeeded him—Juscelino Kubitschek, who was able to achieve the economic development that Vargas had sought. A particularly powerful symbol of the new optimism Kubitschek brought with him was his success in realizing a dream that had gripped Brazil since the mid–eighteenth century (it was even specified in the 1891 Constitution): the building of Brasília, a new capital that would open up Brazil's interior. But Kubitschek's achievements had their downside. Four years after his presidency had ended, the inflation kindled by his growth policies led to a political crisis so grave that the military intervened, taking power for themselves in 1964.

The 1945 Election and the Dutra Period

When the military sent Vargas back to his ranch, they ensured that electoral democracy returned to Brazil. The presidential election was held as scheduled in December 1945, with six million votes cast. This was three times as many as voted in 1930—the last presidential election—making the Brazil of 1945 a far more national polity than the oligarchy that had collapsed in 1930. In this election, party labels had some meaning in the large cities, but in the countryside and small towns, political allegiances (with party labels) still went to one or another local political clan whose origins went back at least to the Old Republic, if not the Empire.

The presidential election of 1945 was primarily a contest between two military officers. It was won by General Eúrico Gaspar Dutra, who ran on the PSD (Partido Social Democrático) ticket—a party composed of state party bosses and some São Paulo businessmen. He had been war minister from 1936 to 1945, serving as a pillar of Vargas's authoritarian Estado Nôvo. Now he had the support of the many state bosses wanting to preserve their influence under the new democratic regime. His chief opponent was air force brigadier Eduardo Gomes, who ran on the UDN (*União Democrática Nacional*) ticket. Gomes, a survivor of the Fort Copacabana revolt of 1922, a hero in the defense against the 1935 Communist revolt in Rio, a prominent opponent of the coup of 1937, and the top officer in the Brazilian air force (established in 1942), was generally recognized to be an upright, highly moral soldier. His reputation appealed to the relatively small middle- and upper-class electorate but failed to reach other voters in sufficient numbers to win.

The major surprise of the 1945 election was the support enjoyed by the Communist party candidate for president, Yeddo Fiúza, who received 10 percent of the vote (exhibit 6-1). The Communists' success is in good part explained by strong worker discontent over the rapid inflation created by World War II. Continuing industrialization, though patchy, had enlarged the working class and the Communist Party had worked hard to recruit within it. The voters chose a new Congress, which, in turn, wrote a new Constitution. Debates over how the new Constitution (Brazil's fifth) should be shaped were dominated by de-

EXHIBIT 6-1
Popular Vote for President, 1945

Candidate	Vote
Eurico Dutra (PSD)	3,251,507
Eduardo Gomes (UDN)	2,039,341
Yedo Fiúza (PCB)	569,818

Source: Walter Costa Porto, *O Voto no Brasil* (Brasília, 1989), p. 262.

mands to restore power to the states and municipalities. Orator after orator identified strong central government with dictatorship, in a concerted effort by the elite to legitimize devolution of power. The Constitution of 1946 reflected this objective. It retained the position of president as head of the national government but restored the power of the purse to Congress. This had the result of returning considerable power to the state political machines, although less than they had enjoyed under the Old Republic.

Although the electoral base in 1945 was a great deal larger than it had been in 1930, socioeconomically Brazil was, in the parlance of the day, still a "backward" country. Its industry was limited to a few large cities. Chronic disease was widespread and regular medical care nonexistent for most of the population. Overall life expectancy was forty-six years, with life expectancy in the Northeast under forty years. The economy continued to depend on coffee exports.

Even so, Brazil appeared to enjoy an enviable economic situation in 1945. It had accumulated significant foreign exchange reserves (during the war, imports had fallen greatly as the Allies restricted civilian industrial production because of the war effort). The Dutra policy makers assumed their economy could take up where it had left off in 1930—relying on sales of primary products such as coffee. This represented somewhat of a return to the traditional liberalism that had, indeed, led to the pre-Depression prosperity based on the rapid world economic growth of the 1870–1914 era. But in 1946–47, a flood of imported consumer goods, along with the buying up of foreign-owned public utilities, soaked up Brazil's foreign exchange reserves. Large-scale worker strikes in São Paulo in 1947 aggravated the situation, alarming both the Dutra government and the São Paulo economic establishment. In the face of the deteriorating economic situation, which led to a severe foreign exchange shortage in 1948, the Dutra government relied on the traditional emphasis on export promotion—greater promotion of coffee sales combined with import controls. There was no serious talk about promoting industrialization.

Reacting to the deteriorating political situation, the Dutra government remembered, and repeated, Vargas's warnings of the 1930s. They depicted the strikers as tools of Moscow, which (not coincidentally) helped justify the almost universal rejection by employers of wage demands by their workers. The growing confrontation between government and business and, on the other hand, the workers looked like a rerun of polarization that had led to Vargas's crackdown on the Communists and most of the left in 1935. Sure enough, the Dutra government resorted to political repression in 1947. The domestic imperatives for this were greatly reinforced by pressure from the United States.

By the late 1940s, the U.S. national security establishment was committed to fighting the Soviet threat everywhere. This included an offensive by the State Department and the Pentagon to convince Latin American governments to break diplomatic relations with the Soviet Union and to repress local Communist Parties. In 1947, the Dutra government broke off relations with the Soviet Union and pushed the Supreme Electoral Court to outlaw the Communist Party. The labor union leaderships and the federal bureaucracy were systematically purged of Communists and militant leftists. In January 1948, the Congress expelled its fourteen Communist deputies and one senator. The shadow of the Estado Nôvo extended over a newly democratic Brazil.

The chief beneficiary of the PCB's suppression was the PTB (Partido Trabalhista Brasileiro, or the Brazilian Labor Party), which now had more room to recruit among workers. The PTB was the third major party (along with the UDN and the PDS) founded in 1945. Its patron was Vargas, who hoped to create a Brazilian version of the European Social Democratic parties. The Communist Party, per se, never regained its electoral influence of the 1945–47 period, although the PTB leaders developed informal pacts with the Communists, many of whom subsequently operated under PTB electoral cover. Communism remained a powerful force among intellectuals and labor unions, however, for the next twenty-five years.

Vargas Returns

As Brazil's participation in the Second World War continued, Vargas had worked on finding a new rationale for keeping power. Beginning in 1943, he and his technocrats had begun to stake out a new political position, the keynote of which was an appeal to the urban working class. Its immediate application was an expansion of the labor union system, where the federal government predominated in managing relations between employers and workers. Vargas left the details to his labor minister, Marcondes Filho, who supervised the codification of the labor laws in 1943 and worked to strengthen government ties with the few leading unions.

That meant using patronage to build a political following among the union leaders. A similar strategy was being followed in Argentina, albeit with a heavier hand, by Colonel Juan Perón, who from 1943 to 1945 was the labor minister in an Argentine military government.

The creation of the PTB in 1945 was an extension of the strategy of cultivating union leadership. Vargas saw this party as the electoral arm of his populist strategy. In the last two years of his dictatorship, Vargas was constructing a direct appeal to urban workers. This effort was cut short in October 1945, when fear of his intentions led to his ouster. Curiously enough, the apparatus of the government labor bureaucracy had hardly penetrated São Paulo. It was to accelerate after 1945.

In the years of the Dutra presidency, Vargas continued to elaborate his populist strategy. He had been elected in December 1945 as a senator from both Rio Grande do Sul and São Paulo, as well as deputy from seven states. He took up his Senate seat only briefly, withdrawing as soon as he had secured a public position from which to spread his message. In his many speeches after 1946, he criticized government policy, particularly for failing to benefit more the working class.

FROM OLIGARCH TO POPULIST

Vargas also worked to maintain his links to the traditional power sectors. Many state political bosses now in power had benefited from his earlier rule, and the São Paulo industrialists owed Vargas much for the business directed their way by his war effort. Finally, as a *fazendeiro* in Rio Grande do Sul, Vargas had the sympathy of fellow land holders, who were grateful he had never threatened the existing system of land tenure. For them, his newly minted populism was purely for urban consumption and was thus a strategy with which they could happily live.

While Vargas worked to transform his image from dictator to democratic politician, his longtime opponents did everything possible to sabotage that effort. The leading São Paulo newspaper *(O Estado de S. Paulo)*, for example, never referred to Vargas by name, but only as the "ex-dictator." They had a ready audience. Vargas, never notably popular in São Paulo, still had the image of the Machiavellian figure who had betrayed democracy in 1937. He was also hated by some state political bosses, who had lost their access to federal power during his dictatorship. Nevertheless, Vargas was relatively successful in shedding the dictator image. By nature a genial personality, he played on the well-known Brazilian inclination to let bygones be bygones in politics.

Political divisions after Dutra's election played into Vargas's hands. The liberal constitutionalists, best represented by the UDN, expected to be the prime beneficiaries of Vargas's overthrow in 1945. They were bitterly disappointed when they lost the 1945 presidential election to General Dutra, the candidate supported by Vargas. They did win respectable representation in Congress, however (29 percent in the Chamber of Deputies, as against 53 percent for the PSD), where they could continue preaching the doctrines of traditional liberalism and prepare for the 1950 presidential election.

As for the left, it had regrouped after the Dutra government outlawed the Communist Party and purged the unions in 1947. The PTB was left as the principal national party with appeal to the urban worker, although that appeal often failed, as in São Paulo, where the PTB remained weak. Thus the government's anti-Communist move of 1947 played into the hands of the populist electoral strategy Vargas had been elaborating since 1945.

By 1949, the international lines of conflict in the Cold War were drawn, with the U.S. government pressuring Brazil, along with the rest of Latin America, to join the United States in confronting the Soviet-led bloc. The intelligence agencies of both the United States and the Soviet Union (and later Fidelista Cuba) gave both financial and training assistance to their favored Brazilian organizations, often in clandestine circumstances. The Communist Party received funds and logistical support from Moscow. A wide range of Brazilian politicians and organizations got money and organizational help from Washington (via the CIA and other agencies). The Brazilian military, for one, readily absorbed U.S. doctrines through such institutions as its Higher War College (Escola Superior de Guerra), created in 1949 with U.S. help and blessing. With the outbreak of the Korean War, the U.S. government pressed Brazil strongly to send combat troops to fight alongside the United States. (The Vargas government successfully resisted.)

The political center was poorly defined in the Dutra years. It was most often identified with the PSD, which represented a wide social spectrum, including landowners, industrialists, and parts of the small middle class. The PSD was the least overtly ideological of the major parties and, therefore, in the best position to bargain.

With the political lines so fluid in 1949, predictions about future trends were especially dangerous. Public opinion research had hardly begun in Brazil (the first poll by IBOPE, the pioneer firm, was in 1945) and voting patterns were too recent to furnish a basis for prognostication. It was in the context of this fluid situation that voters saw Vargas emerging from his "exile" in a new and democratic incarnation.

Vargas's carefully laid groundwork to run for the presidency in 1950 included more than establishing himself as a populist. He also paid attention to the pragmatic task of getting the support of powerful political groups. First, he got assurances that the military would not veto his candidacy or his taking office should he win. This assurance was facilitated by General Góes Monteiro, Vargas's onetime collaborator during the Estado Nôvo and a still influential figure among the generals. Second, Vargas enlisted the support of three key political forces that could form a winning coalition. One was Adhemar de Barros, governor of São Paulo and an early proponent of the populist style in politics (meaning an appeal to urban voters based on public works, social welfare benefits, and an efficient voting machine). Adhemar wanted to run for president but was willing to back Vargas now in return for Vargas's later support of his own bid. Another was the PSD, which had its own candidate, but for which Vargas was able to split the support by wooing its regional chieftains, especially in Minais Gerais. The PTB, which was a growing force in selected states, rounded out the list.

The vote showed the extent of Vargas's skill. In a multiple field of candidates he received 48.7 percent, nearly an absolute majority. His chief opponent once again was Eduardo Gomes of the UDN, who received only 29.7 percent, while Machado of the PSD received 21.5 percent. Gomes, the loser in the 1945 presidential election, seemed to have learned little about Brazil's move toward change. During the campaign he actually went so far as to advocate repeal of the minimum wage law. By contrast, Vargas attacked the Dutra government for having neglected industrialization. In Rio, where the left was comparatively strong, he sounded a particularly populist note: "If I am elected on October 3rd, as I take office the people will climb the steps of Catete [the presidential palace] with me. And they will remain with me in power."

VARGAS'S LEGISLATIVE PROGRAM RUNS INTO TROUBLE

Once back in power, Vargas broke definitively with the liberal economic policies partially reinstated by the Dutra government. Implicit was his assumption that Brazil would need to promote industrialization if it were to overcome the balance-of-payments bottleneck that had become only too obvious during the Dutra years. An able team of young technocrats soon began to develop a plan for national economic development. The first step was creation of the National Bank for Economic Development in 1952. Here Vargas and his technocrats were drawing on the work of the Joint U.S.-Brazil Commission on Economic Development (1951–53), which, composed of technical experts from both countries, had produced an analysis of Brazil's primary economic needs. Since energy supplies were perennially inadequate to support industrialization (government concern on this count went back to 1938), the government proposed to create state enterprises in oil and electricity. Such measures violated the liberal prejudice against state intervention in the economy and provoked heavy criticism from UDN politicians and orthodox economists. The president defended his measures by invoking patriotism, nationalism, and realism in the face of the changing world economy—placing a heavy bet that his nationalist appeal would overcome the elite consensus favoring economic liberalism.

The strategy failed. His proposal for a state enterprise in petroleum became the most controversial measure of his new presidency. The government's original proposal called for a mixed public-private corporation, called Petrobrás, with a de facto state monopoly over the central operations. The proposal was sent to Congress in 1951, and for two years the country was locked in a passionate debate. On the right, supported by U.S. opposition to the proposal, spokesmen attacked it as dangerously interventionist. On the left, the Communist Party (acting partly through surrogates) demanded a full state monopoly. They exploited the public's distrust of international oil companies and charged that government supporters were on foreign payrolls. The U.S. government's opposition to Petrobrás only reinforced the fury of the left. Vargas was caught in the middle.

The danger in this confrontation was compounded by the involvement of the army officer corps. Its nationalist wing passionately supported Vargas's proposal for strategic purposes. They wanted Brazil to develop its own oil supply so it could be self-sufficient in time of war. The other military faction, the anticommunists, attacked the proposal as collectivist state intervention that would move Brazil toward the Communist camp.

The disagreement within the military was ominous for Vargas. He knew that to remain in power he had to retain the support of the top army officers. He had carefully reassured these officers when he returned to the presidency, but now divisions among the military threatened to undermine their support for him.

The fight over Petrobrás did not turn out as Vargas had hoped. The UDN, intending to outflank and embarrass Vargas, switched position and announced in favor of a total state monopoly. By such a reversal they hoped to steal the nationalist flag from Vargas. Congress passed this more extreme version, ruling out the private participation provided for in the government proposal. This outcome saddled Vargas with a more statist law than he had wanted. It also meant that he had lost control over the legislative process.

As the Vargas government devised its new economic strategy, it also faced serious trade problems. World coffee prices had declined sharply in 1953, thereby shrinking Brazil's foreign exchange earnings. The result was a growing balance-of-payments deficit, which the International Monetary Fund (IMF) blamed on Brazil's allegedly inflationary domestic policies. (See exhibit 6-2.) In 1953, under pressure from the IMF and the U.S. government, Brazil launched a stabilization program to correct the balance-of-payments deficit. Vargas turned to his longtime political ally Oswaldo Aranha, who was named minister of finance, to carry out the program. Stabilization was a bitter pill for Vargas to swallow for two reasons. First, it would preclude any economic growth for the rest of his term. Second, it was bound to arouse popular opposition since it in-

EXHIBIT 6-2
Brazil's Balance of Payments, 1947–54
Inflow Minus Outflow (US$ millions)

	Commercial Balance(a)	Net Services	Transfers	Net Capital	Errors & Omissions	Surplus (+) or Deficit (−)
1947	130	−257	−24	12	−43	−182
1948	278	−273	−7	−51	29	−24
1949	153	−232	−3	−74	82	−74
1950	425	−283	−2	−65	−23	52
1951	68	−469	−2	−11	123	−291
1952	−266	−336	−2	35	−26	−615
1953	424	−355	−14	59	−98	16
1954	148	−338	−5	−18	10	−203

(a) Exports minus imports.
Source: IBGE, *Estatísticas Históricas do Brasil*, 2nd ed. (Rio de Janeiro, 1990), p. 581–85.

volved restricting credit and holding down wages. Vargas's ambitious dreams of economic development and support from the working class were under a growing cloud.

SUICIDE

As 1954 began, events were closing in on Vargas. Economic crisis had made his government more vulnerable politically. His enemies, especially in the UDN and military, smelled weakness. The bitter debate over Petrobrás had inflamed ideological opinion in Brazil and aroused military suspicions about Vargas's intentions. A campaign to drive Vargas from office began. It was led by Carlos Lacerda, a venomous journalist and leading orator as a UDN politician, who now devoted his formidable talents to vilifying the president. Lacerda controlled a newspaper (*A Tribuna da Imprensa*) that carried his message on a daily basis. Lacerda's more moderate UDN colleagues (who could not bring themselves to adopt his language) were exhilarated by his attacks and began to see him as a powerful weapon against a president whose return to power they had never accepted.

Vargas's supporters, especially among the PTB, were on the defensive because Vargas had been reelected in 1950 by a loose coalition ranging across the political spectrum. His former supporters among the wealthy now saw him as dispensable, and his support on the left was too weak to neutralize the current scale of attacks. This political impasse reflected the inherent limitation of the populist political strategy which Vargas had increasingly adopted since 1953. Populism, in the form of wage hikes, nationalist economic initiatives, and patronage for the faithful, had not created a political base that could withstand an onslaught of civilian conservatives and a military looking for reasons to mount a coup. The same lesson would be learned by Argentine president Juan Perón in 1955 and by Brazilian president João Goulart in 1964.

Vargas, who had wavered between orthodox and nationalist measures, now swung decisively toward nationalism. The first indicator was wage policy. Vargas's labor minister was a young PTB politician from Vargas's local region in Rio Grande do Sul, João Goulart (the man who would be Brazil's president from 1961 until his own ouster by the military in 1964). Goulart was a Vargas protégée. On the minimum wage, which had not changed since 1951, Goulart recommended a 100 percent increase, infuriating the right, especially the military. This action was in part a response to the massive industrial strikes (such as the "Strike of the 300,000") which had shaken São Paulo in 1953. Put in the proper perspective, Goulart's recommendation was not patently absurd. Such an increase would have represented a real raise (i.e., more than compensated for inflation) over the 1951 level but would have left the minimum wage still far short of many prevailing industrial wage rates. Furthermore, the minimum wage varied widely by region, with São Paulo levels considerably higher than those in the Northeast. Yet Goulart had become a political liability and saw he had to resign.

Vargas accepted Goulart's resignation, leading observers to expect the president to settle on a lower increase. On May 1st, however, he announced as a *fait accompli* exactly what Goulart had recommended: an increase of 100 percent. This act alarmed employers and confirmed military suspicions that Vargas was plotting a thoroughgoing radical populist strategy. Many employers refused to honor the wage decree, even though it had been legitimated by the Federal Supreme Court. The result was a wave of strikes and strike threats across the country. Once again the UDN charged that the president had no commitment to maintaining "order."

The second indicator of Vargas's political swing was a possible organization of rural labor unions. The Estado Nôvo labor laws had never been extended to the countryside, thereby maintaining Vargas's strategy of avoiding any threat to landowners. In February, however, Goulart had proposed, along with the minimum wage increase, regulations to recognize rural labor unions, thereby threatening to expand the Vargas populist strategy to the rural sector.

For Vargas, this strategy came too late. The final chapter of his presidency began in June 1954 with a UDN attempt to remove Vargas by constitutional means. It was decisively defeated when the Chamber of

Deputies rejected an impeachment motion by 136 to 35. The UDN would have to resort to other means. The weapon at hand was Carlos Lacerda, who was also a candidate in the October congressional elections, in which his principal opponent was Getúlio's son Lutero. (Lacerda won.) By early August of 1954, Lacerda's campaign attacking Vargas had seized the imagination of the Brazilian public. Among the more sensational (and utterly unsubstantiated) charges was the claim that Vargas had secretly negotiated an alliance with Argentina's Juan Perón, presumably to fortify a "syndicalist republic" in each country. It was the kind of face-off even the politically uninitiated could understand. Furthermore, Vargas had conspicuously failed to create an effective enough public relations capacity to counter his critics. Those around Vargas were alarmed by the effects of the attacks on the president, who became withdrawn and depressed. The faithful tried to fight back.

One of Vargas's most faithful followers was Gregório Fortunato, the president's Afro-Brazilian bodyguard and chauffeur. As he listened to the voices of alarm in the palace about Vargas's plight, he decided to act—contacting a professional gunman and instructing him to eliminate Lacerda.

The would-be assassin stalked Lacerda in front of his apartment near Copacabana Beach and fired at him from across the street. The bullets killed an air force major, Rubens Vaz, who was acting as Lacerda's bodyguard, but only wounded Lacerda in the foot. (His detractors thought it should have been in the mouth.) The gunman had done the ultimate disservice to Vargas and his chauffeur. Lacerda continued his attacks, now even more dramatic from his hospital bed, and the air force officer corps created a board of inquiry to investigate their fellow officer's assassination. It was not difficult to trace the killer to the presidential palace. Vargas's opponents were now able to accuse the president of harboring an accomplice to murder.

Vargas probably did not know of Fortunato's plot to kill Lacerda, but he certainly knew his palace was out of control. He was shaken by the revelation that Samuel Wainer, his journalist friend and key supporter (as editor of the pro-government daily *Última Hora*), had gotten sweetheart loans from the Bank of Brazil. This confirmation of corruption around the president led Vargas to remark "I feel I am standing in a sea of mud."

Vargas's days as president were clearly numbered. If he did not resign, a military coup was inevitable. Yet if he did resign, he would abandon his long-cherished image of himself as a leader single-mindedly devoted to the welfare of the poor. He described himself as a martyr opposed by powerful and selfish forces, both domestic and foreign.

Vargas's advisers and his cabinet were divided over how he should react. Some wanted him to resist, if necessary with arms. Others called the situation hopeless and warned that the president's safety was in doubt if he did not promptly resign. On August 24th, Vargas held a lengthy cabinet meeting in the Catete presidential palace to discuss his next move. He said nothing about what he intended to do, but his closest advisers were troubled by his mood. They had more reason than they realized to be troubled. What they did not know was that Vargas had talked of suicide in his diary—the existence of which was not revealed until many years later—as early as 1930.

The president left the meeting, retired to his Catete palace bedroom, reached for a revolver, and fired once into his heart. The sound reverberated through the palace. His longtime ally, Oswaldo Aranha, rushed into the bedroom and burst into tears.

The political climate was transformed. Before the suicide, an atmosphere of hostility had been aimed at the president; now, a wave of outrage was aimed at his tormentors. The streets filled with pro-Vargas demonstrators who attacked the offices of the conservative newspaper *O Globo*. Lacerda went from a hero to a hunted man. He soon left Brazil for an extended exile.

By his suicide, Vargas had turned the tables on his enemies in the UDN and the military. He had neutralized what they had planned to be a smashing political victory. They wanted not only the removal of Vargas but the reversal of his policies and the displacement of his political network. That political agenda was now impossible, given the state of public opinion. Vargas may have been dead, but his influence was very much alive.

A brief socioeconomic profile of Brazil around this period is useful context for interpreting the political history of the ten years following Vargas's suicide.

A Socioeconomic Profile of Brazil in the Late 1940s and 1950s

The Brazil of the late 1940s and 1950s was in the midst of a population explosion. It was also a country with major regional disequilibria, large movements of population among regions, and enormous social inequalities. All these factors were catalysts that increased the volatility of Brazil's political life during the period.

By 1945, the long-standing public health campaigns against the epidemic diseases long ravaging Brazil were beginning to pay off. Much of the medical technology and personnel for the campaigns had been furnished by the Rockefeller Foundation, which had started sending specialists to boost Brazil's public health programs in the 1920s—a dramatic example of how relatively small investments in prevention can have large consequences in developing societies. Unfortunately, the payoff included rising fertility rates, from 6.16 (children per mother) in 1940 to

EXHIBIT 6-3
Population and Population Growth Rate, 1940–91

Census Year	Population (millions)	Average Annual Rate of Growth since Last Census
1940	41.1	1.49
1950	51.9	2.39
1960	70.0	2.99
1970	93.9	2.89
1980	119.0	2.48
1991	146.8	1.93

Source: IBGE, *Censos Demográficos.*

6.28 by 1960, putting Brazil's rates among the highest rates in the world. This, combined with a mortality rate that fell by 68 percent between 1940 and 1960, produced population growth rates that put a great burden on Brazil's economy. (See exhibit 6-3.)

This rapidly growing population was increasingly urban. By 1950, the share of the population classified as urban was approaching 40 percent, up from 30 percent in 1940. The process of urbanization was chaotic. In-migrants from the countryside, finding no housing, erected their own shanty towns, sprawling developments (often called *favelas*) that typically appeared on the city edges and often became more populous than the formal city. Although urban services were poor or nonexistent, these in-migrants rightly saw their life chances as better in the city than in the countryside. They found jobs in the service sector, many in the informal economy. And they could also flow back to the countryside when the city economy turned sour.

Of this rapidly growing urban population, the increasing proportion of Brazilians under twelve years of age was a special burden because the infrastructure for education and health care services was thin and grossly underfinanced. Schools, hospitals and clinics were all inadequate. Although the outside world saw a relatively favorable picture through films such as *Black Orpheus*, which romanticized *favela* life in Rio de Janeiro, the growing *favelas* frightened the urban elite within Brazil.

REGIONAL DISEQUILIBRIA AND MIGRATION

The early postwar years saw continuing economic divergence among Brazil's regions. São Paulo's share of national industry had risen from

36 percent in 1940 to 47 percent in 1950, for example, reaching 54 percent in 1960. The largest losers in this concentration of new industry were the Northeast, which fell from 12 percent to 8 percent, and Rio de Janeiro, which went from 27 percent to 17 percent. The concentration in São Paulo was hardly surprising, since it resulted from the same economies of scale that have produced similar patterns in every industrializing country.

Even so, the fact that São Paulo was producing about half of Brazil's GDP and more than half of its federal revenues led the rest of Brazil often to be jealous and critical. Politicians from the poorer areas attacked São Paulo as greedy and selfish, exploiting the rest of Brazil—attacks that had ample precedent in Brazilian political tradition. Politicians from the Northeast, in particular, argued that their region had become a virtual colony of São Paulo, attacking São Paulo's industrial products as overpriced and leading to unfair "terms of trade" between the regions. This argument was given its most sophisticated form by a brilliant economist from the Northeast, Celso Furtado, as in his seminal book *The Economic Growth of Brazil* (first Brazilian edition in 1959). In essence, the Northeasterners were appealing to the conscience of the elite in the south, a case that was strengthened by a devastating drought that struck the Northeast in 1958.

Other lagging regions got far less attention than the Northeast. The most obvious was the Amazon Basin, where Brazilian settlement was still extremely thin. Another was the far West, the Campo Cerrado, where fertile land (its fertility was contested by geographers before the 1960s but amply demonstrated thereafter) was cheap but often inaccessible. The truth was that the Brazilians were still largely following the pattern of their Portuguese ancestors by "clinging to the coast like crabs."

As already discussed, employers in the Old Republic, especially in the Center-South, had concentrated on looking for new workers among immigrants from other countries. Racial and regional prejudices led them to underestimate the value of the labor force already in their country. As large-scale in-migration from abroad declined after World War I, employers looked more seriously for workers from other parts of Brazil. This flow, unlike the earlier flow from Europe, was not organized or subsidized by the employers; rather, it was a spontaneous process of individual Brazilians and their families responding to economic signals across the country.

Although there are no official statistics on internal migration, estimates from census data and population growth rates indicate the trends. In the years from 1940 to 1950, the largest movement was out of Minas Gerais and into Rio, São Paulo, and Paraná. In subsequent years, there was also significant migration from the Northeast to São Paulo.

Such migration had several effects. First, it deprived the sending states of many enterprising and talented citizens. Second, it fed a pool

EXHIBIT 6-4
Immigrants into Brazil by Decade, 1872–1972

Years	Immigrants (absolute numbers)
1872–79	176,337
1880–89	448,622
1890–99	1,198,327
1900–09	622,407
1910–19	815,453
1920–29	846,647
1930–39	332,768
1940–49	114,085
1950–59	583,068
1960–69	197,587
Total (1872–1972)	5,350,889

Source: 1872–1970: Thomas W. Merrick and Douglas H. Graham, Population and Economic Development (Baltimore, 1979), p. 119. 1991: Instituto Brasileiro de Geografia e Estatística, Diretoria de Pesquisas, Population Census.

of surplus labor that helped to keep wages down and thus reduce potential union militancy in the industrial cities. Third, it reinforced the national character of Brazil's culture. In-migrants from other parts of Brazil brought with them their music, folklore, cuisine, and style of life. This influx and its resulting human contact helped to bridge regional differences (although it also produced a backlash, as in the Paulistas' frequent scorn for Northeasterners). Many street corners and *praças* (squares) in São Paulo and Rio, for example, became known for their Sunday night congregations of migrants from distant states. Finally, as the migration of Brazilians increasingly replaced the recruitment of foreigners (see exhibit 6-4), Brazilian society would henceforth be made up primarily of native-born Brazilians. For better or worse, the era of hoping for redemption from Europe was now over.

PATTERNS OF URBAN AND RURAL GROWTH

It was during the immediate post–World War II period that Brazil began to see the emergence of the vast cities that would characterize urban life for the rest of the century. Brazil's urbanization differed, however, from that of Argentina, Chile, Mexico, or Venezuela. Those countries all had a single dominant metropolis, the capital. In Brazil, the official capital of Rio de Janeiro had to share dominance with São Paulo. Brazil was, therefore, saved from focusing the vast majority of its attention on a single city.

Brazil's rapid urban growth, as elsewhere in Latin America, has been criticized for having attracted huge populations that concentrated in the informal sector because the cities lacked the formal sector jobs to support their populations. This was especially true of secondary cities such as Recife and Salvador. Yet it should be remembered that such urban growth had its logic. The rural mass chose to move to the city because they perceived their economic opportunities to be better there and knew they could move back to the countryside if city conditions became bad enough. Their underemployment in the urban economy simply reflected the labor force stratification implicit in the countryside from which they came. These "marginal" inhabitants strove to improve their life by upgrading their shacks or by moving to better housing. This mobility within the marginal population was integral to economic growth. The marginal urban dwellers were nonetheless viewed with wariness by the middle and upper classes. They were seen as potential, if not actual, criminals and thus a threat to public order. They were, in the eyes of the well-to-do, the "dangerous classes," despite the fact that the thousands of domestic servants serving peacefully in the homes of the higher classes came from these very ranks.

Despite the rapid growth of cities, more than half of all Brazilians in the 1950s still lived in the countryside. But rural Brazil was far from homogeneous. Large-scale commercial agriculture, worked by wage laborers, included coffee plantations in São Paulo and Paraná, sugar plantations in Pernambuco and Alagoas, and wheat farms in Rio Grande do Sul.

Rural Brazil also had a large subsistence sector, where farmers cultivated their own small plot or worked as sharecroppers. These small units were farmed by families whose numerous children could be put to work in the field. Subsistence farmers often tried to market a few cash crops, but their ability to do so depended on weather, road conditions, and market prices.

Most rural dwellers had little knowledge of their government. Medical care and schools were usually nonexistent. People communicated by word of mouth. The one regular link to the outside world was a radio. Between 1945 and 1960, for example, the number of radio stations in Brazil had increased from less than 100 to more than 800. Travel to the nearest town was done on foot or horseback. Access to buses, trucks, or automobiles was difficult and expensive.

There were, however, exceptions to the general pattern of low-productivity, low-skill agriculture. One was the network of dynamic

Japanese truck-farming colonies in São Paulo, Paraná, and Pará. Organizing large cooperatives, they pooled their skills to become the largest food supplier to the city of São Paulo. Another exception was the network of settlements by German (along with Ukranian and Polish) descendants in Santa Catarina and Rio Grande do Sul. These farmers mastered medium-scale commercial farming and also provided the public services (especially education) that most of rural Brazil lacked.

Rural Brazil also produced its own cultures. There was a distinctive music and folklore (including humor) for each region. The Northeast become famous for its tales of banditry, the best known hero of which were Lampião and his companion Maria Bonita. Their exploits became celebrated in poetry, song, and film. In southern Brazil, the familiar figure was the *caipira*, or backwoodsman, who was the subject of endless folklore, such as observed in the children's festivals on St. John's day every June. This cultural construction from the countryside became an integral part of Brazilian national culture.

SOCIAL STRATIFICATION

A general picture of Brazil's highly stratified society during this period can be drawn, although the quantitative indicators to document the extent of the disparities are sparse. Income distribution data was not yet gathered in Brazil and wealth data were also nonexistent. Aggregate data for such items as infant mortality and life expectancy are available, but there is no breakdown by income.

The widest social differences were found in the countryside, where a landowner's or merchant's income was many times that of a subsistence farmer. At least equally important, those at the bottom had virtually no hope of mobility. In the city, at least the chances for mobility through public education, though small, were higher.

Urban areas were also strictly stratified, although the divergence between top and bottom was slightly less. At the bottom were the urban workers in the informal market. They had no fixed employment and survived through ad hoc jobs, often as street sellers. One up from the bottom of the scale came the manual workers, such as bus drivers, janitors, factory workers, and mechanics. They fell below the middle classes, not only in pay but also in education. The small middle class consisted of the professions and the government bureaucracy. These were nonmanual workers with at least a secondary education, and attuned to urban values. Above them were the high-income earners and major wealth holders. They held the lucrative positions in commerce, law, industry, and finance, usually coming from families with extensive links to rural landholding.

This social hierarchy retained much of the flavor of Brazil's colonial era. Those at the top were treated with great deference by those below.

The tone of the relationship was captured by the anthropologist Roberto da Matta in the phrase "Do you know who you're talking to?" (as the superior haughtily addresses the inferior). The parallel with the power of the slave-master relationship comes to mind. Life was lived within the hierarchical context of prestige and power. The way to survive was to find a powerful *patrão* (patron) to act as one's protector. Collective action was not a rational option within this world. Rather, the premium was on promoting one's individual fortunes and those of one's family. The devices used reflected the social system. Brazilians relied on such institutions as the extended family (even a distant relative might prove a valuable contact), the network of friends (the *panelinha*) and co-godfatherhood or godmotherhood (*compadresco*).

The political implications of this social ethos were far-reaching. It favored strong leaders, personalistic politics, and minimal collective action. As a cultural atmosphere, it was unfriendly to both the merit system of hiring and promotion and to the creation of loyalties to parties or movements.

A New President, Juscelino Kubitschek, Elected

The public's reaction to Vargas's suicide robbed his opponents of their long-awaited triumph. They could not carry out their plans to disrupt the government. A presidential election was scheduled for 1955, but until then, the federal government was run by caretaker regimes (headed by Presidents Café Filho and Nereu Ramos). They lacked authority to make significant changes, however, even though inflation continued to increase and the balance-of-payments deficit failed to improve. Little foreign capital came into the country, exacerbating Brazil's low domestic savings rate. This boded ill for future growth. In 1955, however, new hope for economic development arrived in the form of Juscelino Kubitschek, who opted for growth with a vengeance as soon as he became president.

Kubitschek was a typical product of the Vargas political system. He had left his initial profession of physician to rise through the PSD party in Minas Gerais, having been mayor of the capital city of Belo Horizonte and governor of the state. His family name was Oliveira, but for political purposes he chose to use the Czechoslovakian name of an ancestor because he thought it would make him stand out among the field of Brazilian politicians. He was an ebullient politician, well used to the wheeling and dealing demanded in Brazil's wide-open politics. He won the presidency by successfully splitting his opposition, the UDN candidate General Juarez Távora, the PSD candidate Christian Machado, and the São Paulo populist Adhemar de Barros, who ran under the banner of the Partido Social Progresista (PSP). Kubitschek thus assumed the presidency with only 36 percent of the vote, which contrasted with Vargas's 49 percent in 1950 and Dutra's 55 percent in 1945. Aside from being a minority president, he was also vulnerable vis-à-vis the military because of his Vargas connections and because his vice presidential running mate was João Goulart, arch enemy of the UDN and the conservative military. His presidency began on an ominous note. A group of air force officers stationed in Amazônia attempted a revolt against the new government in January 1956. The revolt was quashed, but it showed the new president would have little margin for error in dealing with the anti-Vargas military.

POLITICAL STRATEGY

Kubitschek's thin political base required him to maneuver carefully to maintain congressional support. The left painted him as the lackey of imperialism, selling Brazil out for short-term political gain. The right accused him of trying to curry favor with militant labor, giving as proof the large 1958 boost in the minimum wage (set at its highest real level since 1945). His own party, the PSD, avoided overt ideology but had uneven power across the country. Kubitschek's method of solidifying support was to make major concessions to both ends of the political spectrum. An example of his efforts to placate the political left was his reaction to pressure from northeastern politicians, who complained that the South region was gaining unduly from industrialization, leaving the populous low-income Northeast even further behind. To quiet this complaint, Kubitschek accepted a proposal for a new federal authority, SUDENE (Superintendência para o Desenvolvimento do Nordeste)—based on a document ("Operation Northeast") by Celso Furtado—to promote northeastern economic development. The idea was to encourage investment and especially industrialization in selected northeastern areas. A key device was a tax-forgiveness scheme to attract new industry or induce established industry to move from more developed regions. Significantly, land reform was ignored. The U.S. government, alarmed over the growth of peasant leagues in the area, also pledged to help in the transfer of technology and capital.

An example of placating the right was how Kubitschek dealt with the military. Since he knew he was ultra-vulnerable on this front, he decided to spend heavily on new military equipment. The navy wanted an aircraft carrier, and so the government purchased an outmoded carrier from Britain and had it refitted in Holland.

By his maneuvering, Kubitschek tried to protect his government from attacks by both left and right. He was successful enough to complete his term and pass the presidency to a duly elected civilian successor. His economic strategy played an important role in that success.

Once in office, Kubitschek launched an ambitious economic development program, which led to a continuing balance-of-payments crisis and initially to a stabilization program which the International Monetary Fund attempted to force on Brazil. Whether his economic program was worth its cost (especially the building of Brasília) is a question that has been debated for decades.

THE ECONOMIC DEVELOPMENT PROGRAM

The first step Kubitschek and his technocrats took was to draw up a *Programa de Metas* ("Program of Goals"), a set of targets for increased production by sector. The objective was to bring together the state and the private sector in a high-growth strategy whose aim was to accelerate industrialization and the construction of the infrastructure necessary to sustain it.

In ideological terms, the Kubitschek economic strategy was centrist. It included heavy public investment but also many incentives for private investment. In the public sphere, the National Bank for Economic Development was to channel funds to major infrastructure projects. In the private sphere, for example, a government commission solicited bids for the creation of a national automobile industry under favorable foreign exchange terms. Kubitschek and his advisers hoped to finesse the bitter ideological divisions that had helped wreck the Vargas government by the political strategy of providing benefits for everyone.

Kubitschek's economic strategy was very successful in reaching its primary objective of rapid economic development and industrialization. Virtually all of the goals in the Programa de Metas were met. By 1961, when Kubitschek left office, Brazil had an integrated motor vehicle industry (created virtually from scratch) and was on the way to creating the many subsidiary industries vital to vehicle production. There were also impressive gains in electricity generation and road building.

In addition to the direct economic advances, there were also more indirect political benefits from Kubitschek's economic strategy. His enthusiastic political style and personality reinforced the traditional Brazilian sense of optimism. Kubitschek stressed solutions rather than problems. He radiated confidence in the country and its capacity to join the industrial world. Even Brazil's national soccer team cooperated by winning its first world championship in Sweden in July 1958. The team's star was Pelé, who rapidly became known as the world's greatest player. The post-victory Brazilian mood was captured by Nelson Rodrigues, the playwright and sports writer, who observed that the myth of "Brazilian sadness" was on the run because "With this world title . . . sadness is a bad joke."

The ultimate example of Kubitschek's style was the building of Brasília. The idea of a new capital that would open up the interior had long been discussed, but few thought it would ever be built. The Constitution of 1891 had stipulated its construction and a site had been selected as early as 1893. It was located in the state of Goiás, 630 miles from Rio de Janeiro and 700 miles from São Paulo. The spot was 3,800 feet above sea level and situated in a semi-arid highland plain (*not* jungle, as foreign journalists often fantasize). During his presidential campaign, Kubitschek promised to build this new capital, and he meant it. Once in office, he pushed the project hard, calling in the distinguished Brazilian architect Oscar Niemeyer and Lúcio Costa, a well-known Brazilian city planner. Both were profoundly influenced by French architects, especially Le Corbusier. With its futuristic architecture and ambitious urban planning, Brasília was to be a lesson both to Brazil and the world, a symbol of a new determination to settle the interior and leave behind the Portuguese habit of sticking close to the coast. The city was built in record time (even though there was no railway or hard-surfaced road connection and all the construction materials had to be brought in by air), much to the dismay of Rio de Janeiro, which lost its role as national capital when Brasília was inaugurated in 1960.

Brasília quickly captured the world's imagination. The inauguration brought a record number of journalists and photographers from all over the world. All the principal buildings were designed by Oscar Niemeyer, who was given a veto over any subsequent major construction. Lucio Costa's layout of the city was designed to make it look from the air like a sweptwing airplane, thereby symbolizing progress with the residential and business areas along the "wings" of the plane. Along the body of the plane are the government offices (each ministry was given a structure of precisely equal size) and cultural, banking, and hotel areas. In the "cockpit" of the plane is the Plaza of Three Powers, with imposing modern buildings for the executive, legislative, and judicial branches. Brasília proved, predictably, to be a one-industry (i.e., government) town, much like Washington and Canberra, other "new" capital cities built from scratch.

But there was also a negative side to Kubitschek's growth strategy, which stemmed from the way it was financed. Brazil's domestic savings remained chronically low, thereby keeping investment low. And the hoped-for inflow of foreign capital to supplement domestic investment was not sufficient to raise Brazilian investment to the level needed for sustained high growth over the long run. Yet Kubitschek would not scale back his ambitious economic plans, despite growing inflation and mounting balance-of-payments deficits.

Many economists criticized Brazil for what they called "inflation financing"—the financing of public sector deficits simply by printing money—because it inevitably redistributed income and wealth toward high-growth (including high-speculation) sectors. Such a shift could not continue indefinitely, because of the natural limits to such transfers and because eventually the losers in the process would be enraged enough to call a halt. The motto of the Kubitschek era was "fifty years' progress in five." His critics called it "fifty years' inflation in five." Kubitschek's inflation financing, as is often the case, stimulated intervention from outside Brazil.

DEALING WITH THE WORLD ECONOMY

Kubitschek's determination to pursue his economic program ensured a continuing balance-of-payments crisis. Brazil's export earnings, which still came primarily from a few primary products, remained stagnant, even as her imports, including capital goods and inputs essential for industry, had grown. (See exhibit 6-2.) Brazil could sustain a deficit in the trade account only if it got foreign financing to make up the difference, either through foreign investment or through loans and grants.

Pursuit of rapid growth without adequate financing rekindled inflation in Brazil. Rather than slow down the program by reducing the government deficit, Kubitschek's team tolerated rising prices. Inflation and the payments deficit came together in 1958, as they had in the early 1950s, forcing Brazil to negotiate a stabilization agreement with the International Monetary Fund (IMF). Only with such an agreement could Kubitschek draw on IMF funds and cover Brazil's payments deficit. Like most stabilization programs, this one required tighter credit controls and wage restraints, as well as budget cuts.

The proposed IMF-approved stabilization program provoked furious opposition in Brazil. The left now had an ideal issue for attacking Kubitschek. They accused him of sacrificing Brazilian interests to the IMF and the U.S. government. Now approaching his last year in office, the president faced an uncomfortable decision. If he pursued stabilization in the face of opposition from the left, the economy would slow down, his Programa de Metas would be hurt, and his role as the dynamic promoter of Brazil's rush to modernity would be compromised.

Kubitschek took a gamble. He decided to break with the IMF and continue his economic program, at whatever cost. His decision proved widely popular. Congratulatory telegrams poured into the presidential palace. Editorial writers hailed him as the champion of a new nationalism. The left was disconcerted because he had stolen their thunder. The right hesitated, since they did not want to defy the patriotic outcry. Kubitschek's gamble paid off politically but disrupted relations with the world economy. Brazil had the thrill of defying orthodox financial experts, particularly in the United States, but there would be a heavy price to pay in reduced access to future foreign financing.

Any evaluation of Kubitschek's economic record must weigh the benefits against the costs—a calculus that depends on essentially normative judgments about the value of the different components.

On the positive side, Brazil gained invaluable technology, although often only through investment by foreign multinationals. Brazil also saw the growth of a national market, concentrated primarily in the Center-South where the prospect of gaining a foothold attracted foreign firms, even if only through modest investment. Finally, Brazilian industrialists and managers began to believe that they could perform at world standards. This was an important psychological change related to the elite's long-standing doubt that Brazil could ever compete with the advanced nations.

But critics pointed to what they considered important costs in terms of welfare effects. These included increased income inequality, since industrial workers earned more than those in the agrarian or service sectors. Of course, even industrial workers' incomes paled in comparison to that of the upper 2 to 3 percent comprising large landowners, major merchants, bankers, brokers, industrialists, and real estate moguls. Furthermore, the inevitable concentration of industry in the Center-South meant exacerbating the income inequalities between that region and the rest of Brazil, especially the Northeast. Both of these effects—rising inequality among persons and among regions—were cited by those who doubted the appropriateness of orthodox-style industrialization in a country such as Brazil, with a large labor surplus and great regional inequalities. The almost inevitable link for developing countries (at least in Latin America) between rapid economic growth and growing income inequality has been dogging Brazil's economic policy debate ever since.

The Brief Presidency of Jânio Quadros

Kubitschek completed his presidential mandate despite constant predictions that he would fall. The campaign for his successor produced two political figures, each bizarre in his own way. Jânio Quadros was a loner who had built a political career on his charisma in the state of São Paulo. He began as a schoolteacher, later selling his history of Portuguese grammar door to door, but his true vocation was convincing middle-class voters he could clean up politics. He was a wild-looking figure—tall and slim, with a shock of hair falling over his brow, and one bad eye (the result of a childhood accident). He was especially adept at keeping the spotlight on himself by giving out tidbits of a story while successfully spinning out the denouement. His campaign for the presidency in 1960 showcased this talent. His campaign symbol was a broom—to sweep out the corrupt incumbents. Quadros attracted such wide and enthusiastic support that he came across to the public as some kind of messiah. He was the choice of the UDN, which nominated him in the hope that they finally had a winner. But Quadros set little store by party loyalty. In the midst of the campaign he renounced the UDN nomination to dramatize his independence.

Marshall Henrique Lott, Quadros's main opponent, was a former army minister. It was Lott who had played the key role in preempting the January 1956 military coup aimed at stopping Kubitschek's inauguration. Now in 1960 Lott was naive enough to be convinced by the left (including the Communist Party) that he was the hero who could save the country. In fact, Lott was an inept campaigner and no match for Quadros.

Quadros won with 48 percent of the vote, a minority but a larger one than Kubitschek's. His *modus vivendi* could hardly have contrasted more sharply with Kubitschek's. Instead of wheeling and dealing, Brazil would now enjoy transparently honest government, if Quadros could keep his promises.

Brazil's most important short-term problem in January 1961 was the economic crisis. Kubitschek had left the Treasury bare and had avoided the politically painful task of attacking inflation. Quadros assembled a cabinet that included numerous UDN figures and set about producing a new stabilization plan. As always with such anti-inflation plans, implementation had dire political implications for the government. By June, details of the plan were beginning to leak out. The IMF and the U.S. government were pleased by the Quadros regime's willingness to bite the bullet in economic policy. The left, along with some businessmen, was dubious.

Once installed in the presidency, Quadros's charisma proved to be a fading asset. With each passing day, his impressive electoral victory seemed to matter less, as he faced a bureaucracy and a Congress immune to campaign oratory. His bizarre personal behavior did not help. He would spend an inordinately long time obsessively positioning himself exactly in the middle of the rear seat of his limousine, for example. And he would issue without warning highly specific presidential orders (nicknamed *bilhetes* or "tickets"), as, for example, one outlawing perfume bombs at Carnival time (the alleged cause of his childhood eye injury). Political commentators began asking how he planned to govern. In fact, Quadros was making little effort to negotiate his program with the Congress. Instead, he spent his time striking sensationalist poses, such as the awarding of Brazil's highest medal for foreigners (the Cruzeiro do Sul) to the visiting Che Guevara in August 1961. It was becoming increasingly clear that Brazil might have elected a false messiah.

Never a politician given to the arts of negotiation, Quadros's way of tackling the obstacles his stabilization program was facing in the Congress was, without warning, to resign. He evidently assumed it would be rejected and would force Congress to give him emergency powers— as had been given to General de Gaulle in the recent French crisis precipitated by Algerian independence. Unfortunately for Quadros, the Congress accepted his resignation. The former president immediately

EXHIBIT 6-5

Major Party Representation in Chamber of Deputies, 1945–62

	1945		1950		1954		1958		1962	
	Seats	*%*	*Seats*	*%*	*Seats*	*%*	*Seats*	*%*	*Seats*	*%*
PSD	151	52.8	112	36.8	114	35.0	115	35.3	118	28.9
UDN	77	26.9	81	26.6	74	22.7	70	21.5	91	22.2
PTB	22	7.7	51	16.8	56	17.2	66	20.2	116	28.4
TOTAL %		87.4		80.2		74.9		77.0		79.5

Source: Scott Mainwaring, *The Party System and Democratization in Brazil* (forthcoming), table 2.2.

left the capital, heading by plane for the military air base of Cumbica in São Paulo. He sailed for Europe shortly thereafter, proclaiming, "I was compelled to resign, but like Getúlio, I shall return one day, God willing, to show everyone who were the scum in this country." Brazil was left leaderless less than a year after the election of 1960. Brasília went into shock as the political scene degenerated once again into turmoil. The UDN had now lost what they had expected to be their entree to power. The one man with a hope of exorcising the ghost of Getúlio Vargas was gone. Even worse, Vargas's political heir, João Goulart of the PTB, was now in line to be president. He had been elected vice-president because the electoral law allowed split voting and Goulart, as Lott's running mate, had outpolled Quadros's running mate, the UDN leader Milton Campos. In fact, since 1945, the PTB had grown steadily in power in the Chamber of Deputies, largely at the expense of the PSD. (See exhibit 6-5.)

The Succession of João Goulart

The prospect of Goulart's succession to the presidency alarmed the UDN and the military, who considered him a dangerous populist all too ready to accommodate the Communists and thereby help them to power. Goulart's location at the moment of his access to power could not have been a more dramatic confirmation that their fears were well-founded: He was returning from an official mission to the People's Republic of China.

Almost immediately after Quadros's resignation, the three military ministers issued a manifesto denouncing Goulart as a subversive and pledging to prevent his succession to the presidency. This salvo began an intense public debate. Those opposing Goulart were the well-known enemies of Vargas, especially from the UDN, which had just lost its access to power. Goulart's supporters dubbed themselves the "legalists," arguing that he had been democratically elected vice-president and was thereby now the constitutional president. The loudest legalist voice was Leonel Brizola, the governor of Rio Grande do Sul, who happened also to be Goulart's brother-in-law (Brizola had married Goulart's sister). Brizola was a fiery PTB leader who aspired to the mantle of Getúlio Vargas. Fortunately for the legalists, the commander of the Third Army (stationed in Rio Grande do Sul) was on Goulart's side. Brizola decided to defy the military ministers. He invited Goulart to return to Brazil via Rio Grande do Sul, and he won a promise by the Third Army commander to repel any federal forces entering from the North.

Goulart arrived in Rio Grande do Sul and began preparing for the journey to Brasília. The centrist politicians in the Congress were so frightened of the prospect of civil war that they began negotiating with the military ministers to avoid a confrontation. In the midst of a bitter national debate, they struck a compromise. Goulart would assume the presidency, but with greatly reduced powers. The president would now preside over a parliamentary system (by constitutional amendment). Executive power would thus rest with a prime minister and a cabinet rather than the president. Goulart accepted this compromise, but only under protest. He vowed to campaign for the restoration of full powers (a plebiscite was scheduled for January 1963).

What was at stake in this struggle? The answer was the shape of Brazil's future. The country's accelerating population growth rate was increasing the ranks of job seekers. To create those jobs, Brazil badly needed to diversify its economic base. The debate over economic strategy in Brazil was polarized by the Marxists and statists on the left and the neo-liberals on the right. Vargas had tried to combine elements from the two. In the end, his balancing act had failed. Kubitschek had given new life to the trade-off between left and right. But with the succession of Goulart, Brazil now faced a repeat of the confrontation of 1954—a populist president, this time with an unstable political base and limited parliamentary powers, versus the military.

POPULISTS VERSUS THE MILITARY

Goulart lasted less than three years in the presidency. Throughout his presidential years he struggled to gain control over an increasingly divided political scene—a task that was vastly complicated by the heating up of the Cold War. Fidel Castro, triumphant in Cuba in 1959, was determined to export his revolution, and Brazil was one of the natural targets. President John F. Kennedy, elected in 1960, was equally determined to stop the Cuban offensive. The result was a clash of surrogates (Cuban, Soviet, U.S.) who tried, often successfully, to infiltrate, bribe, or otherwise influence Brazilian political parties, state governments, military officers, universities, professional associations, churches and any other institution judged worthy of importance.

The Brazilian left had grown steadily since Vargas's return in 1951, but it had also become much more heterogeneous. One component was the Brazilian Communist Party, with its long experience of both open and clandestine politics. But the Communist Party was still scarred from repression during the Estado Nôvo and burdened by the memory of its abortive revolt in 1935. Furthermore, the Communists now had to contend with the cautious attitude of the Soviet Union (as compared to Fidel Castro) in promoting revolution in Latin America.

In addition, the party was outflanked on several fronts. On the left was the breakaway Chinese-oriented Communist Party of Brazil (Partido Comunista do Brasil), founded in 1962. This small but vocal group drew inspiration not only from the People's Republic of China but also from Cuba, where Fidel Castro had shown how to make a revolution by accelerating the dialectics of history.

Also important on the left were the many and varied "radical nationalists." Most passionate were the left-wing groups affiliated with the Roman Catholic Church. They had attracted many university students and aimed at creating political consciousness among the marginal masses, both urban and rural. The language of the radical nationalists was Marxist and many of their members had close links past or present to the orthodox Communist Party, but they were seldom under control of the latter and frequently followed a strategy that was all their own.

On the right were the traditional wealth-holders of Brazil. Their principal voice was the UDN, and they relied on their links to the police and the military. They included landowners and many industrialists. Their trump card was the capacity of the military to intervene against their enemies.

The right attacked the legacy of Vargas despite the fact that many of their number had benefited greatly from Vargas's economic policies. In theory, they favored orthodox economic liberalism. In practice, they welcomed subsidies or protective tariffs when available, as in the coffee-support program. The right also relied upon the U.S. government as its ultimate support. They knew that pointing to the "Communist threat" would resonate in Washington, and some readily accepted secret U.S. funds for their electoral campaigns and propaganda battles.

Between left and right, the political center was shrinking. These were the politicians who were reformist but not revolutionary, who wanted to maintain the political game, and who often resorted to legalisms to solve social conflict. The centrist par excellence was San Tiago Dantas, a prominent lawyer and intellectual. He tried to relegitimize at least part of the left as consistent with democracy by dividing it into "positive" and "negative" wings. The positive wing, he argued, was ready to participate in democratic political solutions. The negative wing, in contrast, was committed to obstructing and delegitimizing the democratic process—gambling on replacing the existing system with a revolutionary regime. Dantas got his chance to rally the center when he became Goulart's finance minister in 1963.

THE ECONOMIC CRISIS ESCALATES

Along with reduced powers, Goulart inherited a worsening economic crisis. Inflation had risen from 25.4 percent in 1960 to 34.7 percent in 1961, and it was now producing serious distortions in economic decision making. It was also one of two signs to Brazil's foreign creditors that the government was losing control. The other indicator was the deficit in the balance of payments, which could only be covered by running down Brazil's foreign exchange reserves or by increasing the foreign debt. The promises of foreign help Quadros had negotiated were now suspended. Stabilization, that bugaboo of recent Brazilian presidents, was unavoidable.

San Tiago Dantas's arrival at the Finance Ministry offered a glimmer of hope. He was joined in early 1963 by Celso Furtado, the father of SUDENE, and they now set to work drafting a three-year plan for Brazil.

Dantas journeyed to Washington in March 1963 and negotiated new agreements for U.S. and IMF support in return for a coherent anti-inflation program at home. When Dantas returned to Brazil he found himself the target of venomous attack from the left. He was accused of "selling out" in Washington, and memories of Kubitschek's break with the IMF began to flood the heads of the Brazilian public. This time, however, Brazil had no margin of foreign exchange reserves to carry out the Kubitschek strategy. To make matters worse, Dantas was diagnosed with lung cancer and had to resign.

Early 1963 had brought one source of relief to the government: In a national plebiscite, Brazilians voted to revoke the 1961 constitutional amendment that had imposed parliamentarism. Goulart now had full presidential powers. But the price of the change was high, ever deepening suspicions on the right, especially among the army officer corps. Would Goulart now attempt to lead Brazil toward the "syndical republic" which the right had long claimed he favored? Meanwhile, the radical left was even more anxious to demonstrate that the "popular forces" could assume power in Brazil—if not peacefully, then otherwise.

As 1963 continued, Brazil sank further into economic disrepute abroad. Foreign investment virtually ceased. Foreign suppliers were demanding immediate payment for anything they shipped, jeopardizing the adequacy of Brazil's supply of petroleum (more than half of which was imported). The U.S. government had already written off Goulart as unreliable at best and revolutionary at worst, and was limiting its assistance to states with anti-Goulart governors, a policy the State Department described as favoring "islands of sanity." This favoritism reinforced the left's charges that the United States was intervening on behalf of reactionary forces in Brazilian politics. By early 1964, Brazilian financial markets were abuzz with rumors of an impending coup. Some days the alleged attackers were from the left, other days from the right. By March 1964, the annual inflation rate was over 100 percent.

The Goulart government had run out of conventional answers. The left was arguing that the time for conventional answers was over and in March Goulart gave a clear turn to the left. He had already called for measures that threatened elite control, such as enfranchising illiterates and permitting unionization of enlisted men in the military. He now launched a series of national rallies where he was to announce key presidential decrees (a way to bypass the federal Congress, where such measures could not pass). The first rally was scheduled for March 13 in Rio de Janeiro. The decrees to be announced included land expropriation and the nationalization of all private oil refineries.

That rally was followed by frantic organizing on the right to protest Goulart's allegedly anti-Christian, anti-family stance. These marches were organized by right-wing civic groups with links to other rightist groups in South America (some undoubtedly supported secretly by the U.S. government). Brazil was now set for a showdown between left and right.

As so often in Brazilian history (1889, 1930, 1937, 1945), the civilian political confrontation was cut short by a military coup d'état. It was organized by many of the same officers who had forced Vargas's ouster in 1954 and opposed Goulart's succession in 1961. The intent was to end Goulart's presidency and with it, they hoped, the Vargas era. The coup organizers had energetically cultivated support among officers, successfully neutralizing Goulart supporters in their midst. The pro-coup forces also knew they could count on U.S. support, although the American officials were careful to keep any commitments secret.

On March 31–April 1, 1964, military units seized key government offices in Brasília and Rio. The military had expected to meet serious armed resistance—the left had boasted that the popular sectors would never allow the military to take power again, and the coup makers had taken the boast seriously. Goulart's justice minister, Abelardo Jurema, called for government supporters to fill the streets, but his pleas fell on deaf ears. The resistance did not materialize. The military and police quickly arrested key figures in the populist apparatus. Trade union leaders were the first target, but the purge soon expanded to include politicians and bureaucrats deemed subversive or untrustworthy. Violence was relatively limited, being most severe in the Northeast, where at least a dozen peasant league organizers and leftist leaders were tortured or killed.

Within days, the new government had consolidated power. At heart, it was an alliance between the military and the technocrats. The purged Congress promptly elected to the presidency General Castelo Branco, the army chief of staff, who had led the military conspiracy. The technocrats were led by Roberto Campos, a diplomat and economist and a leading critic of the Goulart government in its waning days. Campos brought with him a team of economists and engineers, many of whom had contributed to the creation of an anti-government think tank, IPES (Instituto da Pesquisas e Estudos Sociais), in Rio and São Paulo. They assumed power with clear and conventional ideas about how to contain inflation and restore Brazil to economic growth. The inflation rate for 1964 as a whole was already down from the over 100 percent annual rate prevailing when Goulart left office on April 1. (See exhibit 6-6.)

Politicians from the UDN were the greatest political gainers. Frustrated by years of unsuccessfully fighting Vargas and his heirs, they had gained access to power via military intervention.

EXHIBIT 6-6
Annual Rate of Inflation, 1950–64

Year	Inflation Rate (%)
1950	9.20
1951	18.4
1952	9.3
1953	13.8
1954	27.1
1955	11.8
1956	22.6
1957	12.7
1958	12.4
1959	35.9
1960	25.4
1961	34.7
1962	50.1
1963	78.4
1964	89.9

Source: Werner Baer, *The Brazilian Economy,* 4th ed. (Westport, 1995), p. 392.

The new government had no legitimacy by existing constitutional law—a non-problem for the military. Their high command issued a legitimizing decree on April 9, 1964, called an "Institutional Act." This self-proclaimed law gave the military the power to do anything it wished. Curiously enough, however, it included a self-limiting clause: It was to lapse on January 31, 1996. This was the first example of continuing legal acrobatics by the military to grant itself legitimacy.

The anti-Goulart conspirators had assumed they would get immediate U.S. support—Carlos Lacerda, destroyer of three Brazilian presidents, went so far as to lecture Americans on their need to be grateful to the Brazilian revolutionaries for having saved such an important country from communism—and, in fact, U.S. president Lyndon Johnson recognized the new government within hours after the coup. The State Department, however, remained uneasy about the repression that followed Goulart's ouster and about the depth of the new government's commitment to economic and social reform, which had been a principal goal of the Alliance for Progress. Full credibility abroad would not only depend on the design of the new stabilization plan but also on the government's capacity to stick to it.

The speed and bloodlessness of the coup left Goulart supporters in total disarray. They began to realize how overconfident they had been, which led to much recrimination about responsibility for key errors. One question remained unanswered. How much freedom would the opposition be given to organize? And how would a military government treat its opposition?

This was hardly a question to detain João Goulart. He fled Brasília for his native Rio Grande do Sul. From there he left the country for Uruguay, where he settled into exile and became a highly successful cattle rancher. His former ministers were scattered among distant foreign capitals. The military had cast the populists from power.

7 Rule of the Military: 1964–85

After the coup of 1964, the military held political power in Brazil for 21 years. For the first year or so they formed an alliance with the UDN, the traditionally anti-populist party hungry for power. It was an effort by the military to seem legitimate in spite of their illegal seizure of power. When this alliance lost them two key gubernatorial elections in 1965, however, the military abolished all existing political parties and replaced them with a new two-party system—a government party and a single opposition party that represented another effort to legitimize the illegitimate. They were no more successful with public opinion than they had been before—public opposition was growing, and the patience of the military right wing gave out in 1968. The military became increasingly repressive, censuring the press ever more stringently, provoking an armed guerrilla movement, and using torture in their efforts to stamp out all opposition.

At the same time that political repression was increasing, the country was operating under yet another economic stabilization plan. Along this dimension the news was good, at least on prices. Unlike previous attempts at stabilization within a democratic context, this plan succeeded in reducing inflation and stimulating vigorous economic growth. The Brazilian economy was even able to withstand the oil shock of 1973, when oil prices on the international market drastically increased. Thanks to Brazil's international credit rating, it successfully increased its borrowing from abroad to cover the oil price increase and continue vigorous growth at home. By the second oil shock in 1979, however, things had become more difficult. Credit rating aside, the low interest rates that had been available to Brazil shot up because they were tied to the new rapidly rising world rates. With its foreign exchange virtually exhausted, Brazil defaulted on its foreign obligations to the commercial banks, primarily U.S., in 1981. Once again, the country was in economic crisis— one that could not be blamed on populists, leftists, or democratic rule.

By this time, interestingly, the military had for several years been slowly easing their repression and planning a transition out of power. A military ally of Castello Branco succeeded to the presidency in 1974, began to listen to closet democrats within the military, and authorized contacts with leaders of the civilian opposition (the most important being the Catholic Church). The subsequent internal history of the authoritarian regime was a battle between the military hard line and the military moderates over whether, and how, to make a transition to civilian rule—a battle that was importantly influenced by rising philosophical distaste for authoritarianism among the younger generation of officers. The moderates eventually won out. Civilian rule was reestablished in 1985 with the election of a civilian, a charmer, and a brilliant political negotiator, Tancredo Neves.

The Generals Search for a Political Base

When the military took over the government in 1964, power within the officer ranks lay with the army, much larger than the other two armed forces and ultimately responsible for maintaining public order. The army officer corps, however, was less united than it appeared. The moderates ("soft-liners" in Brazilian parlance) believed their country was in peril because Brazilians had been misled by populist politicians and their left-wing allies. But they also believed the Brazilian public would come to its senses and that democracy could work once the "irresponsible" populists and the Communists were removed from the scene.

The "hard-liners" within the military had a more apocalyptic view of Brazil's political plight. They distrusted *all* politicians, including the UDN. They thought only authoritarian measures could protect Brazil against the threats from the left. The hard-line leaders were led by officers with the most militantly anti-Vargas records, such as (among the older generation) Marshall Odílio Denys and General Jurandir Mamede. These hard-liners allowed the moderate military to take the lead in forming the new government in 1964, but behind the scenes they remained committed to tougher measures.

The military who seized power faced one extremely awkward political fact: They had no firm legal basis for their intervention. This would not have bothered many Latin American militaries, but the Brazilian officers had a strong legalist streak and they wanted legitimacy. The civilian supporters of the coup had lacked the congressional votes to impeach Goulart, just as they and their predecessors had lacked the votes to impeach Getúlio Vargas in 1954. The constitutional path now would have to bend for the new military rulers to be granted emergency powers by the Congress. But the conservative congressional leaders balked.

On April 9th, 1964, the three military ministers took matters into their own hands. They arbitrarily issued an "Institutional Act" (it became the first of many with that title), which had been drawn up, ironically, by Francisco Campos, the author of Vargas's authoritarian Constitution of 1937. The act gave the Brazilian executive extraordinary powers, such as increased authority to gain constitutional amendments, exclusive power to propose expenditure bills to Congress, and the power to suppress the political rights of any citizen for ten years. President Goulart had often complained that he lacked the authority to carry out his presidential duties. The military agreed with the diagnosis and now imposed their own solution.

The military moderates then turned to the UDN, long-time enemies of the populists, as the political party to help them legitimize their takeover of power. Castello Branco, coordinator of the coup and leader of the moderate military wing, was personally close to the UDN leaders and considered them the proper civilian inheritors of power. The UDN were happy to oblige. They had never won the presidency with one of their own (Janio Quadros had accepted their nomination in 1959 but declared his political independence during the succeeding campaign) and were eager to take power at last. The military-UDN alliance elected Castello Branco to the presidency—not an unexpected victory given that the electorate consisted of a Congress which had already been purged of leftist elements.

There were seeds of instability in the alliance, however. First, in joining with the military the UDN was going against its own ideological principles—dedication to legalism, defense of the Constitution, and keeping government small. Second, it was not clear that the UDN had sufficient appeal to win direct elections, even after the purge of the populists. If their electoral power turned out to be weak, the hard-liners in the military could not be counted on to let democracy of any sort continue, and in the event that they did allow some representative government, they would almost certainly look elsewhere for electoral support.

The policy-making arm of the Castello Branco / UDN government was a group of economic experts dubbed the "technocrats." Their leader was Roberto Campos, an extremely articulate neo-orthodox economist who had helped define a new and more conservative development strategy in his extensive writings. Campos was appointed minister of planning. He was joined by Octávio Bulhões, a distinguished conservative economist who became finance minister. Joining them was a cadre of younger economists and engineers, such as Glycon de Paiva, a longtime critic of the government's petroleum monopoly. These technocrats now had the opportunity to reshape policy under the mantle of military power. One of the Castello Branco government's first measures was a decree prohibiting Congress from increasing budget requests from the executive, a practice that had often undermined previous stabilization efforts.

These technocrats launched the same type of orthodox stabilization measures previous governments had tried to implement. They argued they were governing in the name of honesty, common sense, and rationality—in other words, acting neutrally in the public interest. However, their measures did not turn out to be neutral in their impacts on different layers of society, as we shall see.

The new government also claimed a new international role. Brazil's military coup was the first in Latin America since the wave of democratization in the 1950s. It was thus an ominous sign for the U.S.-sponsored Alliance for Progress, which had aimed to strengthen democratic rule in Latin America by promoting economic growth and social reform. The military takeover of democracy in Brazil, Latin America's largest nation, suggested that U.S. strategy might have to be rethought.

In fact, promoting democracy had never been the sole aim of the United States. Another principal preoccupation for Washington was geopolitical: "Stop Castroism." Soviet influence must not be allowed to expand in the hemisphere was the logic. The Brazilian coup-makers's claim on U.S. support rested on this goal.

In the short run, the coup-makers succeeded in gaining U.S. support. The Lyndon Johnson administration recognized the new regime in Brazil less than forty-eight hours after the president of the Congress had declared the federal presidency vacant. The Brazilian congressional action was in fact illegal, since Goulart had neither been impeached and convicted, nor fled the country without congressional permission (the only two ways a living president could constitutionally lose office). President Johnson ignored this technicality in the hope that early recognition would help to strengthen the military moderates to resist a possible turn toward authoritarianism.

When neighboring Argentina, always closely linked politically to Brazil, suffered its own military coup in 1966, the Argentine generals used similar anti-Communist rhetoric to justify their intervention. Officers in both countries saw themselves on a common mission to save Western democracy from the "menace" on the left.

GROWING OPPOSITION, GROWING REPRESSION: 1964–67

Two major issues emerged to coalesce an emerging opposition to the new regime: repression and economic policy.

The military government was quite open in its decision to purge the left wing from the political system. It was not so open about the fact that it also forced the retirement of several thousand civil servants, including a number of distinguished figures who had never been political partisans. Many were simply victims of personal vendettas by rivals promoting their careers by getting the ear of the military security officers. Negative reactions to these purges, plus antagonism to the loss of the democratic principles of liberal constitutionalism, were widespread. It should be noted that the press remained relatively free in this early period. Censorship of the media came later.

The new economic stabilization program was bitterly attacked by the left (and many in the center), which predicted that the anti-inflation program of Campos and Bulhões would create massive unemployment and facilitate sweeping takeovers by foreign firms, especially North American. Once again, the left portrayed Brazil as slipping under the heel of the United States and the International Monetary Fund. The more extreme critics charged that the entire coup had been a U.S. production, with Brazilian officers merely carrying out Uncle Sam's instructions.

The August 1965 elections were the first formal test of the opposition's strength. State governorships were up for grabs, including those in the two key states of Guanabara (greater Rio de Janeiro city, which was then a state) and Minas Gerais. Pro-government candidates won in every state except Guanabara and Minas Gerais, where the winners were traditional PSD politicians of the Vargas stripe. Although both winners had reputations as wheeler- dealers, neither was a full-fledged populist.

Even so, the hard-line military were infuriated by the outcome, interpreting it as proof that Castello Branco's dependence on the UDN would not work. Ominous threats swept through the officers' barracks in Rio de Janeiro. General Costa e Silva, the army minister and a sympathizer of the hard line, brokered an agreement with the president. As a result, using a freshly issued Institutional Act (No. 2), Castello Branco and his advisors decided to replace the old party structure with two new parties. One party, ARENA (Aliança Renovadora Nacional) would represent the government, and the other, the MDB (Movimento Democrático Brasileiro), would represent the opposition. Castello Branco chose this two-party structure out of his admiration for the Anglo-Saxon political experience and for what he saw as Brazil's positive experience during its nineteenth-century (largely two-party) parliamentary monarchy. The trick from the president's standpoint was to ensure a continuing majority for the pro-government party.

TRIUMPH OF THE HARD LINE

The issuing of the new Institutional Act and the reorganization of the party system did not quiet the opposition, but Castello's critics increasingly focused on the effects of stabilization, which were felt through 1965 and 1966. The resulting fall in real wage rates and the public spending cuts provoked ever growing protest from opposition politicians and economists, who predicted that Brazil would never regain its growth path.

Castello Branco had promised he would not extend his presidential mandate, which was the presidential term to which Quadros had been elected in 1960 and which Goulart had assumed in 1961. But back in July 1964 Castello had succumbed to intense pressure from his economic policy-makers, who thought the presidential election scheduled for November 1965 would not allow time for their policies to show results. So he agreed to extend his term by fourteen months, to March 15, 1967.

On that date, Castello Branco passed the presidency to General Costa e Silva, the incumbent army minister and the second military president to be elected indirectly by the Congress.

Relations between the hard line and the moderate military were still tense until April of 1968, when a series of wildcat strikes erupted in Minas Gerais. Worker resentment against the steady fall in real wages had become so intense that the "safe" labor union leaders, appointed by the military in 1964, could not control their members. The hard line let this disruption go. But several months later, the government faced a new challenge to law and order. Students in Rio de Janeiro, always at the forefront of protest, staged noisy protest marches. This time the riot police turned out in force and the clash led to at least one death. These two incidents showed the hard line that the moderate military, although ostensibly repressive, were allowing continued public opposition. The hard-liners were determined to control both workers and students.

As 1968 continued, the political atmosphere became steadily overheated. The spark that started the final fire came from a speech by Márcio Moreira Alves, a young Rio congressman who challenged the honor of the military by suggesting that Brazilian women should protest military rule by withholding their favors from men in uniform. The hard line was livid at this ridicule and demanded Alves's immediate arrest. He eluded the authorities and slipped into exile in Chile and later France.

The hard-line officers decided the time had come for tougher measures. The president now issued in December yet another Institutional Act (No. 5), which, unlike the preceding Institutional Acts, had no expiration date. Brazil was now a genuine dictatorship. Congress was closed (although not abolished) and all crimes against "national security" were now subjected to military justice. Censorship was introduced, aimed especially at television and radio. Several prominent print media, such as the daily *O Estado de S. Paulo* and the weekly *Veja,* became subject to prior censorship (meaning their copy had to be cleared by an army censor).

Wire tapping, mail opening, and denunciations by informers became commonplace. University lectures were monitored and a wave of purges hit the leading faculties, especially in São Paulo, where a future Brazilian president, Fernando Henrique Cardoso, was forcibly retired from his professorship. Numerous other faculty were hit, losing their political rights for ten years. Security forces zeroed in especially on opposition clergy and students, among whom the doctrines of liberation theology were still influential.

The Arrival of the Guerrillas

The military takeover in 1964 had not stimulated any immediate significant armed resistance, but the government's record of growing repression gradually provoked armed opposition, which surfaced in 1969. One guerrilla group tried to apply Fidel Castro's strategy of rural guerrilla warfare to the cities. Their chief theoretician was Carlos Marighela, a former member of the Brazilian Communist Party and a founder of the breakaway Action for National Liberation (ANL) in 1968. In his *Minimanual of the Urban Guerrilla* he argued that a tightly organized cadre could bring down a dictatorship through urban combat.

More than a dozen guerrilla groups emerged in Brazil at about the same time, bearing a variety of labels, such as VAR (Vanguarda Armada Revolucionária—Palmares), ALN (Ação Libertadora Nacional), and COLINA (Comandos de Libertação Nacional). The combatants probably totaled fewer than five hundred, usually in their late teens or early twenties, although there were many others providing logistical support. They included committed Marxists and radical nationalists (many were Catholics attracted to liberation theology), mostly products of pre-1964 leftist politics, but some joining after 1964.

The guerrillas first gained notoriety by robbing banks—forays that, at least initially, were highly successful. The poorly guarded banks were sitting ducks for the young robbers, who left the scene carrying their spoils, shouting revolutionary slogans and scattering anti-military flyers as they ran. The money was badly needed to finance their operations. The actions themselves were needed to prove that the citadels of capitalism were not impregnable.

The guerrillas also resorted to a strategy of kidnapping prominent foreign diplomats. This had two purposes. One was to demonstrate again the weakness of the government. The second was to use the diplomatic hostages to bargain for the release of guerrillas captured earlier by the security forces.

The kidnapping began with the U.S. ambassador, Burke Elbrick, who was snatched from his black Cadillac limousine while riding home for lunch. The kidnappers offered to release Elbrick in exchange for ten guerrilla prisoners. After a fierce debate among the military, the government agreed to trade the prisoners for the ambassador's freedom. The precedent was thereby set for subsequent kidnappings and negotiations.

The guerrillas then turned to other diplomatic targets, including the Swiss ambassador, the German ambassador, and the Japanese consul general. In each case, the captors increased the number of prisoners demanded in exchange for the hostage, thereby gaining more and more publicity at the expense of the generals. In each case, the guerrillas won release of the prisoner.

The publicity did not help them win their case with the country, however. The guerrillas hoped to dramatize the exploitative role of foreign capital by kidnapping foreign diplomats in the order of the size of their country's investment in Brazil (United States, Switzerland, Germany, and Japan). This subtle symbolism was lost on the average Brazilian. It was also typical of the Brazilian guerrillas' tendency to overestimate the capacity of symbolic actions (especially in the face of censorship) to rouse a discontented population.

Although the kidnappings did not provoke an outpouring of public support for the guerrilla movement, they did provoke the security forces into ever more draconian security measures. They resorted to every method of surveillance and torture in their hunt for information. The truth is that even a mediocre military and police force could bring great pressure to bear on a small number of armed opponents. The danger of infiltration became so great that the guerrillas could not recruit new members, and their original number steadily dwindled as the arrests mounted. Within one year of their emergence, the trap was closing on the few guerrillas still at large. Marighela's strategy had been disproved. The cities were not hospitable to the guerrillas. Instead they had become, in Fidel Castro's own phrase, "the graveyard of the revolutionary."

The one major attempt to mount a rural front also failed after a promising start. In the Araguáia region of the Amazon Basin, a group of carefully trained guerrillas infiltrated a peasant area and gained the sympathy of the locals. The army sent in a force of poorly trained regular troops to clean out the area. They were easily routed by the guerrillas. The army then withdrew to train an elite corps of 10,000 counterinsurgency troops. Not surprisingly, they killed or captured all of the 69 guerrillas in the area. But it took two years and repeated assaults, much like Canudos eighty years earlier. There was yet another historical parallel: The guerrilla commander was an Afro-Brazilian, Osvaldo Orlando da Costa, admired by his peers for his bravery. The victorious soldiers displayed his dead body to the locals, much as the Portuguese had done with the head of Tiradentes in 1792.

The armed opposition was totally liquidated by 1974. That did not stop the military hard line from exploiting the claim of a continued guerrilla threat to keep the military moderates off balance and thereby justify its continued repression.

Culture and the Generals

The armed opposition had been one expression of the nationalist energy generated in Brazil since Vargas's 1954 suicide. It accelerated during the presidency of Juscelino Kubitschek, a viscerally optimistic politician determined to establish Brazil's national self-confidence by every means possible.

The supreme symbol of Kubitschek's drive for a new national identity was, as noted, the building of Brasília, which was typically Brazilian in its contradictions. On the one hand, Brasília was to be uniquely

Brazilian, erected far inland (thereby centering attention on the long-neglected interior of the country) and designed to give international attention to Brazil's leading architect and city planner, Oscar Niemeyer and Lucio Costa, respectively. The result was a futuristic new city that proclaimed Brazil's entry into the modern world. On the other hand, the inspiration for Brasília's basic conception was strictly French, which stimulated outspoken criticism. Gilberto Freyre, the most influential commentator on national culture and history, dismissed Brasília as "un-Brazilian." Some residents agreed, condemning the impracticality of glass-sided office buildings under an intense sun. Then there was the city traffic, unconstrained by a single traffic light in the maze of cloverleaf intersections. Intended to be a modernistic model of fluid flow, it soon set a national record for road accidents, thus leading to the tardy installation of orthodox traffic lights.

The new capital did not only have critics; it also had its passionate supporters. Many young families praised its excellent climate, first-rate schools, excellent recreational facilities, and relative lack of crime. It was, they argued, an ideal place to raise children. Even those Brazilians who criticized the "artificiality" of so much perfect symmetry in the midst of a desolate plateau had to admit that their country had caught world attention. Famous European intellectuals such as André Malraux, for example, were calling Brasília "the capital of hope."

Whoever was in favor of or against it, the building of the new capital city and the new surge of industrialization were tangible evidence that Brazil was leaving behind the image of a sleepy tropical enclave. Other indicators of change also entered the cultural scene. Best known was "bossa nova," the subtle musical mixture of samba and jazz. It was born in the late 1950s, along with Brasília, and soon attracted worldwide attention.

Bossa nova musicians such as Antonio Carlos Jobim, Sergio Mendes, and João Gilberto collaborated with American jazz musicians such as Stan Getz. Was Brazilian culture now penetrating the First World? Antonio Carlos Jobim and Vinícius De Moraes, the great lyricist of bossa nova, were even invited to write a symphony for the dedication of Brasília. The title of their work, "The Symphony of Dawn," paid tribute to Kubitschek's symbolism for the new capital. Although not performed at the dedication, the commissioning showed the link between this cultural movement and the ideological atmosphere of the era.

Bossa nova reached a climax in the highly successful Carnegie Hall concert by more than twenty Brazilian musicians in 1962. Their enthusiastic reception in New York (promotion by the Brazilian Foreign Ministry had helped) had great repercussions in Brazil—greater, some said, than their country's dazzling victory in the 1960 World Soccer Cup. Once again, Brazil was being recognized on the world stage.

Yet bossa nova had already faded by the time polarization led to the coup in 1964. Perhaps it was too subtle, too gentle for the turbulent climate shaking Brazil. Or perhaps it was too much a product of the cultural elite and its inevitably small middle class audience. Bossa nova's fame, once brilliant in Carnegie Hall, soon proved ephemeral in Brazil.

There were other cultural fireworks in the early 1960s. One of the most notable was *cinema novo*, or "new cinema." It was closely linked to radical nationalism, one of the ideological currents that gained wide support in intellectual and left-wing political circles during the 1950s. The radical nationalists, as we saw earlier, believed that Brazil's relative backwardness was the result of foreign (especially U.S.) exploitation, which could only be countered by a strong state, a worker/peasant-oriented economy, and strict controls on all foreign economic and political participation. Its theoretical inspiration was Marxist, although its influence extended much beyond the Communist parties.

The radical nationalists rejected Kubitschek's entire economic policy as a sellout to international capital. They ridiculed the moderate "nationalist developmentalist" ideology which the Kubitschek advisors and sympathizers had articulated to legitimize the presidency. Cinema novo showed the influence of the more radical position. *Vidas Secas* ("Barren Lives," 1963), for example, was a powerful portrait of a destitute northeastern peasant family reduced to desperation by a suffocating drought. The social injustice of their plight would be obvious to the Brazilian viewer who knew the facts about the grotesque distribution of power and wealth in the Northeast, then the largest pocket of misery in Latin America.

A later film, *Deus e Diabo na Terra do Sol* ("God and the Devil in the Land of the Sun," but released as "Black God, White Devil," 1964), left the viewer in no doubt. In this case the peasant living in the parched Northeast is cheated out of his allotment of cattle and takes his revenge by killing the landowner. Although the film is hardly a call to revolution and spends most of its time in a complex depiction of messianism, the filmmaker leaves little doubt as to the source of injustice. It was a film likely to alarm the army generals who had the mission of maintaining "order" in the Northeast.

The implicit challenge to authority from the artistic left gained even greater tension in Ruy Guerra's *Os Fuzis* ("The Guns," 1964), where a truck loaded with food breaks down in a drought-stricken town whose starving inhabitants are held at bay by rifle-bearing soldiers. Once again the picture is of stark injustice, with even more radical implications since it is army troops who nervously hold off the hungry townspeople. The generals could not fail to get the message: their own fighting men could be alienated by subversive propaganda films.

The first phase of cinema novo was reaching its climax just as the Goulart presidency was careening toward destruction. Like the radical nationalists pushing Goulart to the left, "the cinema novo directors," in the words of a leading film critic, "searched out the dark corners of Brazilian life—its *favelas* and its *sertão*—the places where Brazil's social contradictions appeared most dramatically."

The coup of 1964 put an end to the increasing nationalist tendency of the Goulart regime, but it did not silence the left. On the contrary, the initial wave of repression (arrest of labor leaders, purge of the civil service, disqualification of politicians) did not immediately result in institutionalized censorship. From 1964 to 1968, the opposition retained space to maneuver. But the cinema novo filmmakers knew a turning point had been reached. They saw that the populist ideology of the early 1960s, increasingly leavened by radical nationalism, had proved bankrupt. Their depiction of Brazil now turned to a critique of the very leftism that had characterized their pre-1964 phase. "Optimism" was replaced by "perplexity," in the words of one critic.

The most famous example was Glauber Rocha's *Terra em Transe* ("Land in Anguish," 1967). The film's events occur in the imaginary state of El Dorado, where a populist provincial governor, Felipe Vieira, chooses not to fight off a coup headed by a rightist politician with the revealing name of Porfirio Diaz (the Mexican authoritarian president). The analogy with Goulart and 1964 is obvious. Most of the film is taken up with a flashback depicting Vieira's political rise, complete with carnivalesque crowd scenes and frenetic behavior by the candidate. Rocha called it the "tragic carnival" of Brazilian politics, where "purity rots in tropical gardens." The film's effect is heightened by novel cinematographic techniques producing fragments that resist narrative synthesis.

After 1968, however, the cultural scene was subjected to strict censorship, including confiscation of suspect materials. Police informers were everywhere, throughout the artistic circles and educational institutions. The penalty for falling afoul of the authorities was arrest, torture, and possibly worse. Many artists now fled into exile, leaving primarily the hacks and the conformists to fill the cultural vacuum.

There were exceptions, nonetheless, especially in music. Perhaps it was the potential for ambiguity that allowed the censors to sometimes approve lyrics which had a double entendre. The master of this game was Francisco Buarque de Hollanda ("Chico Buarque"). Son of a noted intellectual, he had the knack for writing and singing songs that appealed both to sophisticated audiences and the ordinary Brazilian.

Such compositions as "A Banda" (1966) and "Roda Viva" (1967), which preceded the 1968 crackdown, quickly established his fame. He eventually found the more militarized climate intolerable and spent 1968 through 1970 in exile in Italy. Upon returning to Brazil, his first song, "Apesar de Você" ("In Spite of You"), was immediately banned because of its thinly veiled attack on military rule. Although rejecting the label of protest singer (he did not want to be typecast as an outsider), Chico continued composing and singing despite the censors' constant intervention. His success could be traced to his genius for combining traditional samba and bossa nova with his own playful originality.

His survival on the cultural scene after 1970 (he remained highly popular until redemocratization in 1985 and after) was a tribute to his endless ingenuity and the ineptitude of the frustrated censors, who never felt able to ban him outright. It was another sign that Brazil's military regime, although repressive, never reached the depth experienced in the counterpart dictatorships of Argentina and Chile.

The late 1960s produced another musical phenomenon involved in attempting to assert Brazilian identity in an unfree society. The movement was called "Tropicalism" and it owed its origins to a Bahian contingent led by Caetano Veloso and Gilberto Gil. They avoided overtly political messages, but nonetheless soon ran into trouble with the censors. They chose to resurrect themes from the iconoclastic tradition of modernist writers such as Oswaldo de Adrade, whose 1920s avant-garde verse celebrated cannibalism as the only truly Brazilian characteristic. Veloso and Gil experimented with outrageously "tropical" costumes and ostentatiously honored Carmen Miranda, the ambassadress to Hollywood with the tutti frutti hairstyle and the kitsch version of samba. Despite their ostensibly non-political style, the Tropicalistas found the post-1968 atmosphere suffocating and went into exile in London in 1969. Their departure followed an episode of house arrest by the federal police in Bahia in late 1968. The military authorities could abide the (censored) subtleties of Chico Buarque, but they found Carmen Miranda and cannibalism too much to tolerate.

We now need to consider more explicitly the social context of cultural production after 1964. The foregoing discussion of cultural trends includes film, which was greatly restricted in its impact. Brazilian filmmakers were at a great disadvantage vis-à-vis their competitors in Hollywood. The Brazilians were grossly underfinanced and lacking in technical resources. Above all, they were handicapped by poor distribution. Movie houses knew that Hollywood films, surrounded with their massive advertising and international glamour, would draw patrons. The kind of cinema novo films discussed above were often too difficult, too disturbing, and too heavy for the typical Brazilian. Popular music, on the other hand, especially after 1964, was more capable of reaching a mass audience via radio and television. For that reason it drew more attention from the censors.

The cultural medium that achieved the greatest impact during the military regime was television. In 1960, the year Janio Quadros won the presidency, Brazil had fewer than 600,000 TV sets. By 1986, the year after the return of elected government, the total was 26.5 million, or more than a forty-fold increase, aided by government-induced favorable installment terms. The number of stations had increased at an even faster rate. In 1964 there were only 14; by 1985, when the last general left the presidency, there were 150. In addition, a government-built microwave network helped create a nationwide system. This meant that the federal government, through its licensing, could and did shape the ownership of the medium from which most Brazilians got their news and entertainment.

The most famous beneficiary of government favoritism was the Globo organization, the media and publishing conglomerate, which entered the TV field in 1965. Initially, Globo had technical and financial help for its fledging TV enterprise from Time-Life, but the corporation soon dropped this link and emerged on its own as Brazil's most aggressive and professional TV network. Its expansion was openly favored by the military governments, which granted it the most attractive locations and facilitated import of the most up-to-date equipment. In return, TV Globo followed a strictly pro-government programming policy. This was a powerful asset for the generals, since TV Globo's evening news had 80 percent of the audience and its overall ratings far outweighed all the other networks combined.

By 1985, TV Globo had become the fourth largest network in the world, with a viewership of 80 million. Its skillfully produced evening *telenenovelas* (soap operas) developed a fanatical following. These *telenovelas* were exported to more than fifty countries, demonstrating that TV Globo's producers, writers, and actors had fashioned a product of universal appeal. For those who worried about Brazil's identity, it was another sign of success, however one might value it, on the world scene.

The private station owners got a further bonus from the heavy advertising by state corporations and banks. Advertising revenues poured in from every source, and rose from $350 million in 1970 to $1.5 billion in 1979. The sophistication of TV advertising grew along with the revenue. Brazilian ad agencies began winning international awards. The Americanization of Brazilian media, in the sense of ownership structure and production technique, if not of U.S. programs, proceeded apace. If much of the programming was insipid and narcoticizing, could the same not be said of TV to the north?

As for the print media and fiction, military repression had the expected effects. Newspapers and magazines proved easy to control. Direct pressure on the editors and owners was enough to create self-censorship, which made "prior censorship" regularly necessary on less than ten publications. The government had many other weapons, including manipulation of state-sponsored advertising (estimated at 30 percent of total revenue) and court actions against individual journalists, editors, and owners. The stakes were also lower with the print media, since no paper had a circulation of more than a few hundred thousand (such as *O Jornal do Brasil* and *O Estado de S. Paulo*) and Brazil was not known for being a newspaper-reading country.

The more adventurous journalists responded to government pressure by creating an "alternative press," primarily weeklies such as *Opinião* and *Movimento*, which were outspokenly oppositionist and in response suffered frequent and large-scale censorship. These publications did, however, keep alive a critical spirit and were an important alternative to exile for opposition journalists. Interestingly enough, the alternative press died in the freer climate of the transition back to electoral government, thus ending one of the most creative chapters in the history of Brazilian journalism.

When it came to fiction during the military era, the story was similar to that of cinema. The audience was necessarily small, given the high incidence of functional illiteracy and the relatively high cost of books and poor sales distribution. Nonetheless, novelists produced works that gave their version of the experience of dictatorship, such as Antonio Callado's *Bar Don Juan* (1971), which depicted the short-lived guerrilla movement, and Loyola Brandão's *Zero* (1974), which laid out a disconnected series of tableaus located in a mythical country called "América Latindia." Both books were banned, although the censors relented on *Bar Don Juan*, and *Zero* was eventually printed in Brazil in 1985 after earlier publication in Italy. Finally, Ivan Angelo's *A Festa* (1976) was a look back at the height of the repression in 1970. The novel is set in Belo Horizonte, where a supposed influx of peasants fleeing from drought in the Northeast creates upheaval, while the local intellectuals lose themselves in sex and drugs. The parallels with Glauber Rocha's *Terra em Transe* are clear: It is another case of dissecting the illusion that had nourished the left before 1964, as well as showing their inability to deal with the repression that had followed.

Culture in the military years was a reflection of Brazilian artists' confrontation with the realities of power in Brazil. More than a few myths had been destroyed. A large portion of the country's artists and intellectuals had endorsed the populist and often radically nationalist vision of the early 1960s. They realized, as the general-presidents succeeded one another, that those visions were dead for at least another generation.

The military governments did attempt one direct use of the mass media, the promotion of patriotic propaganda on the lines of "O Brasil Grande" ("Vast Brazil"). The theme was the traditional one of Brazil's destiny to become a great power on the world stage. This ambition could be traced back to turn-of-the-century literary figures such as Afonso Celso and Olavo Bilac. These enthusiasts had painted a great future for Brazil as a powerful modern nation, despite its real status as a minor power on the margins of international politics. Now the military, emboldened by their success in the coup of 1964, thought the time had come to fulfill Brazil's destiny. That would also require a media campaign to prepare the public.

Proof of their commitment was to be found in the government's megaconstruction projects: the Itaipú dam (then the world's largest) on the Paraguayan border, the Transamazon Highway (crossing the world's largest rainforest), and the giant atomic energy project (utilizing a German technology never used before). All these multi-billion-dollar government-financed projects were supposed to help launch Brazil into the First World. They were given lavish coverage in the media, accompanied by patriotic music and liberal use of the national colors.

This brand of propaganda may have been effective in the 1968–74 period, when the Brazilian economy was growing by 10 percent a year, but the prolonged economic stagnation triggered by the 1979 oil crisis and Brazil's inadequate reaction to it made the public more skeptical. By the end of the last military presidency in 1985, censorship had finished and the generals had lost control of the media.

THE EFFECTS OF REPRESSION

Brazilians started journeying into exile as early as 1964, but the outflow accelerated in 1968–69. Those who fled included leftist politicians, intellectuals, academics, and artists, all convinced that they had no choice but to reconstruct their lives outside Brazil.

Many went to Chile, a democratic refuge where political pluralism was still a reality (until the military coup of 1973 brought the Pinochet dictatorship, which ensnared numerous Brazilian exiles). Chile was also attractive as a traditional ally of Brazil and as the center which had articulated a Latin American strategy of development. Other fleeing Brazilians joined intellectual and artistic circles in Mexico. Europe, especially France, also got its share of Brazilian refugees. France had long been the ideal refuge for restless Brazilians, and Paris soon had a large Brazilian exile colony. A small number went to Cuba and Eastern Europe, to live under socialist regimes. Some exiles came to the United States, but the number was relatively small because its conservative climate (as symbolized by outspoken U.S. support for the 1964 coup) made it less attractive.

Exile came as a shock to these Brazilians, who were passionate Brazilian patriots. Most felt painfully out of place abroad, where they began reexamining and writing about Brazilian history and the role of the left. Some simply repeated the Marxist or populist analyses they had been producing since the 1950s. Such authors found that Brazil's authoritarian turn merely confirmed what they had long seen coming. The more thoughtful expatriates, however, began to question the assumptions behind the populist strategy of the early 1960s.

They now saw that the left had seriously miscalculated the balance of power in the 1960s. Established authority had not been about to crumble in the face of a populist offensive. On the contrary, the right and the military staged their own coup with ease. These exiles also began to re-think their rationale for opposing the military government. The public backlash against it was weaker than they had predicted; the military were right in thinking they had the upper hand. One ex-guerrilla, Her-bert de Souza ("Betinho"), reflected on his pro-Maoist days, "We had ar-rived at the most extreme political madness. We were incapable of per-ceiving and gauging reality."

Meanwhile, the horrors of repression continued in Brazil. The vic-tims of government torture continued to pile up through 1974. If the Marxist and the populist formulae had been wrong, how could Brazil-ians find a successful alternative to authoritarian rule and all that went with it?

Forced residence abroad had another important effect on the exiles. It plunged some of Brazil's best and brightest into sustained contact with other societies, other cultures, and other political systems. Brazilians liv-ing in welfare states—such as Sweden, France, or Germany, in particu-lar—found a capitalism quite different from that of Brazil. They also got to know societies where there was still room for political debate.

The repression was ostensibly aimed at the armed opposition, but in fact affected the entire society. To understand how, we must take a brief look at the role of repression in Brazilian history.

Although the elite had always preferred to view their country as fundamentally nonviolent, that is a very inaccurate reading of Brazilian history. Slavery, for example, had been based on physical brutality that included mutilation, merciless beatings, and execution, and had contin-ued in Brazil until 1888 (forced labor of Amazonian Indians continued even longer), longer than anywhere else in the Americas. In the Brazil of the early 1960s, physical mistreatment of ordinary citizens by the po-lice was still commonplace. In part, this was a legacy of the violence that surrounded slavery. But it was also inherent in maintaining the highly hierarchical society that the Brazilian Republic inherited. From the be-ginning of the Republic in 1889, governments had repeatedly resorted to declaring a state of siege, thus allowing the suspension of judicial guarantees. During the popular protests against compulsory vaccination in Rio in 1904, for example, the crowds were bombarded by artillery. Over 300 of the detainees were then deported, without any judicial pro-ceeding, to a distant camp in the Amazon. Similar internment tactics were employed in the wake of the 1910 naval revolt.

Police mistreatment of the elite, on the other hand, was rare, not least because the police were members of the non-elite classes and were in awe of their social superiors. Examples of differential behavior were easy to find. Any arrestee who held a higher university degree, for ex-ample, was by law (created by the 1941 Penal Code) entitled to better jail quarters than common detainees. Any elite member who ran afoul of the authorities could count on quick help from his or her web of elite contacts. A prime indicator of the unequal application of justice was the gross leniency shown toward white- collar criminals such as stock market swindlers. Rarely did they suffer any meaningful punishment, while common suspects could usually expect the worst.

This system of differential justice was well understood by all Brazilians. It reinforced a hierarchical social structure that was tight but not impermeable. When Brazil grew economically, its elite expanded. Yet this mobility did not alter the hierarchy itself.

The elite had long been able to remain in ignorance of the true workings of the criminal justice system, but that changed with the highly authoritarian turn in 1968. The reason was that the guerrilla movement was led primarily by disaffected youth from the elite, not by workers. The militant radical nationalists, bitter over the coup, were prime recruiting material for the armed opposition. Many of them came from leftist Catholic youth organizations and university political groups (overwhelmingly elite in origin). The security forces interrogated all guerrilla suspects by methods that were normal for common criminals but not practiced on the elite. One was the "parrot's perch," where the victim was suspended naked on a horizontal pole and subjected to beatings and electric shocks. Another was to submerge the victim in filthy water and shoot just over his or her head whenever the body surfaced. For particularly difficult cases—i.e., where confessions or incriminating evidence were not forthcoming—electricity was applied to the genitals, eardrums, and other body apertures. Elite and non-elite alike were fair game. As word of this brutal treatment leaked out, the elite victims' families were truly shocked. Even the sons of generals faced the horror of torture.

This indiscriminate repression made many in the elite reconsider their support for the military government. Did the security threat really justify the government's barbarity? They had not realized it would come to this.

Slowly, elite institutions began to react. Best situated was the Catholic Church, whose bishops were shocked by the mistreatment of their clergy. Even conservative bishops who had enthusiastically endorsed the coup now denounced torture. A second elite institution that reacted, albeit slowly, was the Bar Association. The few criminal lawyers who defended political prisoners and knew first-hand of the torture now tried to rouse their colleagues to action. The lawyers, the cream of the elite, began to discover a new meaning to the rule of law. Yet neither the Church nor the Bar had leverage against the military. The best they could do was spread a discreet word among the elite or leak information to friends abroad.

Even within the military there were signs of unease. Most officers had bought the official line (admitted internally but never publicly) that torture was used immediately after arrest to get "hot" intelligence that would "save lives". But the torturers sometimes continued their work for weeks or even months after the victim's arrest, when there was not even any tactical purpose to such brutality. The military command flatly denied any excesses, while informally officers made it clear that "war is war." In the short run, there was no recourse against the torturers. But there was a larger question. If military rule should end, would the Brazilian elite recognize that torture was in fact the latest expression of a repressive system sustaining the social hierarchy that had benefited them for so long?

MILITARY RULE AND QUESTIONS ABOUT BRAZILIAN POLITICAL CULTURE

The harsh reality of dictatorship raised another question for Brazilians. Was Brazil's political tradition inherently democratic or authoritarian? The coup of 1964 had ended the democratic era that had resumed in 1945. But 1945 had in turn ended the authoritarian era of 1937–45. What was "normal" for Brazil?

This question is complicated by the need to recognize that torture and repression are not the whole story of the military rule that began in 1964. For the vast majority of Brazilians, the victory of the hard line in 1968 probably made little if any difference in their lives. Some civilian politicians had been banned from public life, but there was no shortage of replacements, albeit of a less independent turn of mind. The higher military had not themselves assumed most of the administration of Brazil. Aside from critical areas such as security and communications, civilians remained in charge of the government machinery. In states such as Minas Gerais, for example, the politicians who allied with the military won much federal investment for their state.

Certain civilian allies (would-be right-wing theoreticians) of the military sought to help solidify the new regime by formulating a new compulsory educational curriculum known as "Moral and Civic Education." It consisted of an omnibus course (combining geography, geopolitics, conventionally oriented Brazilian history, and a dose of conservative civics) that was required at every level of education, public and private, from kindergarten to the doctoral level. The chief beneficiaries were the textbook writers, who rushed in to win a share of the lucrative new market. Nonetheless, the thinking elite worried about Brazil's image in the world. They had long believed military dictatorships in Latin America occurred only in Spanish America. They saw Brazil as an island of legality in the sea of Spanish American *caudillos* (traditional strongmen). They were right to be worried. Brazil's sharp turn toward authoritarianism in 1968 aroused immediate criticism abroad. The U.S. government, which had grown increasingly worried over the hard-line influence, expressed concern (the public language was mild; behind-the-scenes statements were stronger). Liberals and human rights observers in the United States and West Europe denounced the generals' new move as a signal that Brazil had betrayed its commitment to democracy and the rule of law.

However, although foreigners were denouncing the political tactics of the authoritarian regime, they continued to support Brazil's economic policy, which was yielding great dividends in economic growth.

The Economic "Miracle" Wrought by the Authoritarians

By the end of the Castello Branco government in 1967, the stabilization program that began soon after the 1964 coup had achieved its principal economic goal: Inflation had been reduced from 92 percent in 1964 to 28 percent in 1967. (See exhibit 7-1.) Much of the foreign debt had been renegotiated and a foundation laid for renewed growth.

That growth appeared in 1968 and opened the way for a six-year boom, during which economic growth averaged the very high rate of 10.9 percent. The economic architect of this boom, as noted, was Delfim Neto, a young São Paulo economics professor recently appointed minister of finance in the new Costa e Silva government. Delfim eased credit in 1967, and the Brazilian economy responded with healthy growth, centered primarily in the industrial sector. (See exhibit 7-2.)

Financial help from the United States was important in establishing the environment for growth. The United States, as a single actor, could commit loan funds more rapidly than the international agencies. The sums were not large in relation to the size of Brazil's economy and its foreign debt, but the impact of U.S. aid was a powerful symbol, made more so by the praise of U.S. businessmen, along with the U.S. government, heaped on Brazil for its economic turnaround.

A key policy change was in the financial area. Brazil had no central bank in 1964, and its financial system had verged on the chaotic. Bulhões and Campos began a reorganization, which continued under Delfim Neto. Two policy instruments were crucial. The first was indexation (automatic adjustment for inflation), which had begun in 1964 for government bonds and became general in the early 1970s. Given the relatively low rate of inflation at that time (approximately 20 percent per annum), indexation helped maintain stable capital markets and prod the public to think in real rather than nominal economic terms. The second instrument was the "crawling peg," a system of small but frequent devaluations designed to maintain a realistic exchange rate (i.e., one that adjusted for the difference between the inflation rates of Brazil and the rest of the world). These continuous small adjustments avoided the need for any major devaluations, which had always proved disruptive. Both

EXHIBIT 7-1
Annual Rate of Inflation, 1965–85

Year	Inflation Rate (%)
1965	58.2
1966	37.9
1967	26.5
1968	26.7
1969	20.1
1970	16.4
1971	20.3
1972	19.1
1973	22.7
1974	34.8
1975	33.9
1976	47.6
1977	46.2
1978	38.9
1979	55.8
1980	110.0
1981	95.0
1982	100.0
1983	211.0
1984	224.0
1985	235.0

Source: Werner Baer, *The Brazilian Economy*, 4th ed. (Westport, 1995), p. 392–93.

devices were defended as short-term measures to help in the transition to low or zero inflation. In 1974, that goal still seemed reachable.

The industrial boom stimulated by the easing of credit soon improved industrial wage levels. This also had the effect of increasing the earnings gap between industrial and nonindustrial workers. Furthermore, it stimulated rural to urban migration, dramatizing the income differential between the industrialized Center South and the poorer regions, especially the Northeast.

Economists had long argued that Brazil could neither stop inflation nor regain growth until it overcame the bottleneck in agriculture. The solution urged by the pre-1964 "structuralists" was land reform—i.e., redistribution of land ownership. Castello Branco had promised meaningful land reform but was not able to follow through on his commitment. The agricultural bottleneck was broken, however—at least in terms of production—not by land redistribution, but by large-scale diversification away from coffee. Brazil became a major producer (and exporter) of orange concentrate (one Brazilian grower reportedly owned more trees than the whole state of Florida). Another virtually new crop was soybeans. Brazil quickly became the second largest exporter of soybeans (after the United States) and a major supplier to Japan. There was also a steady increase in the production of domestic food crops.

The federal government's generous rural credit policy was one factor behind the increased agricultural production. The government's granting of export subsidies was another. Both policies benefited primarily the large commercial farms and were accompanied by the opening of new lands (Brazil had one of the world's largest reserves of unused arable land). The expansion spread into the *cerrado,* a vast western territory previously lacking transportation facilities. It also moved into western Bahia and the western Amazon Basin, with settlers arriving from states to the South, such as Minas Gerais and Paraná. In 1975, for example, the cerrado produced virtually no soybeans. By 1985 it was producing almost six million metric tons, a third of Brazil's soybean harvest. There was comparable success with rice.

The main beneficiaries of this agricultural boom were the large landowners, who were best situated to take advantage of the easier credit, export subsidies, and other government favors. Federal policy also favored export agriculture, rather than production of domestic food-

EXHIBIT 7-2
GDP Distribution by Sector, 1955–75 (percent shares)

Year	Agriculture	Industry	Commerce	Other	Total
1955	25.1	24.4	16.3	34.2	100
1960	22.5	25.2	15.1	37.2	100
1965	15.9	32.4	15.1	36.6	100
1970	10.1	35.9	15.6	38.4	100
1975	11.0	37.1	17.1	34.8	100

Source: Raymond W. Goldsmith, *Brasil 1850–1984: Desenvolvimento Financeiro sob um Século de Inflação* (São Paulo, 1986), p. 225, 239.

stuffs. Nonetheless, the latter increased sufficiently to prevent food prices from endangering the boom. All of this had a cost: increased income differentials among regions and classes.

THE BENEFITS AND COSTS OF FOREIGN LOANS

The economic boom was also successful in the external sector. The balance-of-payments deficit that was such a major destabilizing factor in 1964 had been reversed by 1968, as Brazil expanded its exports significantly. But the good fortune did not continue indefinitely. The balance of payments went into deficit again starting in the mid-1970s and deteriorated thereafter. (See exhibit 7-3.)

In 1973, OPEC, the price-fixing cartel of oil-producing and -exporting countries, imposed its first steep price increase. The effect on Brazil was immediate. Since it depended on imports for more than half its oil consumption, Brazil's import bill ballooned. Faced with a threat to the economic boom, Delfim Neto and his advisors decided to "grow their way out of the oil shock." To pay the bill they sharply increased their borrowing abroad, which they could do primarily on the accounts of Brazil's state corporations.

When a second OPEC oil shock followed in 1979, they took two additional steps to reduce oil imports. One was a massive program to produce the alcohol fuel from sugar cane for use in passenger cars. Existing gasoline-fueled cars could run on a mixture of 20 percent alcohol and 80 percent gasoline. New car production was quickly shifted to models that burned almost all alcohol. The second step was to accelerate the 1976 program for obtaining German technology to build nuclear reactors. Here again, the goal was to find an alternative energy source for petroleum.

EXHIBIT 7-3
Brazil's Balance of Payments, Selected Categories, 1965–85

Year	Exports Minus Imports	Net Services	Net Capital	Overall Surplus (+) or Deficit (−)
1965	655	−362	−6	331
1970	232	−815	1,015	545
1975	−3,540	−3,162	6,189	−950
1980	−2,255	−10,152	9,678	−3,472
1985	12,486	−12,878	−2,554	−3,200

Source: IBGE, *Estatísticas Históricas do Brasil,* 2nd ed. (Rio de Janeiro, 1990), p. 583–85.

These steps did not ease the need for borrowing abroad, however, because Brazil had now adopted a strategy of "debt-led growth," aided by the availability of "petrodollars" from the oil-exporting economies. The strategy was understandable in short-run terms. World interest rates continued to be lower than the rate of inflation in New York and London, and Brazil could, for the moment, borrow at negative real rates of interest.

What had seemed sound borrowing strategy in the early to mid-1970s turned slowly but surely into a longer-term disaster. In 1979, OPEC again jacked up the price of oil. By 1980, oil was accounting for 43 percent of Brazilian imports. In 1981, a massive credit squeeze, led by the U.S. Federal Reserve Bank, hit the industrial world. Since the interest rates on Brazil's foreign loans were tied to world rates, the interest due on Brazil's loans—the largest in the developing world—shot up. Brazil, like the rest of Latin America, could not make its payments. Latin America went into default on its commercial bank loans, and Brazil's economic boom came to a halt.

THE WINNERS AND LOSERS

What role did labor play in this story? One feature of most developing economies is a relative surplus of labor—the result of the declining demand for labor in agriculture and the high population growth rates in such societies. Surplus low-cost labor can be a benefit or a liability, depending on one's perspective. Such a surplus can be an asset in that it produces a relative wage advantage in producing for export. It can be a liability in that it can depress wages and make union organizing more difficult.

Brazil exhibited both these effects. Its industries recruited cheap labor among rural in-migrants; at the same time, the ready availability of those workers acted as a drag on the wages and working conditions of unskilled and semi-skilled labor. Low wages also kept down the level of consumer demand, especially for clothing and less expensive durable goods. Meanwhile, the thriving economy (until 1982) caused wages for the relatively few high-skilled workers to increase rapidly, creating large wage differentials and relatively little labor-market mobility. Benefits from the economic boom were therefore distributed very unequally. At least half the labor force fell outside the formal labor market altogether, making them (in addition to earning very low cash wages) ineligible for the corporatist system of health care, vacations, and pensions created by Getúlio Vargas.

The lot of individual workers varied greatly by where they lived. Those in the industrializing Center-South had a chance at the better jobs. Those in the countryside were the poorest. They were most numerous in the Northeast, but large pockets of rural poverty existed also in the

South and West. The labor unions could do little in the way of working class mobilization. The existence of a large surplus labor force inhibited union militancy even in an open society. Under the military regime, they were subject to control and manipulation by the Ministry of Labor. How successful they could be in organizing if and when democracy returned was a question no one could answer.

Who got the income and wealth generated by the rapid growth of the 1970s? Any perceptive visitor to Brazil could have given an answer. Every large city had its construction boom, especially of high-rise apartments. The better-off "non-manual workers" (in the demographer's term) were acquiring luxurious quarters—at least compared to those inhabited by 90 percent of Brazilians.

How could this contrast be exposed in the language of economists? The official data on income distribution showed increased inequality (see exhibit 7-4). This data was much cited by critics at home and abroad. But the data also showed that every income group had improved their absolute income level during the 1970s. The shares of the economic pie had grown more unequal but the absolute size of each slice had become larger. The publication of these data provoked great controversy. Critics of the government at home and abroad emphasized the growing inequality; government supporters emphasized the increasing absolute shares.

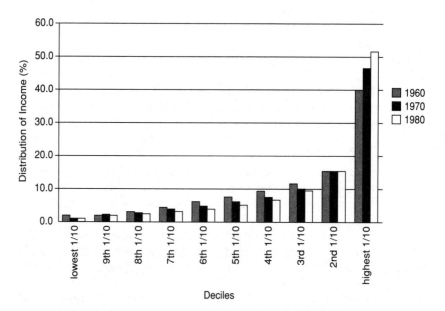

Exhibit 7-4. Distribution of income for the economically active population, by deciles, 1960–80. From IBGE, *Estatísticas Históricas do Brasil*, 2nd ed. (Rio de Janeiro, 1990), p. 77.

Other indicators, except of course civil liberties, showed steady improvement. During the 1960 to 1987–88 period, infant (under five) mortality dropped from 160 to 85 per 1,000. Over the same period, life expectancy increased from 55 to 66. Literacy rates rose, as did the number of homes with indoor plumbing (crucial for improving public health). Finally, access to radio continued to increase and television became a reality for many, transforming the leisure time of millions.

Perceptions of these facts were as important politically as the facts themselves. Brazil was becoming a test case for capitalism in the developing world of the 1970s. Its boosters called it an "economic miracle." Those on the left and left-center cited the data on income inequality as proof that the authoritarian regime was bent on rewarding the rich. (See exhibit 7-4.) They also pointed to continuing urban-rural inequalities. The government defenders, led by Delfim Neto, acknowledged the inequalities but dismissed them as inevitable in a vigorously growing capitalist economy. "The pie must grow before it can be divided up," they liked to note. They pointed to the large inequalities produced by U.S. and West European nineteenth-century growth—inequalities that had even grown in the early twentieth century before subsequently moderating. They argued that Brazil, once farther down the capitalist road, would exhibit more equal income distribution.

The left was in a difficult position with one aspect of this largely ideological debate. They had declared in 1964 (and before) that any stabilization program would plunge Brazil into a long recession. They were proved wrong. With inflation under control, Brazil succeeded in resuming growth, however distorted the distribution of its benefits. Some critics acknowledged this point. Celso Furtado, for example, writing from exile in Paris, published a series of theoretical treatises explaining how, despite dire predictions, the economy had managed to resume growth. He even acknowledged that this growth strategy could continue to operate, however distasteful its social effects.

The debates over economic justice versus growth had their counterparts abroad. The World Bank now saw Brazil as a case of economic growth at the cost of social justice. Robert MacNamara, still smarting from his disastrous experience as U.S. secretary of defense, assumed the presidency of the World Bank in 1968 and made Brazil a priority.

The question to which no one knew the answer was whether this spectacular growth record could only be achieved by an authoritarian regime, or only by one with highly concentrated income distribution. Would the technocrats always need military protection to carry out their unpopular decisions? And would growth—at least of the capitalist variety—always require rewarding the rich so their savings could supposedly finance needed investment? Brazil was on the way to finding out.

The Road to Redemocratization

The initiative for change, surprisingly enough, came from within the military itself. The leader was General Ernesto Geisel, who assumed the presidency in 1974 after his indirect election by the Congress. Geisel had the reputation of being a stern, humorless officer, known for going by the book. But he remained a Castelista (read: *moderate*), a trait which had grown stronger when he headed the military household during Castello Branco's presidency. His political adviser was General Golbery Couto e Silva, a closet democrat whom he made head of his military household. The subsequent internal history of the regime was the battle between the hard- and soft-line factions over a possible transition to civilian rule.

Golbery, a consummate behind-the-scenes maneuverer, started playing a complicated game with the civilian opposition. As of 1974, the Catholic Church was the most important other player. Its human rights advocates had long demanded an accounting for the several hundred missing Brazilians. Golbery met with the Catholic Church and other opposition leaders and promised to return with information from Geisel. At the same time, he was sending emerging signals to labor union leaders in São Paulo. Golbery was widely distrusted, but his influence with Geisel could not be doubted.

The Geisel government accompanied this political maneuvering with an easing of censorship and police surveillance in 1974–75, a move that emboldened opposition groups. The Bar Association, in particular, became more aggressive. A few progressive business leaders from São Paulo called for a return to democracy. And São Paulo metalworkers began spontaneous meetings to protest wage policies.

For the rest of the Geisel presidency, which ended in 1979, authoritarianism was slowly eroded by the interaction of the soft-line military and the increasingly vocal civilian opposition. Neither could have succeeded without the other, but the process was long and frustrating because of hard-line interference.

BATTLES WITHIN THE OFFICER CORPS

Not surprisingly, Golbery's overtures alarmed the hard-line military. They disdained him personally (calling him "the General from Dow" for his earlier highly paid consulting with Dow Chemical, an American firm). They also persuaded their colleagues in the repressive apparatus to begin a new security crackdown designed to discredit Golbery's contacts with the opposition.

The hard line's logic was as simple as it was absurd: They believed Brazil suffered from the malignant disease of "populism," "communism," or "corruption"—terms they used interchangeably. The more fanatical officers saw this malady as a challenge to Christian civilization, of which Brazil was presumably a bulwark. By this logic, pornography was as great a threat as Cuban agents. Unlike the Castelistas, who thought a few years of military rule would be enough of a convalescence to cure the disease, the hard-liners believed Brazil was suffering from an entrenched cancer that could only be cured by decades of harsh treatment. They also made sure to build their own network of cronies to guarantee themselves the best military postings and the best benefits.

The Castelistas also distrusted most politicians, but they came from the "legalist" Brazilian military tradition, believing that ultimately only popular elections gave legitimacy. After a decade of authoritarian medicine, the soft line now wanted a return to democracy, if under carefully controlled conditions.

This strategy, identified closely with General Golbery, implied several important rules of engagement. First, there could be no public admission of torture or other illicit activity. Second, no punishment could be permitted for those, military or civilian, who had served in the security apparatus. Third, all officers must follow the strict rules of retirement, which included a limit on "years in rank" (decreed earlier by Castello Branco). In other words, the Brazilian army insisted upon rotation of its general presidents to ensure that no general was allowed to perpetuate himself in power. This principle, in particular, distinguished them from the Argentine generals, who failed to limit the term of their military presidents, making them perennial targets for overthrow. Finally, seniority by age was to be strictly observed.

The Castelistas had one important factor in their favor. The military government had never completely repressed the main civilian political institutions. The Congress remained open (although partially purged) and remained directly elected. It was also used to elect succeeding general-presidents. This approach contrasted with later military governments in Argentina and Chile, which simply abolished their legislatures.

Brazil's way out of authoritarianism was also influenced by the international context. The elite was highly aware of their country's image abroad, just as they had been since the nineteenth century. As a group, they identified strongly with the North Atlantic democracies. Brazil had been the only Latin American country to send troops to fight Hitler, and identification with the victorious allies was also central to the officer corps's identity. The use of torture and the abuse of human rights since 1964 had brought heavy criticism from churches (including the Vatican), politicians, and intellectuals in the United States and Western Europe. The Brazilian elite's fear of social revolution (which was fading fast after a decade of repressive government) was being overtaken by their desire to return to the democratic world.

United States influence was crucial in this changing calculus, and after the authoritarian turn in 1968, U.S. approval of the 1964 coup began to be mixed with criticism. The economic boom of the 1970s gave the military some added legitimacy in the eyes of the outside world, but did not erase Brazil's repressive image. Thus, the Brazilian elite's desire for international respectability aided the soft-liners in their plans.

MANIPULATING THE ELECTORAL SYSTEM

President Geisel had to worry about winning elections if he was to stay ahead of his hard-line enemies. In his first presidential year, he had decided to change a previous campaign rule that denied the opposition access to television. As a result, both parties were to be given free television time in the 1974 elections. The main opposition party, the MDB, won major victories in every state where voters were exposed to antigovernment TV campaigns. As a result, the government lost its two-thirds majority in the Congress and therefore its ability to amend the Constitution at will.

What had been intended as a minor concession to critics turned out to be a major setback that put Geisel and Golbery in a dilemma. They wanted to change other electoral rules as well (to strengthen the government party's position) but could not now count on automatic congressional support. To deal with the situation, Geisel had to issue a series of arbitrary decrees ("The April Package of 1977"), which were in fact constitutional amendments. The Fifth Institutional Act had given the president this power, and he now used it to pack the Senate with nonelected presidential appointees and to unilaterally amend the constitution. The new senators were quickly dubbed "bionic," demonstrating both Brazilian wit and the influence of U.S. TV programs (the reference is to "the bionic man" on U.S. TV's *The Six Million Dollar Man*) in Brazil. Armed with these new weapons, Geisel and Golbery felt they could guarantee government party electoral victories and prevent the civilian opposition from gaining power. Golbery returned to negotiating with leading groups in civil society.

When Geisel left power in 1979, the path for the transition had been laid out. It was to be "slow, gradual, and certain," in Geisel's words. The fifth general-president was João Batista Figueiredo, hand-picked by Geisel. He apparently thought Figueiredo's genial personality would help give the military government a new face. Geisel, as noted, had been a stiff, rather stereotypically German figure (his father was an immigrant German school teacher). He never held a press conference in Brazil (there was one given abroad) or made any other gesture to woo the public. Yet Geisel played a crucial role in disarming the hard line and managing an extremely tricky transition back toward electoral democracy.

Figueiredo's easy manner made a favorable first impression, and he continued the process of relaxing authoritarian power while keeping the hard line at bay. In August 1979, the Congress passed (knowing the government would accept) an amnesty law which, as was typical in Brazilian history, applied to *all* political crimes, whether by the government or the opposition. The exiles, famous and not so famous, began streaming back home. Golbery remained as chief political advisor to the new president and continued his efforts to shore up the government party. He was aided by the bionic senators' presence, which gave him the two-thirds majority he needed to manipulate the electoral rules in the government's favor.

But the economic scene was daunting. Figueiredo inherited the intensifying debt crisis, which reached a breaking point in 1981–82. He brought back Delfim Neto as finance minister, but Delfim's skills at monetary manipulation could no longer match the world forces working against Brazil.

Figueiredo was, however, helped along on another dimension. A new generation of army officers had emerged who had graduated from the military academy since 1964. No longer necessarily anti-Vargas or even anti-Goulart activists, they were worried about their profession's image among fellow Brazilians. The lurid stories of torture now tarred the entire military. Some military officers had even stopped wearing their uniforms in public for fear of ridicule. They saw the hard line as having dragged their profession in the dust. Nor were these officers as susceptible to the psychology of the "red scare" as their predecessors had been. The hard line was losing support where it counted most—within the army officer corps.

Meanwhile, in the civilian sphere a spirited campaign had begun to restore direct election of the president in 1985, with millions of supporters wearing T-shirts that read; "I want to vote for president!". It began, logically enough, with the PMDB, then picked up endorsement from top Catholic clergy and soon became an enthusiastic movement featuring regional rallies that reached 500,000 in Rio and one million in São Paulo. The rallies featured pop singing stars such as Fafá da Belêm and Elba Ramalho and even Brazil's leading soccer announcer, Osmar Santos. It was an outpouring of civic spirit unprecedented since the military seized power two decades earlier. Unfortunately, the effort fell short in the government-controlled Congress, where, despite enormous public pressure, proponents of the direct election of the president came up just twenty-two votes short of the required two-thirds majority. There was massive public disillusionment. Another president would be elected indirectly.

All attention was now centered on the jockeying for the presidential election, which would take place in Congress. The generals now faced a predictable challenge: The government party wanted to nominate a civilian candidate. The leading contender was Paulo Maluf, the indirectly elected governor of São Paulo in 1979, famous for his tough right-wing stand in Paulista politics. Maluf had inherited great wealth (from both his own family and that of his wife) and was one of Brazil's most aggressive political campaigners. Many observers on the center and left found him crude and unscrupulous, not least for his use of the police, when governor, to suppress strikes and civic demonstrations.

The opposition had united behind Tancredo Neves, the governor of Minas Gerais and a political veteran of high office in the governments of both Vargas and Goulart. His personality and politics contrasted sharply with those of Maluf. He was a quiet, discreet, diminutive charmer who preferred the politics of intimate negotiation to public bombast. And he was known as the ultimate centrist.

Maluf's drive for the official nomination had set on edge the teeth of numerous PDS leaders. They disliked his style and worried that he could not be trusted as president. No longer afraid of the military at the top, they began to defect from the PDS, forming a splinter party (the PFL or Partido da Frente Liberal) with just enough congressional votes to give Tancredo the election. Tancredo was meanwhile negotiating discreetly with the military to assure them that as president he would treat them well. Not least was his promise to increase the military budget, which had lagged badly in recent years. The military's financial situation was certainly desperate. By the early 1980s, units at the Villa Militar, for example, had no ammunition for target practice and the frontier units in Rio Grande do Sul were denied the ultra-modern military vehicles Brazil was exporting.

The defectors' strategy succeeded. The dissenting PDS votes (now under the PFL label) combined with those of the PMDB to make Tancredo the first elected civilian president since Jânio Quadros. His election met with public rejoicing and, more interestingly, minimal concern by the military. He was, virtually everyone agreed, the ideal leader to restore Brazil to the ranks of the electoral democracies.

8 Redemocratization—New Hope, Old Problems: 1985–

An Unintended Succession

The excitement surrounding Tancredo's accession to the presidency was short-lived. Following his tried-and-true methods of maximizing support, Tancredo was keeping the many contenders for office hopeful but in the air about their chances. Negotiations for the new cabinet were particularly intense—with Tancredo making promises left and right and keeping those promises close to his chest—when persistent rumors began to surface about his health. As time passed, it became increasingly clear to those in the know that the president-elect was seriously ill. The public knew that he needed surgery, but the gravity of his true condition was kept a closely guarded secret.

All hell broke loose on the eve of his inauguration in Brasília on March 15, 1985. Tancredo was stricken with such acute stomach pains that he was rushed to the nearest military hospital. Vice president José Sarney was hastily installed as provisional president and Tancredo underwent intestinal surgery. The scene at the hospital was a nightmare. Sterile conditions were impossible because of the crowds of political cronies and hangers-on that filled the operating room. Then, Tancredo's intestine ruptured. If the cause of his condition was an infection, the rupture certainly spread it into his abdominal cavity.

The surgeons declared their work a success and the president-elect was said to be on the mend, but that was not the truth, as the spokesmen must have known. He continued to have dreadful intestinal symptoms, frightening his physicians into sending him by air to Brazil's best hospital, not surprisingly in São Paulo. By the time Tancredo underwent his seventh surgery, on April 12, the gravity of his condition, if not its cause, was widely known, stimulating a lengthy public vigil as millions of Brazilians directed their prayers to his hospital room. Hundreds of religious offerings, both Christian and Afro-Brazilian, surrounded the hospital entrance. As one journalist noted, "It wasn't just Tancredo in intensive care, it was the whole country."

Tancredo died on April 21, 1985, amid recriminations from all sides about the management of his medical care and the news releases about his condition. Had the care been incompetent in Brasília? Was there a cover-up in São Paulo? Was malpractice endangering Brazil's transition to democracy? Rumors still persist that Tancredo died of stomach cancer and that his closest advisers kept it secret for fear that the news might derail the new democracy just as it started. The truth remains a secret. But reaction of Brazilians to his death was certainly genuine. In São Paulo, two million people lined the street to bid adieu as Tancredo's body began its journey back to São João Del Rei, his birthplace in Minas Gerais. Tancredo's funeral was the most massive outpouring of public grief since the funeral that followed Vargas's suicide three decades earlier.

Once again, Brazil was to be governed by a vice-president, José Sarney, Tancredo's running mate, who was suddenly thrust into the spotlight of full presidential power.

Sarney and the New Democracy

José Sarney was a long-time member of the political elite (he was first elected federal deputy in 1958) and PDS national party president from the poverty- stricken northeastern state of Maranhão. He had been put on the ticket as a concession to the PDS congressmen who had defected to vote with the PMDB. Sarney was an old-style politician for whom politics meant little more than getting elected and dispensing patronage. He soon used the patronage attached to the presidency to woo the PMDB, Tancredo's party.

Sarney's presidency faced two gargantuan tasks: rebuilding democracy after a hiatus of almost two decades, and resolving yet another inflationary crisis. To strengthen his own hand, his first action was to push to extend his term from four to five years. Intensive horse trading and liberal dispensing of new television licenses to congressmen who were swing votes achieved the extended mandate he sought.

A return to open politics demanded a new Constitution and free political parties. The drafting of the Constitution was a task for the Congress (constituted also as a Constituent Assembly) that was elected in November 1986. Thus, the Constitution-writing task fell to a set of congressmen elected in the normal cycle of congressional elections. It took over a year to draft the Constitution of 1988, which was the result of one of the most intense lobbying efforts in the history of the Brazilian Congress. Lobbyists representing leftist groups in the Church, the union movement, and the human rights community were especially active. Much of its content represented a victory for populist ideas against many of the principles advocated by the military government.

The Constitution, longer than any previous one, stipulated a long list of citizen rights and reaffirmed such corporatist tenets as absolute job tenure for federal civil servants (Federal University faculty, for example, got tenure after one year of service). It was also nationalist in establishing the inviolability of Petrobrás, the state oil monopoly. These measures were all attempts by the heirs of the populist tradition to prevent another 1964.

The populists failed in their attempt to include a strong agrarian reform provision, however. The provision owed its decisive defeat to conservative congressmen, who were unworried at seeing Vargas-style corporatist measures continue in the urban sector, but wanted no truck with expanding property rights in the countryside. A new organization of rural landowners, the União Democrática Rural, outflanked the agrarian reform advocates through intense and effective lobbying. The conservative message was clear: Guarantees of human rights were harmless, but threatening land rights was another matter.

One of the most important constitutional provisions was a new allocation of federal revenues. The military governments had concentrated more and more spending power in Brasília until 1982, a concentration that caused frustration and resentment among state governors and mayors. Although this trend had reversed by 1985, the Constituent Assembly, whose members largely identified with the states and *municípios*, sought to further correct the balance by increasing the share of the federal revenues for lower levels of government. Before 1988, 44.6 percent of revenues went to the federal government and 55.4 percent to the states and municipalities. Now the division was 36.5 percent and 63.5 percent, respectively. The revenue shift was made without reducing the federal government's constitutional responsibilities, however, thus virtually guaranteeing permanent federal deficits. Seen in a larger context, it was a continuation of Brazil's long alternation between centralization and decentralization, both politically and economically. Previous swings had happened in 1830, 1841, 1889, 1930, 1937, 1945, 1964, and 1969.

Most Brazilian politicians and editorial writers congratulated themselves on their country's new "magna carta," praising its fully up-to-date democratic content. The problems inherent in some of its more exaggerated provisions would take longer to be appreciated.

The political party system presented a more intractable problem because the existing parties were badly fragmented. General Golbery had begun manipulating the electoral laws in the early 1980s in a successful effort to divide the opposition and thus assure a continuous majority for the government party. This fragmentation had now assumed a momentum of its own, however, which threatened the stability of the democracy Golbery had worked to achieve. Ever since the PDS, the government party, had lost its majority in the Chamber of Deputies in 1982, the number of parties had grown and the rules for their operation had become more lax—especially legislation passed in 1985. Castello Branco's 1965 plan for a two-party system had collapsed once military control was relaxed and the military needed to manipulate the vote to remain in power. By 1985, eleven parties were represented in Congress and by 1991 the total had reached nineteen. Such fragmentation, accompanied by weak party discipline, encouraged individual wheeling and dealing by congressmen and made consensus on policy action, especially with regard to the economy, virtually impossible.

The effects of this fragmentation complicated an already delicate moment in the evolution of post-1985 democracy. With the first direct presidential election since the 1964 coup scheduled for November 1989, two major factors combined to make voter preferences unpredictable and potentially highly unstable. First, Brazil now had a huge electorate dominated by relatively young voters who had never faced a genuine choice at the polls. The total vote for president in 1960 was 12.6 million. In 1989, it turned out to be 82 million. Uncertainty about their preferences was aggravated by the fact that the minimum voting age had dropped from eighteen years to sixteen (although voting was only compulsory for those eighteen or older). The second factor contributing to potential instability was the election schedule, with elections at some level—federal, state, or municipal—planned for every one of the next four years. During the military regime the hard- and soft-line officers had disagreed on how unstable a free electorate might be. The answer was now at hand.

THE CRUZADO PLAN

The economic problem facing Sarney as he took office was the continuing foreign debt crisis stimulated by the "debt-led" growth of the 1970s, which finally caught up with the Brazilian economy in 1983. In order to meet payments on its foreign debt, the government resorted both to increased domestic public debt and to inflationary money creation. This meant that servicing the foreign debt had forced the Brazilian government to feed the flames of inflation. Brazilian inflation was therefore increasing and the Sarney government had to do something about it.

Things started off well. In late 1985, a group of young and innovative government economists designed a new stabilization plan. It was a heterodox plan, similar to the Austral plan that was simultaneously being attempted in Argentina. The term "heterodox" was meant to indicate that it differed from the "orthodox" plans long urged by the IMF. The plan began in February 1986 with the introduction of a new currency, the cruzado, to replace the existing unit, the cruzeiro. Prices, the exchange rate, and wages (after an initial adjustment) were frozen, and indexation was virtually eliminated. After this initial phase, a 20 percent annual wage increase was instituted (in line with Finance Minister Dilson Funaro's populist inclinations) and the monetary policy was expansive.

For the next few months the plan appeared to be a brilliant success. Inflation fell to less than 2 percent a month, negligible by recent Brazilian standards. A consumer boom ensued, with labor shortages provoking further wage increases. By mid-1986 the economy was clearly overheating, but the corrective measures urged by the technocratic team were politically unpalatable to both Finance Minister Funaro and President Sarney.

The euphoria lasted through the November congressional and gubernatorial elections, in which Sarney and the PMDB won a stunning victory. Its delegation in the Chamber of Deputies went from 201 to 261 (out of 487) and its number of senators rose from 23 to 45, giving an even larger majority in that body. The PMDB also swept the gubernatorial elections in the most populous states. It looked as if the democratic opposition had finally won a decisive vote of confidence against the authoritarians. In fact, it was the swan song of the PMDB, which was about to begin a long and inglorious decline.

Inflation was already accelerating in December, as excess demand was leading merchants to violate the official price freeze with under-the-table price increases. Their action was ratified when the government began increasing utility prices in late November. There was also trouble on the balance-of-payments front. The officially frozen exchange rate was becoming increasingly overvalued, as imports were favored and exports discouraged. The unmistakable sign of panic came in February 1987 when, with foreign exchange reserves rapidly falling, Funaro suspended interest payments on the foreign debts owed to private banks. It was the unilateral moratorium that Brazilian finance ministers had long been avoiding. It was also the last populist gesture of Funaro, who was struggling with terminal cancer.

By 1987, the Cruzado Plan had become just another failed stabilization program. Prices shot up, indexation was reinstated as a way to live with inflation, and the public once again turned cynical about all government plans. We will never know for certain, of course, but there is a pretty fair consensus among experts that, if politics had not beaten the technocrats—if Sarney had put on the economic brakes at the right time—the Cruzado Plan stood a good chance of beating inflation and setting Brazil on a steady growth path.

Such was not to be the case. The last two years of the Sarney presidency saw the economy go increasingly out of control. Inflation for 1988 reached 1038 percent. Brazilians had always (since World War II) lived with inflation rates that seem unimaginable to Americans, but never anything as high as this. (See exhibit 8-1.) A poll in mid-January 1989 in greater Rio and São Paulo registered a 70 percent "no confidence" rating for the president. The obvious question was, would Brazil be able to limp along until a new president was inaugurated in March 1990?

EXHIBIT 8-1
Annual Rates of Inflation, 1950–89

Year	Inflation % Variation
1950	9.2
1960	25.4
1965	58.2
1970	16.4
1975	33.9
1980	110.0
1985	235.0
1987	416.0
1988	1038.0
1989	1783.0

Source: Werner Baer, *The Brazilian Economy*, 4th ed. (Westport, 1995), p. 392–93.

The Debt Crisis and the Economy

The effects of the 1982 debt crisis were to linger for many years. Brazil was obligated to spend much of its scarce foreign exchange on servicing its foreign debt. Financing the resulting transfer of capital had a serious effect on the domestic economy. The only solution for the debt to the foreign commercial banks was to roll it over, which meant paying more interest in the future. Furthermore, new loans (aside from the rollovers) were unavailable at any price, since the commercial banks had stopped making new commitments.

As discussed in the previous chapter, Brazil, like the rest of Latin America, was hit by a debt crisis that was compounded by the unprecedented rise in interest rates triggered by the U.S. Federal Reserve and the ensuing world recession, which reduced demand for Brazilian exports, putting further pressure on its balance of payments.

All this was accompanied by an inevitable drop in both public and private investment in Brazil. Real investment as a share of GDP averaged 23 percent in the 1970s but dropped to 17 percent in the 1980s. Public investment fell because government deficits led to budget cuts, and private investment fell both because of high interest rates and because of the bleak outlook for consumer demand. This low investment had the short-run effect of reducing economic activity and the long-run effect of reducing Brazil's potential future growth.

There was still another source for Brazil's economic problems, which had to do strictly with Brazil's past economic policy decisions, especially since the 1930s. With the loss of export earning capacity after the 1929 crash, Brazil concentrated on "inward looking" development. The years of high tariff protection (identified with "import-substituting industrialization") had encouraged inefficiency in Brazilian industry. A notable example was the computer industry, where the government had banned both imported products and foreign-owned domestic producers. The logic for this policy came initially from the Brazilian military, who opposed dependence on foreign suppliers for technology crucial to weapons systems. The policy was quickly embraced by the economic nationalists in the civilian sector. The result was a domestic computer industry known for high prices, low quality, and out-of-date technology. Meanwhile, smuggling of foreign-made equipment became a major industry.

This industrial protection had been accompanied by an inadequate effort to import up-to-date technology more generally. A prime example was the automobile industry. Although its wage rates were low, Brazilian car makers had total costs that rivaled or exceeded those of Western Europe. Finally, the public sector continued to be highly inefficient. State enterprises such as Petrobras and the ports were infamous for their overstaffing and inflated salaries. Poor management of the state-owned electric utilities and telephone companies, along with the badly maintained rail and road system, also added to the cost of doing business in Brazil (foreign investors called it *custo Brasil*, or "the Brazilian cost").

These factors more than explained why Brazil was in economic trouble. There was no shortage of suggested solutions as the economists in and out of government offered their formulae. In the end, however, they all depended for their implementation upon political leadership, and leadership was in short supply in the Sarney years.

LOST INVESTMENT

The mid to late 1980s saw Brazil lose two types of investment. The first was reduced investment in the physical capital that was key to growth in the economy. The second was lost human capital from a brain-drain out-migration of Brazilians looking for better lives abroad.

Domestic investment in Brazil's business and public infrastructure was a major loser in the economic slowdown of the 1980s in Brazil. An obvious culprit was low consumer demand in the economy. With low wages, workers had less money to spend. Given the government's inability to cure inflation and resume growth, few sensible businessmen wanted to risk expanding their productive capacity. On the contrary, in many sectors (especially where competition was weak) businesses maintained high prices in order to compensate for low volume.

Sluggish demand was not the only culprit, however. The government's decision to reintroduce indexation in late 1986 also contributed. In the short run, indexation, first introduced in the mid-1960s, had proven highly effective in neutralizing many of the price distortions produced by inflation and forcing economic actors—individual and corporate—to think in real, not nominal terms. But indexation produced its own distortions because it was not applied uniformly across the economy. By the late 1980s, there were scores of different indexation tables (with different rates of adjustment) applied to contracts.

The one type of contract for which full indexation was guaranteed was government debt. In order to finance the federal deficit, the Central Bank had to sell bonds to the public. In order to make the bonds attractive, they had to include full indexation and a high rate of real interest. The Central Bank also needed to make the bonds attractive in order to induce wealthy Brazilians (and foreigners) to keep their money in Brazil rather than sending it abroad. Thus, the need to finance the deficit, along with the need to prevent capital flight, encouraged the use of indexation. The government achieved its purpose, at least partially. It was able to market its bonds, although by the late 1980s it was no longer able to stem large-scale capital flight.

The price of the Central Bank's decision on indexation policy was high, however, because it greatly encouraged financial speculation. Investors could routinely earn double-digit real returns on their capital by simply investing in government bonds. This helped make the banking sector the most profitable in the economy. It also resulted in a substantial diversion of capital from productive investment to financial speculation. The consequences were serious for Brazilian industry, which was not getting the capital it badly needed for modernization. Brazil was turned into a tropical paradise for financial manipulators. Finally, indexation had the effect of "institutionalizing" inflation. Its critics noted that indexation rarely achieved a reduction in the inflation rate, but rather, at best, perpetuated the current rate.

Public investment also suffered. One reason was that current tax revenues were swallowed up by government deficits. A second reason was the irrational pricing policy of the state enterprises. The weak federal and state governments of the 1980s kept prices down on such utilities as petroleum, electricity, water, and telephones, in a desperate attempt to slow inflation and win popularity. Unfortunately, however, prices lagged behind costs, pushing the major state enterprises into deficit and eliminating the surplus needed for investment. Successive governments postponed public-sector investment in the hope that it could be made up later. The quality of the utility services inevitably declined and the quantity failed to keep pace with the growth in demand.

This serious lag in private and public investment had dangerous consequences for future stable growth. Should growth resume, industry would soon find itself operating at the limits of its capacity. Furthermore, Brazil's relative productivity was increasing little in this climate of stagnation and low investment. In the ranks of emerging capitalist countries, especially when compared to the dynamic East Asian economies, Brazil had become a conspicuous underperformer.

THE BRAIN DRAIN

The brain drain during the 1980s of some of the best and brightest from Brazil was perhaps the strongest symbol of how low Brazil's morale had sunk. At less than one percent of the population, the size of the outflow may have been modest, but the fact that Brazilians were choosing to leave was the startling point. Brazilians had long been famous for their fierce loyalty to Brazil. Foreigners marveled at the patriotism of their Brazilian friends. Even in difficult times, Brazilians had kept alive the belief that theirs was the country of the future.

Doubt had begun to set in during the military government, yet there was no major exodus then, aside from the political exiles whose circumstances forced them out. The economic boom of the 1970s undoubtedly provided an economic incentive to stay, even for Brazilians who may have been repelled by the repression. When Brazil returned to civilian government in the mid-1980s, genuine loyalty and optimism revived. The Brazilian pattern continued to be staying close to the home state. Going abroad was always temporary.

The disorganization, corruption, and economic chaos of the Sarney government sapped the usual patriotism. Brazilians began voting with their feet. Their prime destinations were the United States (610,000) and Japan (170,000), with a smaller number heading for Portugal, whose membership in the European Community made it attractive. Given its ill-defended borders and generally ineffectual immigration controls, the United States—and especially such cities as Miami, New York, and Boston—was a favorite destination for growing Brazilian exile communities. These Brazilians were leaving not for political reasons but because they wanted a better life. Thousands of their counterparts went to Japan for similar reasons. They were Brazilians of Japanese descent who could earn more in a menial job in Japan than in a skilled profession in Brazil. The Japanese government strengthened the appeal by granting Brazilians of Japanese descent special visas. Japanese social welfare agencies even had to open offices to counsel the Brazilian arrivals, who were of Japanese ancestry but became disoriented because they could not speak a word of Japanese and because the Japanese did not accept them as authentic Japanese.

This loss of Brazilians to foreign countries was particularly painful because it often involved the most energetic and talented of Brazilian

EXHIBIT 8-2

Income Inequality in Brazil, 1960–90*

	1960	1970	1980	1990
Lowest 20%	3.5	3.2	3.0	2.3
Next 60%	42.1	34.6	30.9	31.6
Top 20%	54.4	62.2	66.1	66.1
	100	100	100	100
Top 10%	39.7	47.8	51.0	49.7
Top 5%	27.7	34.9	33.8	35.8

*Percent of economically active population with nonzero incomes.

Source: Susan Kaufman Purcell and Riordan Roett, eds., *Brazil Under Cardoso* (Boulder, 1997), p. 73.

citizens. Furthermore, they were taking their talents away from Brazil primarily to the two leading world economies—an ominous sign of what critics called the "reversal of development" in Brazil. The fact that it was occurring under the new democracy made it particularly dispiriting.

As already discussed, the economic boom of the 1970s had increased income inequality in Brazil. (See exhibit 8-2.) Income for all income groups increased, but the rich got richer much faster than the poor got

EXHIBIT 8-3

Hungry Persons* in Brazil, 1990

Region	Total	Percentage of Region's Total Population
North	685,204	13.9
Northeast	17,288,528	40.9
South	4,082,314	18.1
Southeast	7,982,453	12.4
Center-West	1,640,597	16.1
Brazil	31,679,095	21.9

*"Hungry" is defined as those persons whose income is inadequate to buy sufficient food.

Source: Anna Maria T. M. Peliano, ed., *O Mapa da Fome* (IPEA: Documento de política No. 14: Brasília, 1993).

less poor. In the years of stagnation during the 1980s, however, absolute incomes fell for some groups, especially those at the lower end of the distribution. This was caused, at least in part, by what economists call the "inflation tax." Those at the bottom had to operate primarily in cash, the value of which deteriorated sharply (often by 50 percent or more) between pay periods. Wealthier individuals could use checking accounts, which were corrected (indexed) for inflation and often added a small real interest rate. Thus, these better-off Brazilians saw the value of their pay retain its value between pay periods. Furthermore, with liquid assets of even a few thousand dollars, they could invest in government bonds, which paid a very high real interest rate. Finally, as always in Brazil, the effect varied greatly by region. (See exhibit 8-3.)

Widening Gaps Between Rich and Poor

A major factor contributing to the drain of Brazilians in search of a better deal abroad were ever-widening economic and social disparities within an environment of declining public investment. Income, education, health, housing, transportation—all are facets of Brazil's "social debt."

Employment measures were unreliable in Brazil, making it hazardous to measure unemployment among the lowest sectors. There were, however, other symptoms. An important one was crime. Crime rates in the major cities rose in the 1980s and any visitor from abroad could see the effects. The gracious entries to the apartment buildings of Rio de Janeiro were now surrounded with elaborate metal gratings to stop vagrants from camping on the steps. Wealthy Brazilians withdrew to expensive new apartment complexes surrounded by electronically controlled fences and guarded by 24-hour patrols.

The epidemic of kidnappings in Rio de Janeiro was a prominent example. They were committed by gangs, often in collusion with the police. And, although millionaires were the obvious targets, even small businessmen fell victim. The response of the wealthy was to hire more bodyguards and ride in armored cars.

Shop owners, annoyed by the presence of hordes of street children committing petty theft, periodically hired off-duty policemen to scare them away and, sometimes, to kill them. In mid-1993, such persecution reached a chilling climax. During the early morning hours of July 23rd, a contingent of well-armed Polícia Militar attacked a group of fifty street children sleeping on the sidewalk in front of Rio's Candelária cathedral. Seven children and one young adult were killed. In São Paulo, the violent hunt for "marginals" was delegated to an elite paramilitary police unit. These heavily armed and smartly uniformed police roamed the São

Paulo streets in late-model Jeep Cherokee wagons looking for suspicious street people. They did not hesitate to shoot to kill, and they helped give São Paulo the doubtful honor of having the world's highest homicide rate by a police force.

Brazilians and foreign observers often asked whether this upsurge of crime represented the beginnings of a social upheaval. The opposite seems more likely. Ordinary crime did not represent any threat to the established economic order. At most, it was a minor redistribution of income by non-economic means—i.e., coercion. In no sense did it represent collective mobilization against the established order. Revolution was never likely to come to Brazil at the hands of small-time kidnappers or car thieves.

In fact, the rise in crime probably worked against any greater awareness of social inequality. Violent crime reinforced the Brazilian elite's image of the lower classes as threatening. The result was a shifting of focus from the *trabalhador* (the worker who had a job and was contributing to society) to the *marginal* (the hustler who lived by his street smarts). Focusing on the marginals ("mere criminals") made it easier to ignore the plight of the many millions of hard-working Brazilians at the bottom. It also helped to strengthen the elite's long-time image of the lower classes as "dangerous" rather than "deserving." This effect on the perceptions of the elite was ironical, since it was the poor who suffered most from crime. Police seldom entered the urban slums except as "SWAT teams." In Rio, the hillside shantytowns (*favelas*) became centers for narcotraffic, with its attendant violence. The resulting firefights often killed or wounded innocent residents. But the rich and middle-class victims of crime got the favorable publicity, both because they made better TV and newspaper copy and because they were victimized in the best sections of town, which in turn became major (negative) news for the international press, affecting the potential tourist trade.

EDUCATION AND HEALTH CARE

Brazil's record in education was one of the worst in the developing world, and the 1980s saw a deterioration even in that dismal record. In major cities where public schools had once educated middle class children, school systems were in physical decay and educational decline. Teachers' salaries were abysmally low (commonly less than $200 a month and often less than $100 a month in the Northeast—in today's prices), and working conditions often equally bad. Brazilian schoolchildren were repeating elementary grades at a higher rate than in any other country. The wealthier middle class reacted by sending their children to private schools, which increased educational segregation by social class and undermined the creation of a cohesive sense of citizenship to which public school systems are dedicated.

The strange thing was that, in this area of public services, the deterioration could not be traced to budget cuts. In 1989, for example, United Nations statistics showed that Brazil was spending almost 18 percent of total public expenditures on education, a respectable share by international standards. The same could be said of Brazil's educational expenditures as a percentage of GDP. The problem clearly was bureaucratic incompetence or fraud. Far too little of the money reached the schoolroom. The results were high dropout rates and an army of half-literate children, most of whom entered the labor market before reaching the normal age for finishing grade school. Public schools had become so overbureaucratized, corrupt, and archaic in their pedagogy that business firms were routinely spending large sums to make up for the training their employees should have received at school. At a time when the East Asian tigers were reducing illiteracy to zero, Brazil was still struggling to bring its illiteracy rate (defined generously) below 20 percent.

Health care—another measure of investment of human capital—was also in a dreadful way in the 1980s in Brazil. Inadequate financing combined with structural disorganization to produce public health care significantly worse than it had been in the 1970s. As in education, what public money there was in the system—much of it in the form of numerous publicly funded, privately run clinics with questionable financial practices—was not reaching the patients. The better-off Brazilians were fleeing the public health care system in the same way as they fled the public schools, and joining private health insurance plans that gave them access to special clinics, thereby reinforcing a two-tier delivery system. The super-rich could always fly to Miami or New York for the ultimate supplement in health care.

HOUSING AND COMMUNICATIONS

Brazilians were getting more segregated with respect to their housing during the 1980s—not as a result of budget cutbacks but, rather, because of the reaction of the middle and upper classes to the sharp increase in urban crime discussed earlier. To protect themselves, they built massive iron barriers around their apartment buildings and hired private security guards to protect their entrances. On the outskirts of São Paulo and Rio de Janeiro, for example, new housing complexes (one was called "Alphaville" in São Paulo) were complete with internal recreation areas so the residents did not have to leave even to have fun.

The final major areas of deficiency, starved into decay because of shrinking funds available for public investment, were roads and the telephone system. Deficits at every government level had reduced road maintenance, leaving gaping holes in the main inner-city streets (a Rio newspaper of the 1980s showed a Volkswagen disappearing into a pothole) and hazardous conditions on the highways (the main artery connecting São Paulo and Curitiba became known as the "death run"). This lack of road maintenance was dangerous because Brazil depended overwhelmingly on road transportation—a dependence that was aggravated by a government decision in the 1950s to concentrate on highways rather than the rail system, which was little updated or expanded from then on.

The capacity of the telephone network, into which the military government had poured funds in the 1970s, had fallen far behind demand by the late 1980s. Residential telephone numbers were regularly advertised for sale in leading newspapers of the major cities at thousands of dollars each. Low investment due to the squeeze on government budgets seen in other fields combined with failure to raise telephone rates to reduce the funds available for the telephone utility's needed expansion.

This delayed investment in transportation and communication increased the "Brazil cost" and damaged the country's competitiveness on an international scale.

Public Health: The Fish That Swam Upstream

In sharp contrast with the deteriorating public services, Brazil's human-development indicators (monitored by the United Nations) show steady improvement through the 1980s. Between 1960 and 1990, for example, as we saw earlier, life expectancy rose from 55 years to 66 years. Over the same period, the mortality rate of children under five years fell from 159 to 83 per 1,000 live births. A key variable explaining these health trends was the access of Brazilians to safe water supplies. That rate rose from 62 percent of the population in 1975–80 to 87 percent in 1988–90. The education data, generally considered less reliable than the health data but still reflecting trends, showed adult literacy rising from 66 percent in 1970 to 81 percent in 1990.

These figures are best interpreted by putting them into international perspective, based on the data gathered by the World Bank and the United Nations. First, Brazil was participating in a favorable worldwide trend. The average absolute improvement in life expectancy for *all* developing countries over the period was 17 years, compared to Brazil's 11 years. Brazil's reduction of the mortality rate of children under five years was 48 percent compared to 52 percent for all developing countries. In terms of increased access to safe water and increased literacy, Brazil also showed percentage improvements less than the average for all developing countries. These improving trends, which were achieved regardless of the type of government or economic system, reflected certain global factors at work. One was urbanization, which made health services and safe water supplies easier to deliver than in rural societies.

A second was modern technology, especially in medicine, which made it possible to control epidemic disease and infection at relatively low cost. A third factor was the role of international institutions, which in recent decades directed major aid to health and education, furnishing technology, capital, and expertise. The World Bank, for example, played a crucial role in expanding the safe water system in the Brazilian Northeast.

Compared to the average for all developing countries, as discussed above, Brazil lagged. This is all the more significant in view of the fact that Brazil has exceptional resources. Its 1989 per capita income ($4,951) was more than double the 1989 per capita average ($2,296) for all developing countries. Brazil was not using the resources it had to foster human development as effectively as other parts of the developing world—not an unexpected conclusion given that its income distribution was one of the most unequal in the developing world.

There was one demographic indicator that brought good news for Brazilian planners: The population growth rate, which had been among the world's highest in the 1950s, had been falling steadily. In the 1970s it reached an annual rate of 2.48 percent. In the 1980s it fell to 1.9 percent and by 1997 the annual rate for the 1990s was estimated to have been only 1.3 percent. A prime cause for the decline was urbanization, which increased from 35 percent in the 1950s to 78 percent in the mid-1990s. Another was the widespread recourse, often in government-supported clinics, to sterilization (usually tubal ligation) as a means of birth control.

This drop in population growth rate meant that the strain on over-stretched public services such as education and health would be eased as there would be fewer children requiring schools and hospitals. That meant lower requirements for investment in infrastructure. Eventually, there would be a negative side if the trend continued, because there would be fewer workers in the labor force to support the ever larger retired population. This made reform of the existing pension system even more urgent.

Changes Affecting Women

Brazilian women have traditionally played a small role in Brazilian public life, even though they won the right to vote sooner than in France or in most Latin American countries.

When Congress approved female suffrage in 1932, it followed decades of lobbying by a small but dedicated band of middle- and upper-class suffragettes. But this expansion of the voter rolls did little to change the overall position of women in Brazilian society. The dominant middle-class feminine stereotype continued to be a passive, submissive being whose existence was defined as a dutiful daughter and patient wife, and who faced a male-dominated society that blocked her professional advancement in all fields except a few "female" roles, such as teaching and nursing. The reality was, of course, even harsher for the vast majority of working-class women. They had to combine child rearing (often as single parents) and paid work at miserable wages in order to survive.

The coup of 1964 highlighted the fact that the status of women had changed little in the intervening thirty years. In the polarization leading to military seizure of power, women appeared primarily as the middle- and upper-class demonstrators in right wing demonstrations such as the "March of Family with God for Liberty," the caricature of the traditional "housewifely" role. The military government, through its subsequent manipulation of politics and the media, made it clear that it intended to reinforce that role. Meanwhile, the few feminist organizations became virtually invisible, experiencing the general repression of the left.

Ironically, two consequences of military rule after 1964 helped provoke women to challenge their traditional role, with the Catholic Church proving an invaluable ally throughout subsequent struggle. The first stimulus was the harsh repression of 1968–75, which took the greatest toll among the young guerrillas of primarily middle- and upper-class background. This was exactly the social sector that had supported the coup most strongly. Now their sons and daughters were being tortured in the police and military dungeons. This brutality brought rising protests, especially from the mothers, whose maternal indignation created a natural solidarity. As censorship eased in the late 1970s, these mothers organized widely noticed protest rallies that were the harbinger of a new brand of political activism among elite women. It was also at this time that many of these white middle-class women were gaining entry into the male-dominated professions (their numbers rose from 18,000 in 1970 to an estimated 95,800 in 1980) thanks to the growth of the technocratic state and the rapid increase in female university graduates.

The second consequence of the military regime for the women's movement was economic. The economically active female population had increased from 18.5 percent in 1970 to 26.9 percent in 1980. The rapid growth of the economy after 1968, however, was achieved in part by compressing real wages. This "squeeze" aroused indignation among urban workers, especially the working-class wives whose household budgets were buying less and less at the supermarket. In the 1970s, these women organized a movement called "Against the Cost of Living" which directly challenged government economic policy. This movement helped break down the women's fear of authority and gave them a sense of confidence in working together. This spirit could be seen also in major cities, where working-class women were instrumental in organizing neighborhood associations (Sociedades de Amigos de Bairros or SABs) that demanded improved services such as fresh water, paved roads, and functioning schools.

Another government policy stimulated a rural counterpart to this urban organizing effort. This was a set of financial incentives, especially low-cost credit, paid to the owners of large farms, which enabled them to go in for capital-intensive agriculture and to get rid of their tenant farmers and squatters. Many of these were women who then turned to wage labor, often on the all-female agricultural work crews of *bóias-frias* (the term referred to the cold lunches they carried). These women labored (often cutting sugarcane to be processed in the alcohol program) hard and long, and were badly paid. The miserable working environment and the propinquity of the women to one another led them to organize powerful rural unions. In 1984, 60,000 *bóias-frias* cane cutters demanded and got union recognition. They then bargained successfully for better pay and benefits such as school instruction and medical assistance for themselves and their families (many had to bring children with them to the job). Thus, the generals were succeeding, unintentionally, in politicizing women of all classes.

The feminists, who were primarily middle class, raised their own range of issues, many of which had been simmering for years. One of the most important was reproductive rights. The existing legal system had been designed by male lawgivers. Under its constraints, access to information about (and availability of) contraception was expensive, and abortion was illegal (except to safeguard the life of the mother—a waiver rarely granted). Rich women had access to both at private clinics, but ordinary women found family planning very difficult. Feminists demanded free and accessible contraception, as well as free legalized abortion. They also wanted free community-based daycare.

The feminist campaign had mixed success. It must be pointed out that, when push came to shove, feminists turned out to be very ambivalent about public subsidization of family planning for the poor. For example, daycare facilities were created in several Brazilian cities, a large number of them in São Paulo. There were no changes in the abortion law, however, leaving women with lower incomes vulnerable to dangerous back-alley abortions. In 1981, when São Paulo governor Paulo Maluf—a right-wing anathema to the feminists, most of whom were left or center-left—launched a privately-funded (through Japanese and American sources!), state-administered family-planning program, feminist organizations opposed it. They said that such programs were "genocidal," intended to manipulate poor (and especially nonwhite) women for the benefit of the white elite. By the early 1990s, the federal government had followed in São Paulo's footsteps with a comprehensive family-planning program. Under the banner of protecting the health of the mother, government clinics carried out tubal ligations, often in connection with cesarean births. Feminists, among other critics, claimed that the female patients were deliberately misled, that the "sterilizations" were part of a conspiracy to reduce the "inferior" population. Program defenders replied that all surgical procedures were voluntary and that the women were merely taking advantage of an opportunity to act on a long-felt desire to limit family size or to use sterilization as a solution to serious health problems.

Violence against women was another issue for Brazilian feminists. Wife (or female companion) abuse was widely known to be a serious problem among all Brazilian social classes, but the police and courts traditionally refused to recognize such behavior as criminal. Charges were routinely dismissed, even in cases when abuse by the man turned literally to murder. Judges routinely excused husbands actually convicted of murdering their wives from penalty by accepting a plea "in defense of honor," the claim that the wife was (or intended to be) unfaithful. In 1980, in São Paulo alone, 772 women were reported to have been killed by their husbands or lovers, who escaped penalty. This abuse of justice had become so common in Minas Gerais that a group of middle class women organized an educational campaign called Quem Ama Não Mata ("He Who Loves Doesn't Kill"). Their efforts included visits to judges to convince them of the injustice of accepting the "defense of honor" plea when sentencing convicted wife murderers.

The campaign to stop court acceptance of wife-battering assumed greater visibility in 1985, when feminist groups convinced the governor of São Paulo to create a division for the protection of women in the state police. Specially designated officers (normally women—their office was dubbed the "women's police station") were posted at police stations to handle abuse complaints from women. In dealing with the state authorities, feminist leaders were soon caught up in party politics where corruption and loss of militancy was a constant threat. Although social attitudes on such a basic question were slow to change, at least the feminist campaign had altered somewhat the public discourse.

The ultimate target in question by the feminist campaign was the dramatic underrepresentation of women in leadership of such major institutions as state and national government, professional associations, and labor unions. For example, the Constituent Assembly elected in 1986 (which wrote the Constitution of 1988) had only 26 women. Once sworn in, they protested their minority status to the assembly president, pointing out that "we represent only 4.9 percent of the Constituent Assembly, while we are 54 percent of the population and 53 percent of the electorate."

Yet some progress was made. For the 1994 municipal council elections the federal government fixed a minimum female candidate quota of 20 percent. Such a measure would have been unthinkable in the even more sexist atmosphere of the 1964–85 authoritarian regime. Women were still conspicuous by their complete absence on the directorship level of such important professional associations as the Ordem dos Advogados do Brasil (the Bar Association), with 52 percent female membership; the Associação Brasileira de Imprensa (the Press Association), with 40 percent female membership; and the Conselho Nacional de Medicina (the National Medical Association), with 31.5 percent female membership. And although by the late 1990s significantly more women were completing secondary school (42 percent as compared to 26 percent), women on the whole were earning 40 percent less than men. On the other hand, women had made real inroads in certain professions, especially in the more developed Center-South. In São Paulo, for example, 44 percent of the newly registered doctors and 63 percent of the practicing dentists were women by 1997.

Pressure by women workers did lead to significant institutionalization of their interests in the two largest labor union conglomerates: the Central Única dos Trabalhadores (the CUT, or Central Union of Workers) and the Força Sindical (Union Power). In 1986, the CUT created a commission on the question of the woman worker, and in 1993 established quotas for women in executive positions. In 1992, the Força Sindical created the National Secretariat for Women, Adolescents, and Children. As one woman union leader active in pursuing these demands put it, "We were educated to be sensitive, affectionate, maternal, everything that means being servile, accepting domination and thinking it's all wonderful. Now we're breaking with this, and we don't want to be anymore wives, mothers, housewives because we are entering public life. We are now going to have 'equal relations and an equal participation in the public world.'"

Despite its failures, such as the failure to legalize abortion, the Brazilian women's movement became the largest, most radical, most diverse, and most effective of women's movements in Latin America. How did it happen? What does it tell us about Brazilian history? Sonia Alvarez, an expert in the field, suggests there were four factors: (1) Church support for community organizations, especially among the poor, both urban and rural; (2) the Brazilian left's intensive organizing of opposition groups in which women were prominent; (3) the military government's deliberate opening of political space (a policy known as *abertura*); (4) the government's granting women more organizing latitude than other elements of civil society because they saw women as less threatening.

From a historical perspective, two points are significant. First, a dissenting sector of the white elite had emerged to challenge politics as usual in the white male–dominated world. Second, there had been genuine mobilization among working-class women, both urban and rural. At times the two movements converged and cooperated, but more frequently they were drawn apart by issues of class, race, and ideology. It was a familiar story among the grass-roots organizations that flourished at the end of the military regime. Once electoral democracy was restored, the political parties, with their patronage and animus toward ideology, filled the public space. The receding of the women's movement from the spotlight (although it is still much alive, if at a reduced level) reflects a familiar Brazilian dilemma: how to incorporate genuine citizen participation in a political system created for top-down government by a narrow white political elite.

Race Relations

Race relations since democratization in 1985 have continued to revolve around the question of Afro-Brazilians, with the status of the Asian-Brazilians and Indians gaining much less attention. Very little has changed in race relations since slavery's abolition in 1888. Brazil continues to be a multiracial rather than biracial society, with an inherent ambiguity. The ambiguity, which dates back to the colonial era, is furnished by the mulatto, who supposedly (by the prevailing myth) enjoyed greater social mobility than the black. In fact, however, mulattos have found little room for movement, especially in the twentieth century.

In 1991, Afro-Brazilians were 44 percent of the population, yet positions of authority were dominated (with rare exceptions) by whites—Congress, the Foreign Office, church hierarchy, military and police officials, and the prestigious professions such as law and medicine. Of the thousands of undergraduate and graduate students at the University of São Paulo (Brazil's most distinguished) in the early 1990s, for example, less than a dozen were Afro-Brazilian. There were even fewer Afro-Brazilian faculty members, and this in a state with a 20 percent Afro-Brazilian population. The record was somewhat better at the Federal University of Rio de Janeiro, where an affirmative action program in the 1980s had brought over one hundred Afro-Brazilians into the student body.

Until the late 1970s, discussions of racial discrimination had remained necessarily anecdotal. There was simply no firm quantitative data. In 1976, however, the Census Bureau, generously funded by the military government, carried out an ambitious national household survey, generating the first reliable national data on race, employment, education, income, etc. They revealed a clear pattern of discrimination against persons of color, both black and mulatto. Yet it should be remembered that this discrimination occurred in the absence of any legal or institutional support. This lack of formal barriers made it easier for the white elite to continue describing Brazil as a "racial democracy," free of the racial conflict that, for example, constantly shook the United States.

Visitors to modern-day Brazil, especially North Americans, often ask why Afro-Brazilians have done so little to protest their plight. Why have they (aside from a very small band of militants) not demanded intervention to counter discrimination? The question reveals a basic misunderstanding of the dynamics of Brazilian race relations, which have proved remarkably stable because all the actors—blacks and mulattos, as well as whites—have believed in key elements of what might be called the "Myth of Racial Democracy." The first element is the belief that race is only a secondary variable in determining life chances. More important variables, in the view of most Brazilians, are social class and education or the luck of the clientalistic culture. Second, Brazilians know the patrimonial system militates against any mobilization from the bottom up. Afro-Brazilians, who are mostly at the bottom of the socioeconomic scale, are therefore doubly affected (class and race) by that deferential mindset. Third, anyone trying to organize Afro-Brazilians on racial line faces a problem unique to Brazil: the almost complete lack of nonwhite solidarity. This can be explained in part by the absence, at least since the eighteenth century, of any formal segregation or other form of official discrimination. The kind of parallel nonwhite institutions, such as produced by United States segregation, are missing in Brazil. The pervasive Brazilian aspiration for "whitening" (and therefore the denigration of blackness) has further undermined efforts of solidarity. Mulattos, for example, have proved notoriously difficult to recruit for any racially oriented political project because they tend to see themselves as completely separate from the black community. In this respect they have implicitly accepted the myth of the "mulatto escape hatch," even though census data of the 1970s showed that mulattos did only marginally better than blacks (and much worse than whites) in employment, education, and income. In São Paulo in 1980, for example, median monthly earnings of white workers equaled 2.3 minimum salaries, while those of blacks were 1.5 and those of mulattos 1.7. The 1980 data for illiteracy showed white men having a rate of 24 percent, while blacks were 47 percent and pardos ("brown" often used to mean "mulatto") were 48 percent.

All these factors have combined to cripple Afro-Brazilian organizing efforts. That could be seen in the fate of the Afro-Brazilian mobilization of the late 1970s. Afro-Brazilians took advantage of the climate of relaxed government control then to organize the Movimento Unificado de Negro Brasileiro (Unified Black Brazilian Movement). They protested incidents of veiled discrimination and demanded punishment of the alleged white offenders. They got considerable publicity, but had little political effect.

Other Afro-Brazilians chose a different path in those years. Rejecting political protest, they called instead for recognition of Brazil's *cultural* legacy to Africa. They celebrated African-style art, music, language, and the Afro-Brazilian religion expressed in such rituals as *candomblé*.

In effect, these "culturalists" were emphasizing the separateness of Afro-Brazilians, not their possible status for integration into a white-dominated society. Their net effect, however, was to divert attention from the fledgling Afro-Brazilian protest movement.

At the same time, some leaders of elite culture began to show increased awareness of the problem of racial discrimination. President Fernando Henrique Cardoso, who earlier in his career had authored pioneering research works on the history of Brazilian race relations, made a historic statement in 1995 acknowledging the existence of Brazilian racism and authorizing the creation of an Advisory Council on Race Questions. Other action on the elite level was equally noteworthy. *Veja* magazine, the fourth largest newsmagazine in the world, has recently run numerous articles on incidents of racial discrimination, and *A Folha de São Paulo*, a leading São Paulo daily, has followed the same pattern. As late as the 1980s, these archetypal organs of elite culture had been virtually ignoring the subject. Finally, the Federal University of Rio de Janeiro in the late 1980s mounted a major affirmative action admission program (the racial dimension was downplayed in the public discussion, although it was a deliberate objective) which, by emphasizing economic need for applicants, sharply increased the Afro-Brazilian enrollment.

By the late 1980s, it was nonetheless clear that this more enlightened elite attitude lacked the active support of Afro-Brazilians themselves. It is doubtful if the initiative of the Cardoso government (admittedly very modest) will gain much public acceptance without strong pressure from the Afro-Brazilian community. But, for the reasons discussed above, that community is far from united, and, equally important, it is notably nonmilitant.

Contemporary Culture

We have seen in the preceding chapter how cultural life reacted to military government. The period after democratization in 1985 proved to be quite different. The intense mobilization of the late 1970s and early 1980s seemed to have drawn down the energies of Brazil's artistic minority. In 1988, the leading novelist Ignácio de Loyola Brandão proclaimed "There is a crisis of creativity affecting the older writers, who are producing nothing, and which is blocking the young."

Bookstores that had few new literary works on their shelves now overflowed with books on self-help. They ranged from how to succeed in business to how to tolerate your mate. *Veja* magazine expanded its weekly best-seller list from fiction/nonfiction to include the new category of self-help. Many titles had a mystical ring. The guru Paulo Coelho was especially popular. The Brazilian reader had turned inward, away from the confusion and tension of contemporary politics and the endless social problems.

Yet there was one constructive reaction from the authorial ranks. Writers—especially journalists—published a series of outstanding biographies of leading historic figures. There was Jorge Caldeira on Baron Mauá (1995), the legendary (if failed) nineteenth-century entrepreneur; Fernando Morais on Assis Chateaubriand (1994), the twentieth-century newspaper and TV magnate; Ruy Castro on Nelson Rodrigues (1992), Brazil's preeminent playwright of the 1940s and 1950s; João Maximo and Carlos Didier on Noel Rosa (1990), the famous Rio samba composer of the 1930s; and João Ubaldo Ribeiro with his epic *Viva o Povo Brasileiro* (1984), a novel encompassing all of Brazilian history.

These books, all bestsellers, reflected a common desire to recapture the past through some unique personality. It was as if these authors were engaged in a common enterprise to reach beyond the nightmare of military rule to find the roots of a more authentic Brazil. The novelists also joined in the effort, as could be seen in Moacyr Scliar's *Sonhos Tropicais* (1992), a fictional portrait of turn-of-the-century public health hero Oswaldo Cruz, and in Rubem Fonseca's *Agôsto* (1990), a novel based on the last days and suicide of Getúlio Vargas in 1954.

As for film, the Brazilian industry had been in decline in the 1980s and became virtually moribund when the Collor government eliminated federal subsidies to film producers. But there was a revival in the mid-1990s, led by historically oriented films such as *Bananas Is My Business*, a documentary on the career of Carmen Miranda, and *Que É Isso Companheiro?*, a filmic reconstruction of the kidnapping of the United States ambassador by Brazilian guerrillas in 1969. Like the biographies and historical novels, these films met a public desire to connect with important moments in the past, thereby perhaps putting the post-military era in perspective. But none of this equaled the creativity and originality of the cultural scene of the 1950s and 1960s. Now Brazilian writers and artists, like most Brazilians, are not sure where Brazil is headed.

The Political Spectrum in the New Democracy

With the return to democracy, all parts of the political spectrum—left, right, and center—turned out to have changed during the military regime. Some understanding of the political landscape is useful in explaining the post-Sarney political world in Brazil.

The traditional left had been shattered by the intense repression of 1968–74. The left's most important point of reference had traditionally been the Brazilian Communist Party (PCB). As we have seen, the Communist Party had adopted a cautious strategy in the radicalized climate leading to the coup of 1964, outflanked on the left by the radical nationalists, especially those coming from the Catholic youth movements. Nonetheless, the PCB remained a key target for the government security forces, which killed, hounded into the underground, or forced into exile virtually its entire leadership. By the late 1980s, there was almost nothing left of the traditional PCB, now also suffering from its identification with the crumbling Soviet regime. By the mid-1990s, the party disappeared, having renamed itself (as the Partido Popular Socialista) and struggled to assume the guise of a social democratic party.

The militant guerrilla groups of the 1960s had not fared much better. The PC do B (the Maoist breakaway from the PCB), once dominated by João Amazonas, suffered heavily from the repression (its older leaders had been killed in the government repression), and its few survivors also sought a more moderate socialist image. The MR-8 (the Eighth of October Revolutionary Movement, named for the day of Che Guevara's execution in 1968) was a guerrilla group that as an armed force was exterminated by the government but survived as a left-wing party. The remaining force on the left were the Trotskyists, who retained their intellectual position (radical Marxist but anti-Stalinist) and operated mainly within the PT (explained below). They had always been powerful critics of the PCB and were now concentrated in a new group on the left, the Convergência Socialista. They were a constant force for militant (not armed) action and fierce opponents of the trend toward "moderate" social democracy. Virtually all the left now agreed on one thing: They could not hope to overthrow the state by force; the illusions of the 1960s were gone. The left would now walk the electoral road, wherever it led.

Remains of the populist left, strengthened by the huge PMDB victory in the 1986 elections, still existed by the late 1980s, wielding considerable influence in the constituent assembly of 1987–88. Yet their long-run electoral appeal was uncertain. Only two of the surviving first-rank pre-1964 populist leaders of the left were still active: Leonel Brizola, who reentered public life as the governor of Rio de Janeiro in 1982 and won the governorship again in 1990, and Miguel Arraes, who had been deposed as governor of Pernambuco in 1964 and now won back that post in 1986 and again in 1994.

Brizola commanded a strong emotional following, especially in the city of Rio de Janeiro, with a discourse that was unchanged since the 1960s. He advocated a militant economic nationalism, liberal benefits for government employees, and a generous education policy (emphasizing a new all-day public school program). He was also the only major politician of this era to recognize racial discrimination and call for its end. Brizola had earlier tried to capture the old Vargas party label of PTB but was blocked by government maneuvering. He then founded his own party, the PDT (Partido Democrático Trabalhista), with major strength in Rio de Janeiro and Rio Grande do Sul.

Yet Brizola failed to recruit fellow politicians in other states. Most of the public saw him as an aging *caudilho* (traditional strongman) whose discourse no longer matched post-populist Brazil. Nonetheless, he could not be counted out as a campaigner. Still the most charismatic political orator on the Brazilian scene, he was unmatched in his mastery of television as a medium for campaigning.

The newest party on the left was the Partido dos Trabalhadores (PT). Born in the labor union activism of the late 1970s, it had become a genuine national party through dedicated grassroots organizing across the country. Its greatest strength did not lie among industrial workers, however, as its name and origin might suggest. Its largest numbers were drawn from government workers, teachers, and middle-class professionals. Catholic activists were highly important PT members and were dedicated to directly attacking Brazil's huge social problems in both the city and the countryside.

The PT grew steadily in the 1980s, despite predictions that such an ideological party would not prosper in Brazil. Its representation in the Chamber of Deputies went from eight in 1982 to forty-nine (almost 10 percent of the Chamber) in 1994. Much of its appeal was its promise to behave as an accountable movement that would not sacrifice its principles for the sake of individual political egos.

In fact, the PT was less unified than it advertised. Moderate PT leaders knew that a truly radical message would be rejected by most Brazilian voters. The moderates' solution was to advocate policies similar to the social democrats of Western Europe. At the other extreme within the PT were the militants (often dubbed "Shiites") who wanted more radical confrontation with the economic and political establishment. They favored "political" strikes—i.e., strikes for other than specific economic claims, for example—and were given to anti-capitalist rhetoric. At their most exuberant, the PT militants recalled the radical left on the eve of the coup of 1964.

Notwithstanding its problems, the PT actually came close to capturing the presidency in 1989. Their candidate in the presidential election was Luís Inácio Lula da Silva (known as "Lula" for short), the leader of the São Paulo auto workers' strikes of the late 1970s. The PT ran an effective presidential campaign in 1989, capitalizing on the free television time allocated to all parties to display the many pop stars who supported Lula and draw attention to the myriad social injustices they planned to correct. The ineffectual Sarney government, paralyzed by surging inflation, offered a perfect target for this message. Lula was also aided by the personality of his opponent, Fernando Collor de Melo, who aroused mistrust among middle-class voters.

Collor proved to have a powerful appeal to the poor and to industrial workers, however. In the end, during the run-off between the top two candidates, Lula lost to Collor in a close race (37.8 percent to 42.7 percent, the remainder being spoilt or blank ballots). Collor carried both the state of São Paulo and its capital city—the birthplace of Lula's "new unionism" had failed to mobilize for him. But Lula had gained a huge nationwide vote. Whether this indicated a real move to the left by the Brazilian electorate was unclear.

The left also included other important groups. One was the CUT (Central Única dos Trabalhadores), an unofficial confederation of labor unions, closely linked to the PT, that was given to militant rhetoric and a readiness to call strikes. And the Catholic Church still furnished some important leaders for the left. Many served in human rights organizations and land reform groups, especially the Movimento Sem Terra. Many also operated through the PT. Finally, there were the progressive think tanks, such as IBASE (Instituto Brasileiro de Análises Sociais e Econômicas), devoted to research and advocacy on such social questions as street children, the environment, education, and police violence. The dominant intellectual in these ranks was the sociologist and social activist Herbert de Souza (known by the affectionate diminutive of "Betinho"), who organized massive civic efforts such as the Campaign Against Hunger, which collected food for distribution to the poor. There was also a myriad of other nongovernmental organizations, many supported by foreign funds, researching and lobbying on social issues from a perspective that reinforced a leftist critique of Brazilian capitalism.

The electoral right in the late 1980s grew out of the PDS, the government party created and nurtured by the military regime after 1965 and first known as ARENA. It had split when a dissident wing formed the PFL in order to vote for Tancredo Neves's presidential candidacy in 1985. But both the PDS and the PFL incarnated the tradition of the political "ins"—i.e. the establishment politicians who had always lived off the status quo of the Brazilian capitalist system.

After 1985, the PFL emerged as the main rightist party. It was strongest in the Northeast, where the traditional political machines gave it a natural home. Many of its leaders had been beneficiaries of the military's manipulation of electoral rules between 1965 and 1985. It had not, therefore, been tested in truly free elections.

The right also included splinter parties, such as the PPB, (Partido Progressita Brasileiro), which was formed in 1995 to bring together smaller conservative parties. In addition, there were ad hoc political movements such as the UDR, organized by the landowners in 1987 as a movement to block land reform. Their urban counterparts were the small businessmen who often faced daily harassment by street children and vagrants, especially in Rio de Janeiro. To rid themselves of this nuisance, merchants joined together to hire off-duty police to remove (and sometimes kill) the children. Both the UDR and the merchants represented the dark side of the Brazilian establishment, ready to use violence to protect their property rights. Both groups routinely collaborated with the police, who turned a blind eye to their vigilante activities.

Finally, the right included many former anticommunists who remained opposed to the few remaining populists or militant leftists. The ideology of these rightists was free market economics. They promoted the writings of such First World conservative economists as Friedrich Hayek and Milton Freedman. Prominent among their spokesmen was Henri Maksoud, a hotel baron and avid promoter of neo-liberal ideas.

The right, therefore, consisted of a large body of traditional politicians, a smaller cadre of zealots prepared to use violence, and a band of wealthy lawyers and businessmen who longed for a free market (although not always conscious of what it might cost them).

The center had a more uncertain fate as of the late 1980s than either the left or the right. Its predecessor was the MDB, renamed the PMDB after the government's party reorganization of 1979. This was the coalition that had opposed the military dictatorship, serving as an umbrella for a wide range of pro-democracy voters. Yet the PMDB had never been a coherent party. Its raison d'être had been the fight against authoritarianism. When civilian government returned in 1985, the PMDB had no clear vision for Brazil. What should be the social and economic policies in a restored democracy? How much maldistribution of wealth and income were PMDB leaders prepared to try and change? And could their policies be sold to the voter, especially given the uncertain nature of the hugely increased and much younger electorate?

Before a start could even be made to face these questions in 1985, the party was caught up in the political misadventure of the Sarney presidency. It began with Tancredo's death and the succession of Sarney, Tancredo's non-PMDB running mate. The initial success of Sarney's stabilization program, the Cruzado Plan, caused the PMDB to enjoy a smashing victory in the November 1986 congressional elections, as noted earlier. But inflation was again rampant by 1987 and the elections at the end of that year showed that the public was greatly disillusioned with the PMDB, which never recovered politically. Henceforth, its image was set by figures such as Orestes Quercia, a São Paulo governor whose alleged corruption was of record proportions.

The PMDB therefore entered the 1990s having squandered the moral advantage it had gained from fighting the dictatorship, even though it remained the largest party in Congress. Virtually without ideas, dominated by irresolute politicians, it offered a weak alternative to the establishment on the political right.

Its decline also led directly to the creation of a new party on the center-left: the Partido Social Democrático Brasileiro (PSDB), whose main founders were disaffected PMDB politicians from São Paulo. The leaders included Mário Covas, a Paulista senator, and Fernando Henrique Cardoso, an ex–university professor and also a senator from São Paulo. Joining them was Franco Montoro, a former Christian Democrat and subsequently a PMDB leader as well as a former senator and governor of São Paulo.

The new PSDB defined itself as a social democratic party in the Western European tradition. Its founders looked to the example of Felipe González, the then highly successful premier of Spain, who had led that country's transition to democracy. They also admired the Portuguese socialists, who had eventually achieved the same transition after the fall of the Portuguese dictatorship. Roughly speaking, they accepted Brazilian capitalism but wanted to moderate its excesses through government reform. As their party symbol, they chose the toucan, the colorful Brazilian parrot-like bird with the huge beak, a symbol that delighted the cartoonists.

The political center also included many public figures and institutions wanting simply to avoid either extreme. A centrist view was typically taken by clergy, intellectuals, and businessmen, who hoped Brazilian capitalism could evolve toward the more egalitarian societies of the North Atlantic world. But these centrists were vulnerable to manipulation by extremist politicians. They and the voters they represented could be attracted by extremists if the issues were polarizing. Rising crime, uncontrolled inflation, decaying public services, cynical displays of wealth by corrupt politicians—attractive schemes that claimed to cure any of these ills could push centrists to either side. As always in Brazilian history, maintaining a center position was a delicate balancing act.

One long-term political actor, the military, was notably absent from the scene. We have seen how they had played a key role at every juncture in Brazilian history since the 1880s. By the mid-1980s, however, the officers were tired, demoralized, and longing to return to a more "professional" role. Many observers thought this transition would be difficult and perhaps even stormy. They were proved wrong. Although the military retained their claim to authority in a few areas (such as Amazon policy), in general they assumed an increasingly lower profile after 1985. Their declining influence was seen most dramatically in their share of the federal budget. With the exception of one year (1990) the military lost budget share every year between 1985 and 1993, suffering a decline of one quarter of their share over those years. Clearly, Brazil had entered a new era. If the civilian elite failed to make democracy work now, they could hardly blame it on the men in uniform.

The Collor Debacle

Into this uncertain political atmosphere stepped Fernando Collor de Melo. He was virtually unknown nationally in Brazil until early 1989, when he began a television blitz to win the presidential nomination. Between March and early June, his approved rating in the national polls shot up from 9 percent to 40 percent. He had increased his TV exposure by buying the free TV time (apportioned under the electoral law in proportion to votes won in the previous election) of several small political parties. Although technically legal, this tactic was typical of the many questionable practices of the Collor campaign.

Collor was young, athletic, handsome, and highly telegenic. He came from the poor northeastern state of Alagoas but had grown up largely in Rio de Janeiro and Brasília, where his politically powerful family maintained residences. His father's family belonged to a powerful clan, the Arnon de Melos, which had long dominated politics in Alagoas. The father had taken his northeastern political ways to the Federal Senate, where, in an argument, he had shot dead a former substitute senator on the Senate floor. But the older Collor was also attuned to modern politics, as shown by his close relations with television network magnate Roberto Marinho (of TV Globo) and his proprietorship of the TV Globo station in Alagoas. Collor's mother was the daughter of a prominent Rio Grandense politician, Lindolfo Collor, who had once served as labor minister under Getúlio Vargas.

Fernando Collor de Melo began his national political assault by assuming the mantle of a crusader against corruption. His targets were high civil servants (*marajás*, or "maharajas"), whom he accused of living luxuriously at the cost of the Brazilian taxpayer. This strategy proved popular with the national electorate, who believed him despite the fact that Collor himself came from the Northeast, a region of notorious political corruption. His other principal message was a pledge to apply neo-liberal economic policies in Brazil—i.e., to shrink government and to privatize Brazil's labyrinth of state enterprises. This, he assured his TV viewers, would bring Brazil abreast of such countries as Argentina, Chile, and Mexico, which were already jettisoning protectionism and selling off their largest public companies. Soon, he promised, Brazil would be entering the First World.

Most important, Collor struck the pose of a messiah who could solve Brazil's problems by the force of his personality. In this he resembled Jânio Quadros, who had won the 1960 presidential election by running as a political messiah. Such a strategy clearly fit the mood of the many Brazilians who were becoming disillusioned with the return to democracy and were thus susceptible to a politician promising miracles. At the same time, his neo-liberal message appealed to business leaders, who sought a candidate committed to reducing the role of government in the economy.

THE ELECTION

With the reinstitution of direct popular election of the president, new electoral regulations provided for a new procedure. The president was to be elected in a two-stage process. In the first round, entry would be relatively easy (there were twenty-two registered candidates in the 1989 first round). If no candidate won a majority in the first round then a second round (a runoff) was held between the top two vote-getters from the first round.

Since Collor was running so far ahead in the polls, it was assumed he would be one of the top two in the first round. Speculation therefore centered on the second spot for the two-person runoff in the final round. When the votes came in, Lula had defeated Leonel Brizola in the first round by running second to Collor. The nature of Collor's appeal as a messiah became even clearer as the runoff campaign proceeded. Lula expected to benefit greatly by the decline of the PMDB, thereby picking up many centrist voters. Lula was a kind of an anti-messiah, the factory worker from São Paulo with fractured grammar and an unmistakably proletarian appearance (he was missing one finger because of an accident with factory machinery). On TV, Lula lacked the slickness of Collor but projected a reformist zeal that touched many viewers worried about Brazil's yawning economic inequalities.

The confrontation between Lula and Collor then took a more ideological turn, as Collor tried to frighten voters by calling Lula a dangerous radical who would expropriate their property. This tactic proved very effective in São Paulo. The PT predicted (correctly, as it turned out) that Collor, if elected, would run an unscrupulous government that would be disastrous for Brazil.

After a hot contest and numerous charges of illegal campaign practices, Collor triumphed by a margin, as we have seen, of 42.7 percent to 37.8 percent. Collor's scare tactics proved to resonate better with the electorate, especially in São Paulo, the homeland of Lula's labor movement. They also frightened wealthy businessmen (industrialists, contractors, etc.) into contributing enormous sums to Collor's campaign.

Collor assumed the presidency in March 1990 amid highly favorable publicity. The media had overwhelmingly supported him, with the foreign press largely following their lead. The U.S. government was especially delighted with Collor, believing he would adopt the neo-liberal policies the United States was preaching for all developing countries.

THE POLICIES

Collor began his government with an economic bombshell. His advisors had warned that Brazil was on the verge of runaway inflation, now approaching 100 percent a month. The only solution, they argued, was a shock treatment, beginning with the freezing of all Brazilian savings accounts. Accompanying steps were a price freeze and the abolition of indexation. The public's initial reaction was disbelief. Many savers were furious that they were suddenly denied access to the money they had carefully put aside. Large business firms were paralyzed because the financial reserves they had used to meet current payrolls were frozen.

Economists doubted the long-run viability of the policy since it depended on inherently temporary instruments such as price controls and a savings freeze. For a few months, however, the therapy seemed to work. Inflation dropped to zero, and the fiscal deficit was dramatically reduced.

This dramatic attack on inflation was accompanied by the dismissal of thousands of federal workers, many of whom had been appointed in Sarney's flurry of patronage, on the grounds of redundancy and the government's fiscal emergency. The civil service unions protested, and the dismissed workers sought court orders to restore their jobs, which had been guaranteed by the liberal job tenure provision of the 1988 Constitution. Eventually, many won back their jobs through court action.

Collor also slashed Brazilian tariffs, among the world's highest. His government announced a phased schedule of tariff reductions that would bring Brazil from having some of the higher tariffs in the world to being in the 10 to 20 percent range found in other Latin American countries such as Argentina, Chile, and Mexico. This policy understandably worried those São Paulo industrialists who were not internationally competitive and would be hurt by cheaper imports. It was particularly embarrassing to those businessmen who had praised neo-liberalism in principle but now realized how it could hit them in the wallet.

Finally, the Collor government moved toward privatization. Brazil had over two hundred state enterprises, most of them money-losing. Many had become refugees for patronage appointments and had lost any ability to establish prices that both covered costs and provided for future investment. Collor announced that the government would begin auctioning off state enterprises to private buyers, including foreigners. Opposition to this came from several sources. Most vocal were the economic nationalists, especially in the PT, who defended the state sector as a bulwark of national sovereignty against foreign interests. The business community followed close behind. For sectors such as capital goods, purchases by state enterprises were crucial to their businesses, which had formed close relationships with such enterprises, often including non-competitive bidding. Privatization would end these cozy relationships and endanger future profits.

Collor implemented these economic policies through a flood of presidential decrees (*medidas provisórias*, or "provisional measures") in 1990, showing little inclination to negotiate with the Congress. He stuck to this imperial style on the assumption that his majority vote in the runoff presidential election would itself legitimize his boldness. By late 1990, however, his approach had aroused strong opposition. Although presidential decrees were only valid if ratified by Congress within thirty days, Collor simply issued them again if Congress refused. His opponents contested the constitutionality of this tactic, and in February 1991 congressional opposition, led by the PMDB, threatened to limit the presidential decree power. He now had no alternative but to negotiate with the Congress. From his inauguration in March 1990 through January 1991, the president averaged 14 decrees per month. For the rest of his term, January 1991 to September 1992, he averaged less than one.

Unfortunately for the president, however, his economic program, like so many before it, was falling apart. Numerous exceptions had been made to the savings freeze, and the price freeze was also collapsing. The finance minister, Zélia Cardoso de Mello, tried a second shock treatment in early 1991, but it was too late. The government's gamble on breaking inflationary expectations had been lost.

The president was able, nonetheless, to show some accomplishments. He signed a historic non-nuclear pact with Argentina, which laid to rest the fears of an atomic arms race in southern South America. At the same time, he scotched an apparent attempt by the Brazilian military to carry out a clandestine atomic weapons program. Further, he showed sensitivity to the long-standing problem of the indigenous peoples in the Amazon, designating huge new areas as exclusive reserves for the Indians. Finally, his measures on privatization and tariff reduction were important first steps toward making Brazil an internationally competitive economy. Perhaps these successes could have been sustained through his term, but something else was eating into his public reputation: Throughout 1991, growing tales of corruption at the highest levels of the government were leaking out.

THE END

By early 1992, Collor's arrogance and unwillingness to negotiate with congressional party leaders—combined with the suspicions of corruption—had left him without any means of mobilizing political support. As had happened frequently in the past, the lack of strong ties among the Congress, the political parties, and the president was making Brazil ungovernable. In January 1992, the president turned to the center to organize a new cabinet, jettisoning his corruption-tainted minister of labor and social security, Antonio Magri, and his health minister, Alceni Guerra. The new ministers included several PSD figures with the image of technical skill and honesty. The cabinet was further strengthened in May when Marcílio Marques Moreira, a respected banker-diplomat, became finance minister. It was dubbed the "last-chance cabinet." The hope of centrists was that Collor would be able to finish his term, if for no other reason than to secure the foundations of the democracy.

Their hope was soon overtaken by a burgeoning scandal involving the treasurer for Collor's presidential campaign. Journalists in Brasília had long described many in the Collor government as abnormally greedy (as opposed to usual political practice) in demanding payoffs from anyone dealing with the federal government. Such rumors had abounded about previous governments, but proof was almost always lacking. In the case of the Collor government, proof became abundantly public. The villain of the piece was P. C. Farias, a political fixer from Alagoas who had amassed a fortune, several mansions, and a jet plane (called the "black bat") through brokering political favors for many. As the treasurer for the campaign, he had successfully pressured so many wealthy donors that funds were still abundant three years after the campaign. Some said Collor and Farias were planning to use to money to found a long-term political dynasty.

In mid-1992, Collor and his collaborators became targets for a relentless Watergate-style investigation. The heaviest blow was a magazine interview in May 1992 by Collor's brother Pedro in which he accused the president of drug use, extortion, and sexual improprieties. The press and the congressional opposition joined to keep the issue alive. Eventually, the congressional investigators extracted bank records that proved exactly how the millions had circulated within the presidential circle. Collor fought back via television speeches. Like former U.S. President Richard Nixon, however, who had once faced a similar personal challenge (although of a graver constitutional nature), Collor dug himself into a deeper hole with each TV appearance. As the evidence mounted, the Congress, many of whose members were no strangers to corruption, began to consider impeachment. They were given further momentum by the massive street demonstrations against Collor in the major cities.

The Collor circle tried to buy off the congressmen involved, but to little avail. In July, a national poll gave Collor a "no confidence" rating of 69 percent. Almost as many (59 percent) thought he should resign the presidency. The Chamber of Deputies voted overwhelmingly (441 to 38) to impeach the president on September 29, 1992, and the Senate met and prepared to convict the president on December 29. Only hours before the Senate voted, Collor resigned, thus hoping to escape the final stage of legislative condemnation. But the Senate was not deterred, voting against Collor (76 to 5) and suspending his political rights for eight years.

It was a historic moment. For the first time, a Brazilian president had been forced out of office not by military coup or military ultimatum, but by orderly vote of the Congress. Collor had done one great favor for Brazil: He had prodded the political class into proving that they could live up to their constitutional responsibility.

Another Vice-President in Command

Yet another vice-president had to assume the Brazilian presidency. Once again, as in the case of Sarney, the new president was a minor politician never considered to be presidential material. Itamar Franco was from the state of Minas Gerais, where he had been a leading political figure in the city of Juiz da Fora. His only national visibility had come via two terms as a nondescript senator. His party identification was PMDB, but he was a decidedly nonideological figure.

Although few had any idea of the policies Franco might adopt, he was initially given the benefit of the doubt by the press and by most Brazilians, who were grateful to see Collor gone and normal succession procedures followed. His early moves were hardly reassuring. His first appointment as finance minister was Gustavo Krause, a little-known federal deputy from Recife. The rest of his original cabinet was hardly more distinguished in terms of national visibility or political clout, although it did cover the political spectrum.

The most pressing economic issue was inflation. Collor's stabilization policies had failed and inflation was again accelerating, but the new president showed little understanding of the economic forces at work. He preferred to look for villains among producers who raised prices on specific goods, such as pharmaceuticals. He also seemed indifferent to the burgeoning fiscal deficit. Above all, he had no stomach for undertaking the tough policies that stabilization required. Brazil was apparently condemned to continued drift.

Franco also expressed strong doubts about the wisdom of privatization and consistently threw roadblocks in the path of Collor's neoliberal policies generally. His rhetoric often sounded like the economic nationalists on the left. He was also suspicious of reducing tariffs and liked to talk, à la the developmentalists of the past, about the autonomy of the domestic market. Franco's image was not improved by his sometimes bizarre behavior—he frequently contradicted his own statements and was unwilling to engage in sustained discussion of major issues. Finally, he restricted his political consultations to a narrow circle of longtime cronies from his hometown of Juiz da Fora, confirming his image as an incurably provincial politician with little capacity to lead the country.

The hapless Franco was rescued by a late appointment to his cabinet. After constantly reshuffling his ministers, in 1993 he appointed Fernando Henrique Cardoso as minister of foreign relations. The choice seemed ideal because the highly intelligent, multilingual Cardoso was well known internationally. After a brief sojourn in the Foreign Ministry, Cardoso was soon to be called to greater things. In early 1994, the president invited Fernando Henrique to assume the Finance Ministry, which had proved a Waterloo for so many incumbents over the last fifteen years. Fernando Henrique accepted the post and assembled a team of outstanding economists, including Persio Arida, Edmar Bacha, André Lara Resende, and Gustavo Franco, many of whom had helped draft the Cruzado Plan back in 1986. They knew the mistakes made earlier and were anxious to demonstrate their competence under more favorable political auspices. They drew up yet another stabilization program that would give Franco's presidency the chance it badly needed to resurrect its reputation.

Back to Stabilization: The Plano Real

When Fernando Henrique was appointed finance minister, Brazil stood out as the only Latin American country that had failed to control inflation, and it was now said to be world champion in signing unfulfilled agreements with the IMF. The problem was fundamentally not one of economic diagnosis, although the treatment of the disease did demand considerable economic sophistication. Rather, it was political leadership. The politicians knew that every stabilization attempt since 1953 had produced short-run political pain, as real wage declines and shrinking credit brought on a recession. President after president had backed away from stabilization: Vargas, Kubitschek, Quadros, Goulart, and Sarney. Only Castello Branco, fortified by an authoritarian regime, had pursued stabilization long enough to reach a successful conclusion.

Itamar Franco had seemed as unlikely as his predecessors to tackle stabilization. He had little understanding of economics and demonstrated an impatient attitude toward unpopular economic measures. The difference between the fate of his stabilization plan and previous efforts turned out to be his timing and his choice of Cardoso as finance minister.

Cardoso's team formulated a complex strategy to fight inflation. First, they ruled out any shock treatment, such as a price and wage freeze. Second, they drew up a balanced budget for 1994, which the Congress passed. Third, they created a two-stage transition to a new currency. The first stage, which began in March 1994, was to last for four months and involved the creation of a new unit of value, the URV (Unit of Real Value), into which all previous values were converted. Meanwhile, the cruzeiro continued as currency, thus creating a dual set of prices. The objective here was to force the public to stop thinking in the currency values that had historically eroded so rapidly. This was also to be the stage for slowing down the "inertial inflation" (the inflation that was self-sustaining, without any new inflationary pressure), which all observers agreed had made rising prices a self-reproducing phenomenon.

The second stage, which began on July 1, was the introduction of a new currency, the *real*. The choice of name was ambiguous (it could mean either "royal" or "real"). In order to dramatize the government's commitment to stability, metallic coins were introduced. Soon, Brazilians were using coin-operated dispensing machines, a phenomenon unknown in Brazil for a generation.

In order to strengthen this approach, the government adopted a mildly overvalued exchange rate and imposed high real interest rates. The first measure was in order to fight inflation (with cheap imports). The second was to prevent the kind of runaway consumer boom that had occurred under the Cruzado Plan. Also scheduled was the gradual elimination of indexation over the following year. Finally, workers were left to negotiate wage increases as defined in the URVs. Thanks in part to the strong economy and good harvest in the last half of 1994, real wages did not decline—as had happened during virtually all previous stabilization efforts—but instead showed increases.

The Plano Real met much initial skepticism. With Brazil's track record on stabilization, the doubts were certainly legitimate, but both stages worked smoothly. The success of the second stage—the transition to a new currency, the *real*—was particularly striking, given the enormity of the challenge. The success was both logistical (getting the new currency to thousands of banks across a huge country) and psychological (getting the public to accept yet another new form of currency for their transactions). The morale of Brazilians could not have provided a better context. Just as the *real* was introduced, Brazil was on its way to winning an unprecedented fourth championship in the World Soccer Cup. Incredibly, Brazil had earlier beaten the U.S. team on the fourth of July, 1994. Could there have been a better gift for the Cardoso team?

Inflation began dropping immediately, going from 913 percent in 1994 to 19 percent in 1995. Consumers went on a buying boom. The last quarter of 1994 and the first quarter of 1995 saw industrial production surge (14 percent for the latter period, when GDP grew 10.4 percent), with inflation continuing to drop. By December it had reached a monthly average of only .96 percent. Obviously, there had been considerable excess capacity in mid-1994. By early 1995, the short-run success of the Plano Real was assured. (See exhibit 8-4.)

Serious challenges remained about the longer term, however. One was whether the government would slow down the boom, which threatened to rekindle inflationary pressure. This is where previous governments had lost their nerve. The second was how to deal with the balance of payments. The Finance Ministry had slashed tariffs on imported vehicles in late 1994, leading to a car import boom that cost the Central Bank several billion dollars in foreign reserves in only a few months. The third was the question of whether Brazilian workers would be content with their real incomes under the plan.

These questions were successfully answered, at least in the short run. The Central Bank imposed new credit controls in April 1995 to slow

EXHIBIT 8-4
Annual Rate of Inflation, 1986–97

Year	Inflation Rate (%)
1986	65.0
1987	416.0
1988	1038.0
1989	1783.0
1990	1477.0
1991	480.0
1992	1158.0
1993	2489.0
1994	929.0
1995	22.0
1996	11.0
1997	4.0

Source: 1986–1992: Werner Baer, *The Brazilian Economy*, 4th ed. (Westport, 1995), p. 393. 1992–1997: Economic Commission for Latin America.

down the boom. The Finance Ministry quickly reinstated high tariffs on over a hundred items, including vehicles, to protect the balance of payments. Finally, possible worker discontent was undercut by the distributional effects of the plan. The price of basic food necessities remained stable, aided by an exceptional harvest. Other prices important to the workers, such as bus fares, also remained stable. The middle class, however, was hit hard. The largest price increases came in services (restaurant meals, hairdressers, domestic airfares), which were, in economic parlance, "nontradables," meaning they did not compete with imports. Maintaining an overvalued exchange rate (thereby making imports cheaper) was a deliberate government device to stop domestic producers of tradables from raising their prices.

There were several reasons for the early success of the Plano Real. The plan was intelligently conceived and implemented. It was helped by the high level of foreign exchange reserves which the Cardoso team had inherited, which (topping $40 billion in July 1994) gave Brazil the largest reserves in its history and among the largest in the world. Such ample foreign exchange gave Brazil a cushion as it cut tariffs. In fact, it lost $10 billion in reserves over the first eight months of the plan when the premature tariff cuts led to an import boom, but it had a large enough cushion to weather this loss. The large agricultural harvest of 1994, which kept food prices down, was another massive piece of luck.

There was good luck on the political side as well. Most of the Brazilian public turned out to really want an end to volatile inflation. In addition, the most likely opponents of the plan—the economic nationalists on the left—were disorganized, demoralized, and reduced in number. Their heart was no longer in the kind of IMF-bashing so successful in the Kubitschek era and in the mid-1960s. The PT had discredited itself by having immediately rejected the Plano Real as a cynical electoral maneuver. Understandable as this response was, it became more and more self-defeating as the plan's continued success became obvious. Finally, the well-informed knew their country was seen as the economic pariah of Latin America. The traditionally successful discourse about Brazil being too big or too special to conform to conventional economic cures was now falling flat. Furthermore, the stable cost of basic goods (especially food), combined with wage increases, had undercut much of the worker discontent that might have been tapped by the government's opponents. Finally, the Cardoso team made liberal use of the *medida provisória*, the executive decree power that allowed the president to temporarily bypass the Congress. In 1994, for example, the presidency issued 397 such decrees (Collor's maximum was 163 in 1990), often to implement unpopular economic measures. In subsequent years, Cardoso—now president himself—had frequent recourse to this decree power, using it to help break some of the paralysis in Brasília that had appeared to render the country ungovernable only a few years earlier. His success showed his political skill, but it also showed a greater opposition willingness to tolerate frequent presidential recourse to exceptional measures.

The Presidential Election of 1994

The election for Franco's successor was set for November 1994. The campaign ended up dominated by the apparent success of the Plano Real, although it had not started out that way. In the early months of 1994, Lula, once again the PT candidate, enjoyed a huge lead in the polls, enticing his supporters to believe they were going to avenge Lula's defeat in 1989. The PT had, after all, predicted that Collor was an adventurer who would do his country no good, and Collor's fall from power amply confirmed their prediction. By their logic, Lula now deserved a turn at power. Furthermore, in early 1994 there was no strong figure from the right or center willing to contest Lula's lead. Cardoso was widely rumored to be a candidate, but he did not confirm it until he resigned from the Finance Ministry in early 1994 (resignation was required under the "incompatibility law" for all candidates who were already holding office). Until July 1994, therefore, the PT was still brimming with confidence. They considered Lula virtually a president-elect.

Cardoso did finally decide to enter the race in March 1994 and was immediately faced with some difficult choices. Because his party, the PSDB, lacked truly national strength, he knew he would have to seek an election alliance with one or more of the major parties. He first contacted the PT, exploring the possibility of a center-left coalition. Such a combination would have been formidable. For obvious reasons, however, the PT was unreceptive. They saw no reason to sacrifice their own candidate (relegating him to be Cardoso's running mate) when Lula was so far ahead. Cardoso then sounded out other parties on the center-left, such as Brizola's PDT, but Brizola was determined to maintain his own candidacy for the presidency, despite his declining standing in the polls.

Cardoso finally succeeded in attracting support from the PFL, a remnant of the official party from the dictatorship and an unlikely bedfellow for Cardoso, given his political philosophy. A link with the PFL would identify him with one of the most traditional (and one of the most reactionary) political images in Brazil, opening him up to fierce attacks from the left. On the other hand, the PFL was now controlled by Antonio Carlos Magalhães, the governor of Bahia and acknowledged political boss of the entire Northeast. In a close election, the PFL might be able to deliver the winning margin by drawing on their political machines in the Northeast. Finally, the PFL was known to favor the neo-liberal reforms in Cardoso's platform. Their support could help counterbalance the economic nationalists on the left who opposed such neo-liberal measures as privatization. The PFL's ability to deliver a large regional vote was probably the most important factor in Cardoso's decision.

The PT was jubilant, believing that his alliance with the PFL would alienate enough centrist voters to ensure Cardoso's defeat. But the election did not turn on the question of the PFL. It turned, instead, on the Plano Real.

The PT had expressed immediate skepticism about the Plano Real. They saw it as government manipulation in favor of the government candidate. Once the campaign began, Lula and his advisors decided to launch an all-out attack on the Plano Real, charging that instead of ending inflation it would worsen the economic plight of the poor. Their decision was based on their assumption that the plan would either fail or at least that it would alienate many voters. Incredibly, this decision was made despite early warnings that the public was reacting favorably to the plan. The decision was reached as part of a larger conflict within the PT. The more militant wing wanted an aggressive campaign, believing that was the only way to maintain Lula's early lead. The more moderate wing of the party did not wish to present too radical a face to the Brazilian voter, fearing the militants' zeal might alienate the average

Brazilian. The militant wing won out—a decision that did not seem as unreasonable in late July 1994 as it does in hindsight.

The plan proved a rapid and continuing success, and Lula's poll numbers began to drop. Fernando Henrique Cardoso was elected president with an absolute majority (54 percent of the valid votes) on the first round. By the second round in November, which was restricted to runoffs for the posts for which no candidate had received an absolute majority, Fernando Henrique's party's triumph became even broader in that PSDB candidates won the governorships in the key states of São Paulo, Minas Gerais, and Rio de Janeiro. The congressional picture was more mixed, however. Despite Lula's defeat, the PT had once again increased its congressional delegation (from 35 to 49), and the PMDB, despite its visible decay, remained the largest party in the Congress.

The political nature of the new Congress was actually quite uncertain, however. There was extreme party fragmentation (eighteen parties represented in the Chamber of Deputies), suggesting that getting any coherent program through Congress could be a Herculean task. Fernando Henrique had won the largest electoral majority of any president since 1945, but as Collor had demonstrated, electoral majorities can be perishable assets when it comes to governing.

THE POLICIES OF THE CARDOSO GOVERNMENT

For its first three years, the Cardoso government's top priority remained stabilization. Presidential policy-makers knew that conquering inflation, after so many failed attempts, would take time. Yet success came much faster than most expected. In 1993, inflation had reached 2,489 percent, the capital market virtually disappeared, and the average Brazilian found personal economic planning to be impossible. By the end of 1994, with the Plano Real in place for only six months, inflation had declined by more than half, to less than 1,000 percent. Even more dramatic results came in 1995, with inflation falling to 22 percent; in 1996, with inflation at 11 percent; and in 1997, with inflation at about 4 percent.

This remarkable record, equal only to President Castelo Branco's success from 1964 to 1967, required continuing battle, especially over the federal budget, where the structure favored continuous deficits. Other areas also needed constant attention. The balance of payments had run a surplus in the half-dozen years before 1994 because continued protection and low growth had depressed imports, while exports remained strong. Now that Brazil was beginning to reduce tariffs, the long-run outlook for the trade balance was more doubtful.

Another area of worry was the financial system. It had overexpanded during the 1980s, with much of its profits coming from the "inflationary float" the banks earned from financial transactions. The rapid fall in inflation after 1994 reduced this float and thus threatened bank profits, forcing several major bank failures (including some of the largest, such as the Banco Nacional and the Banco Econômico). This process required costly government bailouts.

Finally, there was the problem of inflationary expectations. Brazil had lived through one of the most pervasive inflationary experiences in the world, with the Brazilian public becoming sophisticated in defending itself financially. Policy-makers knew that any significant recurrence of inflation would signal the economic actors that stabilization had failed again. The Cardoso government thus had to fight against extreme public skepticism about its ability to hold the price line. Based on stabilization experience elsewhere in Latin America, the government realized it might well take the rest of Cardoso's term to squeeze inflation out of the economy. This was hardly a welcome prospect and could land Cardoso with the label Castello Branco had readily accepted: the president of "between harvests."

The stabilization battle necessarily involved a campaign to reduce deficit spending, which had become a way of life at every level of government. The most obvious confrontation was in the federal Congress, where members were always interested in enjoying the fruits of federal patronage. The battle also went on at the state level, especially with the state banks, notorious for running up large debts (usually incurred to fund political campaigns or pet projects of incumbent officials) and then blackmailing the national government into bailing them out. The leading example was Banespa, the São Paulo state bank, which by 1994 had run up a debt of more than $25 billion. After years of wrangling, the São Paulo state government and the federal government reached a complex agreement in November 1996 whereby the latter helped refinance the debt of the bank (and the state of São Paulo) in return for the forced sale of state assets (including the railways and the electricity system) and the temporary takeover of the bank by federal authorities.

The Cardoso government also faced a vast federal, state, and local bureaucracy with a remarkable talent for reproducing itself. The largest single increase in government expenditure during the Sarney presidency, for example, had been for personnel, representing a fiscal time bomb for the future because the generous government pension system would have to fund them when they retired. As of March 1998, the government had succeeded in getting the preliminary two-thirds Congressional vote to reform the notoriously generous federal pension system. Yet such reform would take time to show results.

A further priority of the Cardoso government was privatization of state enterprises, which under Franco and Collor had been subject to numerous delays. In this area, the Cardoso government had continuing trouble. The process of auctioning off ownership of large public corporations proved more difficult than anticipated, with establishing appraisals of the corporations' value especially controversial. It was also difficult to find satisfactory buyers since few private interests had the large-scale capital needed. As a result, domestic pension funds were at first often the winning bidders, with substantial foreign buyers ready to bid only in such areas as telecommunications. They often hesitated because of uncertainty over the potential profitability of the privatized enterprise. One of the government's motives in pushing privatization was the prospect of gaining cash that could help reduce federal deficits, which had given stabilizing governments an important boost in Argentina and Mexico. But this was just beginning to occur in Brazil, where most of the buyers in the early 1990s had paid in nonnegotiable government bonds. Nonetheless, by mid 1998 the government could show considerable success, having privatized (by sale or lease) more than fifty firms in such areas as steel, fertilizer, and iron ore. In almost every case, efficiency immediately increased.

Finally, there was the question of measures to improve the social welfare of the ordinary Brazilian. Few Brazilians—save the wealthy—needed to be reminded of the decay in public services and the increase in economic inequality that had occurred over the last decade and a half. The need for public investment in education, health, transportation, and communications was enormous. Unfortunately, however, the necessary federal funds were not available in the short run (although tougher tax collection helped raise revenues) and the urgent need to balance the budget meant that they could not be expected soon. Cardoso's government had to content itself with essentially token gestures such as putting computers in school classrooms, a measure that was much cheaper than raising teachers' salaries.

Agrarian reform was one area of social policy that would not wait. In recent years, landless workers had organized a protest movement (Movimento Sem Terra) that organized land invasions, especially in the South and in the Amazon Basin. Landowners fought back, usually with the support of local police. In April 1996, military police killed twenty-three workers in a bloody confrontation in the Amazonian state of Pará.

Nationwide indignation over this incident provoked the Cardoso government to promise a complete investigation, but the workers could expect little relief. Local landowners and their sympathetic military police had almost invariably proved beyond the reach of federal authorities, as shown in the reaction to a similar wave of killings in the Amazon during the previous August. Furthermore, the Cardoso administration had rejected a policy of simply handing out land, especially in small units, on the grounds it was counterproductive economically. Nonetheless, by mid-1998 INCRA, the land reform agency, had made record-breaking distributions of government-controlled land.

Human violence was not the only ill plaguing the Amazon. The relentless destruction of the rain forest had also disturbed thoughtful

Brazilians and became a prime issue in the international ecological movement. Since 1960, fires and chainsaws had stripped an area of Amazon vegetable cover larger than all of France. After a drop in the rate of destruction in the early 1990s, there was an increase in 1995 and an even greater upsurge in 1996. Inadequate budgets for the environmental ministry, combined with indecisive leadership in Brazília were giving the loggers (many illegal) and the slash-and-burn settlers near free rein. Even with the best will in the work, Brasília, with its few hundred inspectors, could not have established effective control over an area larger than Western Europe. The problem was compounded by the fact that Amazonia was simply not a priority for the Cardoso government.

The government was also well aware of how little it could do on social welfare. The first response was to launch a "community solidarity" program directed by the first lady, Ruth Cardoso. The strategy was to identify the needy *municipios* in Brazil and deliver strategic assistance to local governments and organizations. This had an important symbolic (and probably political) value, and could also serve to stimulate self-help efforts on the local level. On the other hand, as its supporters acknowledged, it could never substitute for satisfying Brazil's massive deferred social investment.

On the latter, the Cardoso government was stronger on rhetoric than action. One obvious reason was lack of funds, a plight produced by the urgent need to reduce the federal deficit. Modest steps were taken in education, such as raising public teachers' salaries (pitifully meager in the primary and secondary schools) and establishing an educational TV network for all schools. But knowledgeable observers argued that the biggest problem continued to be the waste, diversion, and mismanagement of whatever funds were appropriated. That had much to do with corruption and perverse incentives existing on the state and local level— ills that would take much more than a few years to cure.

In one respect, the Cardoso government scored a victory for the poorest Brazilians: The rapid decline in inflation had suddenly raised the average buying power of consumers who dealt only in cash (such as the poor) because the deterioration of their income between pay periods was now less. (The better-off, in contrast, had been able to keep their liquid funds in fully indexed checking accounts.) Furthermore, abundant harvests helped to keep food prices down. A 1996 government study showed that between July 1984 and January 1996, the percentage of poor in the six largest metropolitan regions had declined from 33 percent to 25 percent. By the end of 1997, it was estimated that the real value of the minimum wage had risen 27 percent since 1994. This reflected a deliberate government policy of using minimum wage policy to target the poorest.

As always, the rich had protected themselves during these years. The greatest squeeze was felt by the middle class, which in Brazil means roughly the fifth to the thirtieth percentile from the top of the income distribution. This class was especially hit by the price increase in "non-tradables"—i.e., the goods and services that were not in international trade and were therefore not subject to price competition from imported substitutes. Most prominent were rent, school tuition, restaurant meals, and all personal services.

CARDOSO'S PROSPECTS

Perhaps because Cardoso realized how limited his accomplishments would necessarily be by the end of his term in 1999, he chose the unexpected course of bidding for another term. To make himself eligible to run in 1998 he would need to amend the Constitution, which required a two-thirds vote, twice, of each house of Congress. Between January and June of 1997, the Congress, succumbing to a political blitz, from the presidential palace (which allegedly included bribes for two congressmen), approved the necessary amendment. In campaigning to lift the constitutional prohibition of a second successive term, Cardoso was following the successful precedents of Presidents Menem in Argentina and Fujimori in Peru, both of whom had been widely criticized for their authoritarian tendencies. Yet Cardoso encountered little significant opposition, either inside his party or out, and his chances of winning in 1998 were obviously enhanced by the apparent lack of other attractive candidates.

As of mid-1998, Brazil seemed in suspended animation both economically and politically. The Real Plan had proved a brilliant success as to its original purpose—drastically reducing inflation, inducing the public to think in real economic terms, and sanitizing a bloated financial system—yet it had not put the Brazilian economy back on the strong growth path that was essential if the country's enormous social needs were to be met. Nor was it clear, despite Brazil's record foreign exchange reserves, that Brazil had the competitive capacity to expand its role in world trade. All of these questions were essentially on hold, as the Cardoso government appeared determined to stick to the stabilization-oriented economic strategy begun in 1994.

Nineteen ninety-seven did not prove so easy, however. Trouble had been brewing in East Asia, the region of rapid economic growth since the 1960s. The crisis was financial: plunging stock markets and plunging currency values. First hit was Thailand in July, but the virus soon spread to Malaysia, Indonesia, the Phillipines, and South Korea. In every case, investors dumped equities, at the same time demanding hard currency for whatever local currencies (the Korean won, etc.) they held. The cause of the panic was the belated recognition that many East Asian financial institutions lacked accountability, transparency, and professional management. Many had made bad loans, resulting in bank portfolios of dubious quality. Furthermore, some East Asian currencies were overvalued.

Most important in the short run, however, was the self-reinforcing nature of the panic. The faster currency traders demanded hard currency, the sooner the countries under siege ran out of foreign exchange. It was a vicious circle. It was also a repeat of the financial crisis that had hit Mexico in 1994.

Brazil soon began to show signs of catching the Asian virus. A sell-off hit the São Paulo stock market, which fell 22 percent in the last two weeks of October. At the same time, speculation battered the *real*, causing the Central Bank to spend approximately $8 million in foreign exchange reserves. Rumors flew about possible bank failures. The New York investment house of Morgan Stanley warned its clients that Brazil had become the number-one global risk. Was yet another Brazilian stabilization plan about to go down the drain?

The fears turned out to be exaggerated. The São Paulo stock market stabilized (by the end of 1997 it was still up 34.8 percent for the year) and the *real* had survived attack, with the Central Bank by December still holding more than $55 billion in foreign exchange reserves (the total reached over $70 billion by June 1998). But the government's successful counterattack required extreme measures. First was a huge jump of 93 percent in interest rates to 40 percent per annum in real terms. This was aimed at holding the "hot money" of investors who might be tempted to withdraw their dollars from Brazil. It was also designed to reduce demand for imports, which were contributing to a dangerously increasing deficit in the balance of payments—by October running at 4 percent of GDP, well ahead of the government target. The second action was a package of fifty-one reform measures, which included budget cuts and tax increases designed to produce a net saving of $18 billion.

However effective in staunching the immediate crisis, these measures also had negative effects. The ultra-high interest rates would be deflationary, possibly driving the economy into negative growth in 1998, an election year. This would inevitably set back the effort to improve living standards, which depended above all on rapid growth. Higher interest rates would also be costly to the government, because they would raise the cost of financing the large domestic public debt. Finally, continuing to maintain an overvalued exchange rate—a key element of government policy—would postpone facing up to a basic cause of the disequilibrium in the external sector. Brazil had thus reduced its short-term international vulnerabilities by making itself hostage to short-term capital movements and a large-scale domestic economic slowdown.

President Cardoso reacted vigorously to the crisis, pledging that Brazil would never give in to the speculators. Finance Minister Malan was even more optimistic. He argued for the chance to "emerge from the crisis better than before." As for the once famous East Asian Tigers, he predicted that the "Latin American economy is beginning a new phase, while Asia is finishing a cycle." It was a curious way to introduce Brazilians to yet another bout of austerity. The irony was that Brazil, three years after successful stabilization, was again having to postpone rapid growth and increased investment in human capital, the only viable paths to greater social justice. Cardoso's challenge was compounded by a renewed speculative attack on the Brazilian currency which began in August 1998. By early October Brazil's foreign exchange reserves had fallen from 73 billion dollars to 47 billion.

Politically, the strategy had not changed since 1994. That strategy was an ad hoc approach, weaving together a shifting coalition of party and regional support. Given the fragmented party system, this style was probably inevitable, but it did involve one unforeseen consequence: a steady weakening of Cardoso's own party, the PSDB, as the president relied for support increasingly on the conservative PFL. Instead of investing in the strengthening of his party, which had been created with such fanfare in 1988, Cardoso invested in himself as Brazil's political solution. By commandeering the passage of the constitutional amendment that legitimized a second successive presidential term, Cardoso was in effect deferring until after the 1998 election (which he won), an attack on such outstanding problems as slow growth and the country's shocking social inequalities.

Epilogue

Since Pedro Cabral's ship first reached Bahia, Brazil has been seen as the "land of opportunity," yet the effort by Brazilians to seize that opportunity has often fallen short. Not for a lack of diagnoses. Since the early nineteenth century, Brazil's best minds have tried to discover how their country could become a respected nation on the world scene. The formulae were many: monarchism, liberalism, positivism, anarchism, republicanism, socialism, democracy, corporatism. But a commitment to capitalism was the real theme. Private property, with few limitations, was elevated as the key to Brazilian development. This was the real meaning of Brazil's long love affair—since the late eighteenth century—with economic and political liberalism.

Brazil's greatest twentieth-century test came in its second half. The politicians and the elite bet on industrialization, embracing its icons of consumption, such as the passenger car, the television set, and the high-rise apartment. Until the mid-1960s, the formula appeared to be working. Brazil was recording one of the world's highest economic growth rates. Unfortunately, however, it was undermined by high population growth, negative world trends, and persistent economic mismanagement.

As a result, Brazil's economic performance has been disappointing for the last twenty years. The boom of the 1970s was followed by the stagnation of the 1980s and early 1990s. The degree of Brazil's disappointing performance could be seen when measured against the record of the "East Asian Tigers"—South Korea, Taiwan, Hong Kong, and Singapore—which, although all far smaller than Brazil, had succeeded since the 1960s in achieving impressive per capita growth and improving income distribution. These countries were all poorer than Brazil in per capita terms in 1960, but all had far outpaced Brazil by 1990. Between 1965 and 1990, the four Tigers grew at almost 7 percent per capita, while Brazil's rate was 3.3 percent. They had done so by controlling inflation, promoting exports, stimulating domestic savings, and investing heavily in human capital. Brazil had been remiss on all four. On other dimensions, however, the Tigers suffered by comparison: They had achieved their economic progress under authoritarian regimes, which included repression deeper and more sustained than that of the Brazilian military. And several of the Tigers ran into financial crises in mid- and late 1997 due to unwise lending practices, inadequate regulation, and excessive international borrowing.

The most unfavorable standard by which to measure Brazil's progress, as well as probably the most unrealistic, was the standard of the Alliance for Progress launched in 1961. This multilateral commitment called upon Brazil, with the rest of Latin America, to achieve rapid economic growth, profound social reform, and lasting democracy. Furthermore, the United States was to supply generous amounts of capital and technology to speed the process. Many Brazilians hoped the Marshall Plan was finally arriving south of the border, but the Alliance for Progress proved to be largely a tissue of illusions. For complex reasons, economic growth sputtered, social reform ended in rhetoric, and democracy soon gave way to military rule. Janio Quadros's resignation in 1961 shattered the hope for political stability and the coup of 1964 frustrated the hope for social reform. If democratic capitalism were to succeed in Brazil, it would have to be built by Brazilians, not by planners from the north.

By the early 1990s, Brazilian spirits had been badly battered. An increasing migration of Brazilians abroad showed the discontent. Endless revelations of political corruption had soured many on democracy. The creativity and spontaneity long typical of Brazilians seemed to be missing.

Why? In a phrase, it was lack of leadership matched by a lack of civic spirit. The Brazilian elite had chosen to enjoy the good life, virtually abandoning any pretense of commitment to societal welfare. This mood was not helped by the sudden and unexplained resignation of Janio Quadros. Goulart proved to be weak, inept, and confused, and the succeeding military presidents never dared expose themselves to a direct election. Then followed a series of mediocre presidents, triggered by the agonizing death of Tancredo, and then came the self-serving performance of Sarney, the tawdry and mendacious government of Collor, and the erratic behavior of Itamar Franco were less than the Brazilian people deserved. The lower political ranks were not much better. There was a dearth of political talent. The years of military government had not favored the rise of new democratic leaders.

There was more hope in the civic movements, such as the 1992 public campaign leading to Collor's impeachment and the 1984 campaign for direct election of the president. These ad hoc mobilizations were complemented by the many nongovernmental organizations campaigning vigorously on behalf of street children, ecological awareness, and human rights. Yet this voluntary activism could never substitute for the political leadership needed to attack the major economic and social needs of Brazil.

By mid-1998, there was the promise of such leadership having arrived. Cardoso had assembled one of the most technically qualified cabinets in recent Brazilian history, and for once the shadow of corruption did not hang over the presidential palace. In its first three-and-a-half years, the Cardoso team succeeded, against most expectations, in reducing annual inflation to less than 5 percent without creating a recession. On the contrary, growth had averaged a healthy 3 to 4 percent for 1995 and 1996, although the restrictive fiscal and monetary measures imposed after the 1997 Asian financial crisis will undoubtedly slow growth, as already occurred in 1997. Furthermore, the government had largely restructured the private financial system and restored the previously defunct capital market. Equally important, there was a real effort to negotiate with the Congress, something seldom seen in recent decades.

The fate of the 1994–98 Cardoso government would first of all turn on its continuing success at stabilization. Second would be its ability to reform the structural features that stood in the way of a modern economy. The targets included regulations on job tenure and pensions, allocation of tax revenues, rules on foreign capital and patents, deficits of runaway state banks, and distorted public financing for education. All had contributed to fiscal deficits and distorted investment patterns.

Despite the stabilization success of the government, there were serious questions about the future. Brazilian economic development had continued to show an ugly side. Income distribution remained the most unequal in the world. Every industrializing nation has encountered this problem and faced the need to temper distributional excesses exacerbated by economic development. North America and Western Europe created varying versions of the welfare state with its safety net for the less fortunate. The East Asian Tigers had, despite their authoritarianism, followed policies that reduced inequality, especially through access to education.

Brazil, on the other hand, like Mexico, seemed incapable of facing up to the darker implications of its strategy for economic development. The elite repeatedly showed indifference to the need to invest in human capital, except for their own children. They seemed to be consciously turning their backs on the historic lessons from the North Atlantic and East Asia. Could Brazil expect to become a modern nation with its small minority of rich and super-rich inside their barricaded apartment blocks, while most Brazilians could barely enter the national market?

These economic excesses have become more obvious at a time when criticism from the left has become weaker. The old-line Marxist parties have disappeared. The PT suffered a stinging defeat in 1994, which was repeated in the 1998 election. Bookstores that once overflowed with critiques of Brazil's economic development model are now awash in volumes on how to make money or find inner peace, or both.

Has Brazil's moment come and gone? The answer will not come from presidential speeches or public demonstrations. It will have to come from the realization that Brazil amounts to more than today's profit margins and tomorrow's pleasures. The ordinary Brazilian is no stranger to hard work—after all, he or she can't afford to be. But it is the incentives they are given that make the difference. Brazilians deserve a leadership that can come to understand why a viable capitalism requires genuine democracy. Only when the participation of all Brazilians becomes a reality can Brazil achieve the just society for which its citizens have long striven.

Suggestions for Further Reading

Of the vast bibliography on Brazilian history, what follows is a selective listing of titles that proved especially helpful in preparing this volume. Many important works and subject areas have been omitted for reasons of space. It also covers only books—readers who wish to explore the periodical literature should consult current and back issues of such journals as the *Hispanic American Historical Review*, the *Luso-Brazilian Review*, *Americas*, the *Latin American Research Review*, the *Journal of Latin American Studies*, the *Bulletin of Latin American Research*, the *Journal of Inter-American Studies and World Affairs*, *Dados*, *Estudos Históricos*, *Revista do Instituto Histórico e Geográfico Brasileiro*, *Revista Brasileira de Ciências Sociais*, *Revista do Instituto de Estudos Brasileiros* and *Revista de Historia*. The emphasis, as in the text, is on the nineteenth and twentieth centuries.

General

Brazilian scholars have produced an important collaborative survey of their history in Sérgio Buarque de Hollanda, ed., *História Geral da Civilização Brasileira*, 10 vols. (São Paulo, 1960–81). Brazil also figures prominently in Lesley Bethell, ed., *The Cambridge History of Latin America*, vols. 1–8; 10 (Cambridge, 1984–95). The most often consulted single-volume histories in English are E. Bradford Burns, *A History of Brazil*, 3rd ed. (New York, 1993); and Rollie E. Poppino, *Brazil: The Land and People*, 2nd ed. (New York, 1973). Recent readable Brazilian surveys are Boris Fausto, *História do Brasil*, 2nd ed. (São Paulo, 1995); and Jorge Caldeira, *Viagem Pela História do Brasil* (São Paulo, 1997). For stimulating collections of essays covering all of Brazilian history, see Carlos Guilherme Mota, ed., *Brasil em Perspectiva* (São Paulo, 1968); and Maria Yedda Linhares, ed., *História Geral do Brasil* (Rio de Janeiro, 1988). Influential general works which put Brazil's past into perspective include Jacques Lambert, *Os Dois Brasís*, Clotilde da Silva Costa, trans. (Rio de Janeiro, 1959); Roberto da Matta, *Carnivals, Rogues and Heroes* (Notre Dame, 1991); Darcy Ribeiro, *O Povo Brasileiro* (São Paulo, 1995); Vianna Moog, *Bandeirantes and Pioneers*, L. L. Barrett, trans. (New York, 1964); Sérgio Buarque de Holanda,

Raízes do Brasil (Rio de Janeiro, 1989); Michel Debrun, *A Conciliação e Outras Estratégias* (São Paulo, 1983); Charles Morazé, *Les Trois Ages du Brésil* (Paris, 1954); Raimundo Faoro, *Os Donos do Poder*, 2nd ed., 2 vols. (São Paulo, 1975); Francisco Iglésias, *Trajetória Política do Brasil: 1500–1964* (São Paulo, 1993); and Mary Del Priore, ed., *História das Mulheres no Brasil* (São Paulo, 1997). A general intellectual history is available in Wilson Martins, *História da Inteligência Brasileira*, 7 vols. (São Paulo, 1976–79).

The Colony (1500–1822)

The colonial era has seen extensive scholarship, with recent work emphasizing social and intellectual history. A useful synthesis is given in Arno Wehling and Maria José C. de Wehling, *Formação do Brasil Colonial* (Rio de Janeiro, 1994). The acknowledged pioneer in the field is Capistrano de Abreu, *Capítulos de História Colonial: 1500–1800*, 5th ed. (Rio de Janeiro, 1969). The background to Brazil's discovery may be found in Sérgio Buarque de Holanda, *Visão do Paraíso* (São Paulo, 1969); Bailey W. Diffie and George D. Winius, *Foundations of the Portuguese Empire, 1415–1580* (Minneapolis, 1977); and Charles R. Boxer, *The Portuguese Seaborne Empire, 1415–1825* (New York, 1969). Boxer has produced a series of magisterial works on colonial Brazil, including *The Golden Age of Brazil: Growing Pains of a Colonial Society, 1695–1750* (Berkeley, 1962), and *The Dutch in Brazil, 1624–1654* (Oxford, 1957). See also Dauril Alden, *Royal Government in Colonial Brazil* (Berkeley, 1968). An outstanding analysis of the northeastern sugar civilization is given in Stuart B. Schwartz, *Sugar Plantations in the Formation of Brazilian Society: Bahia, 1550–1835* (Cambridge, 1985). The classic work on that subject, first published in 1933, is Gilberto Freyre, *The Masters and the Slaves*, Samuel Putnam, trans., 2nd ed. (New York, 1956). The colonial economic system has been given an influential interpretation in Fernando A. Novais, *Portugal e Brasil na Crise do Antigo Sistema Colonial: 1777–1808* (São Paulo, 1979); and Richard Graham, ed., *Brazil and the World System* (Austin, 1991). The fate of the Indians in the colonial era is treated in John Hemming, *Red Gold* (Cambridge, Mass., 1978). John Manuel Monteiro, *Negros da Terra* (São Paulo, 1995), is a pioneering study of Indian slavery in South-Central Brazil. The classic analysis of the colonial system is Caio Prado Junior, *The Colonial Background of Modern Brazil* (Berkeley, 1967).

African slavery is one of the most studied topics, although much is yet to be done. An imaginative reconstruction of its human dimension is Katia M. De Queirós Mattoso, *Ser Escravo no Brasil* (São Paulo, 1982). Brazil is placed within the Latin American context in Herbert S. Klein, *African Slavery in Latin America and the Caribbean* (New York, 1986). For a vigorous critique of "revisionist" scholarship, see Jacob Gorender, *A Escravidão Reabilitada* (São Paulo, 1990). The same author has produced his own synthesis in *O Escravismo Colonial*, 5th ed. (São Paulo, 1988). A useful overview of recent publications is Stuart B. Schwartz, *Slaves, Peasants, and Rebels* (Chicago, 1992). Luiz Mott, *Rosa Egipcíaca* (Rio de Janeiro, 1993), tells the remarkable story of a female slave who attained popular sainthood. Robert Edgar Conrad, *Children of God's Fire*, 2nd ed. (University Park, 1994), is a collection of reprinted excerpts documenting the entire history of Brazilian slavery. Slave resistance is surveyed in Clovis Moura, *Rebeliões na Senzala* (São Paulo, 1959). The link between slavery and modern race relations is analyzed in Carl N. Degler, *Neither Black Nor White* (New York, 1971). The same theme was treated in an international context by José Honório Rodrigues, *Brazil and Africa*, Richard A. Mazzura and Sam Hileman, trans. (Los Angeles, 1965).

Social history of the colonial era has produced notable works such as A. J. R. Russell-Wood, *Fidalgos and Philanthropists* (Berkeley, 1968), Thales de Azevedo, *Povoamento da Cidade do Salvador* (Bahia, 1949), Laura de Mello e Souza, ed., *História da Vida Privada no Brasil* (São Paulo, 1997); the same author's *Desclassificados do Ouro* (Rio de Janeiro, 1982) and her *O Diabo e a Terra de Santa Cruz* (São Paulo, 1987), Ronaldo Vainfas, *Trópico dos Pecados* (Rio de Janeiro, 1989); João Adolfo Hansen, *A Sátira e o Engenho* (São Paulo, 1989), Evaldo Cabral de Mello, *Olinda Restaurada* (São Paulo, 1975), and the same author's *Rubro Veio* (Rio de Janeiro, 1976).

The transition from colony to independence has been the subject of extensive study. Kenneth Maxwell, *Conflicts and Conspiracies* (Cambridge, 1973), remains a fundamental work, along with the same author's *Pombal, Paradox of the Enlightenment* (Cambridge, 1995). For an important revolt in Salvador, see Affonso Ruy, *A Primeira Revolução Social Brasileira: 1798* (Bahia, 1951). Useful collective works include Dauril Alden, ed., *Colonial Roots of Modern Brazil* (Berkeley, 1973), Carlos G. Mota, ed., *1822: Dimensões* (São Paulo, 1972); and A. J. R. Russell-Wood, *From Colony to Nation* (Baltimore, 1975). The story is continued into the early Empire in Roderick J. Barman, *Brazil: The Forging of a Nation, 1798–1852* (Stanford, 1988).

The Empire (1822–1889)

For the Empire, there is the dated but still useful C. H. Haring, *Empire in Brazil* (Cambridge, Mass., 1958). The first monarch of an independent Brazil has received an able biography in Neill Macaulay, *Dom Pedro* (Durham, 1986). The most reliable biography of Pedro II is Heitor Lyra, *História de Dom Pedro II*, 3 vols. new ed. (São Paulo, 1977). The same monarch is the subject of an intriguing fictional autobiography in Jean Soublin, *D. Pedro II: O Defensor Perpétuo do Brasil*, Rosa Freire d'Aguiar, trans. (São Paulo, 1996). The most convincing analysis of the imperial political system is José Murilo de Carvalho, *A Construção da Ordem: A*

Elite Política Imperial (Rio de Janeiro, 1980), and the same author's *Teatro de Sombras: A Política Imperial* (Rio de Janeiro, 1988), and is also spelled out in his *A Monarquia Brasileira* (Rio de Janeiro, 1993). For valuable detail one should consult also Richard Graham, *Patronage and Politics in Nineteenth-Century Brazil* (Stanford, 1990). The finest overall interpretation is Emília Viotti da Costa, *The Brazilian Empire* (Chicago, 1985). The fall of the Empire is the theme of two important older works: Heitor Lyra, *História da Queda do Império*, 2 vols. (São Paulo, 1964); and Oliveira Vianna, *O Ocaso do Império* (Rio de Janeiro, 1925). Much imperial history unrolls in Joaquim Nabuco, *Um Estadista do Império: Nabuco de Araujo*, 3 vols. (Rio de Janeiro, 1897).

The topic of nineteenth-century slavery is treated in Mary C. Karasch, *Slave Life in Rio de Janeiro, 1808–1850* (Princeton, 1987), Sidney Chalhoub, *Visões da Liberdade* (São Paulo, 1990), João José Reis, *Slave Rebellion in Brazil* (Baltimore, 1993); Emília Viotti da Costa, *Da Senzala à Colonia*, 2nd ed. (São Paulo, 1990); and Ciro Flamarion S. Cardoso, *Escravo ou Camponês?* (São Paulo, 1987). The slave trade, which goes back to the sixteenth century, is documented for the eighteenth and nineteenth centuries in Joseph C. Miller, *Way of Death* (Madison, 1988); and Leslie Bethell, *The Abolition of the Brazilian Slave Trade* (Cambridge, 1970). For concise histories of the trade, see Philip D. Curtin, *The Atlantic Slave Trade: A Census* (Madison, 1969); and Robert Edgard Conrad, *World of Sorrow: The African Slave Trade to Brazil* (Baton Rouge, 1986).

The long struggle leading to abolition is analyzed in Robert Brent Toplin, *The Abolition of Slavery in Brazil* (New York, 1972); and in Robert Conrad, *The Destruction of Brazilian Slavery, 1850–1888* (Berkeley, 1972). See also Ciro Flamarian Cardoso, ed., *Escravidão e Abolição no Brasil: Novas Perspectivas* (Rio de Janeiro, 1988); Maria Helena Machado, *O Plano e o Pânico: Os Movimentos Sociais na Década da Abolição* (Rio de Janeiro, 1994), and João José Reis, ed., *Escravidão e Invenção da Liberdade* (São Paulo, 1988). The classic argument for abolition was given in Joaquim Nabuco, *Abolitionism*, Robert Conrad, trans. (Chicago, 1977), first published in 1883.

Valuable social history of the empire may be found in Gilberto Freyre, *The Mansions and the Shanties* (New York, 1963); Frédéric Mauro, *La vie quotidienne au Brésil au temps de Pedro Segundo, 1831–1889* (Biarritz, 1980); Katia M. de Queirós Mattoso, *Bahia, Século XIX* (Rio de Janeiro, 1992); Sandra Lauderdale Graham, *House and Street* (Cambridge, 1988); Eul-Soo Pang, *In Pursuit of Honor and Power* (Tuscaloosa, 1988); João José Reis, *A Morte é uma Festa* (São Paulo, 1991); Spencer Leitman, *Raízes Sócio-Econômicas da Guerra dos Farrapos* (Rio de Janeiro, 1979); Thomas H. Holloway, *Policing Rio de Janeiro* (Stanford, 1993); Eduardo Silva, *Prince of the People*, Moyra Ashford, trans. (New York, 1993); and in accounts by such travelers as Prof. and Mrs. Louis Agassiz, *A Journey in Brazil* (Boston, 1868); and Rev. D. P. Kidder and Rev. J. C. Fletcher, *Brazil and the Brazilians* (Philadelphia, 1857). The military and its role in the Paraguayan War is treated in John Schulz, *O Exército na Política* (São Paulo, 1994); Wilma Peres Costa, *A Espada de Dâmocles* (São Paulo, 1996); and Ricardo Salles, *Guerra do Paraguai* (Rio de Janeiro, 1990).

The Old Republic (1889–1930)

When we come to the Republic, the reader will find a rapidly growing literature, recently enriched by much archival research. For three leading figures who span the late Empire and the early Republic, see Luiz Viana Filho's three volumes: *A Vida do Barão do Rio Branco* (Rio de Janeiro, 1959), *A Vida de Joaquim Nabuco* (São Paulo, 1952), and *A Vida de Rui Barbosa* (São Paulo, 1949). Other important biographies are Afonso Arinos de Melo Franco, *Um Estadista da República*, 3 vols. (Rio de Janeiro, 1955); and Stanley Hilton, *Oswaldo Aranha: Uma Biografia* (Rio de Janeiro, 1994). A political history of the entire Republic is available in Ronald M. Schneider, *"Order and Progress": A Political History of Brazil* (Boulder, 1991).

The economic context is crucial in understanding the era, as can be seen in Steven Topik, *The Political Economy of the Brazilian State, 1889–1930* (Austin, 1987); Peter L. Eisenberg, *The Sugar Industry in Pernambuco, 1840–1910* (Berkeley, 1974); Stanley J. Stein, *Vassouras: A Brazilian Coffee County, 1850–1900* (Princeton, 1985); and Richard Graham, *Britain and the Onset of Modernization in Brazil, 1850–1914* (Cambridge, 1968).

For three fine studies of regional change during the Old Republic, see Joseph L. Love, *São Paulo in the Brazilian Federation, 1889–1937* (Stanford, 1980); John D. Wirth, *Minas Gerais in the Brazilian Federation, 1889–1937* (Stanford, 1977); and Robert M. Levine, *Pernambuco in the Brazilian Federation, 1889–1937* (Stanford, 1978); which can be complemented by Joseph L. Love, *Rio Grande do Sul and Brazilian Regionalism, 1882–1930* (Stanford, 1971); Maurício A. Font, *Coffee, Contention and Change* (Cambridge, Mass., 1990); and Ralph della Cava, *Miracle at Joaseiro* (New York, 1970). Local-level politics are treated in Linda Lewin, *Politics and Parentela in Paraíba* (Princeton, 1987); Eul-Soo Pang, *Bahia in the First Brazilian Republic* (Gainesville, 1979); and Victor Nunes Leal, *Coronelismo: the Municipality and Representative Government in Brazil*, June Henfrey, trans. (Cambridge, 1977).

The 1890s revolt at Canudos was immortalized in Euclides da Cunha, *Rebellion in the Backlands*, Samuel Putnam, trans., 5th ed. (Chicago, 1957); and in a more recent treatment in Robert M. Levine, *Vale of Tears* (Berkeley, 1992). An equally significant although less well-known revolt is recounted in Todd A. Diacon, *Millenarian Vision, Capitalist Reality* (Durham, 1991). For an account of popular resistance in the city, see Teresa A. Meade, *"Civilizing" Rio* (University Park, 1997); Boris Fausto, *Trabalho Urbano e Conflito Social* (São Paulo, 1976); and Paulo Sérgio Pinheiro and Michael M. Hall, *A Classe Operária no Brasil, 1889–1930* (São Paulo, 1979–81). For a work that bridges labor history for the Old Republic and post-1930, see Joel Wolfe, *Working Women, Working Men* (Durham, 1993). The urban context is further treated in Gilberto Freyre, *Order and Progress* (New York, 1970); June E. Hahner, *Poverty and Politics* (Albuquerque, 1986); Sidney Chalhoub, *Cidade Febril* (Rio de Janeiro, 1996); Dain Borges, *The Family in Bahia, Brazil, 1870–1945* (Stanford, 1992); and Rosa Maria Barboza de Araújo, *A Vocação do Prazer* (Rio de Janeiro, 1993). Studies of the monarchists and the jacobins can be found in Maria de Lourdes Mônaco Janotti, *Os Subversivos da República* (São Paulo, 1986); and Suely Robles Reis de Queiroz, *Os Radicais da República* (São Paulo, 1986). The series of military revolts began in Rio in 1922 and culminated in the rebel force known as the "Prestes Column." Whatever the possible historical influence of the rebels, they unquestionably stimulated a huge bibliography. Recent titles include Anita L. Prestes, *A Coluna Prestes* (São Paulo, 1990); and Vary Pacheco Borges, *Tenetismo e Revolução Brasleira* (São Paulo, 1992).

Intellectual history of the Empire and the Old Republic is covered in João Cruz Costa, *A History of Ideas in Brazil*, Suzette Macedo, trans. (Berkeley, 1964); Roque Spencer Maciel de Barros, *A Ilustração Brasileira e a Idéia de Universidade* (São Paulo, 1959); Roberto Schwarz, *Um Mestre na Periferia do Capitalismo* (São Paulo, 1990); Brito Broca, *A Vida Literária no Brasil: 1900*, 2nd ed. (Rio de Janeiro, 1860); Jeffrey D. Needell, *A Tropical Belle Epoque* (Cambridge, 1987); L. Hallewell, *Books in Brazil* (Metuchen, 1982); Barbosa Lima Sobrinho, *Presença de Alberto Tôrres* (Rio de Janeiro, 1968); Francisco de Assis Barbosa, *A Vida de Lima Barreto*, 5th ed. (Rio de Janeiro, 1975); and Sergio Miceli, ed., *História das Ciências Sociais no Brasil*, vol. 1 (São Paulo, 1989). A useful source collection may be found in Djacir Menezes, ed., *O Brasil no Pensamento Brasileiro* (Rio de Janeiro, 1957). On public health, see Nancy Stepan, *Beginnings of Brazilian Science* (New York, 1976).

The Republic since 1930

Post-1930 political history has generated a burgeoning bibliography, partly because the social scientists (political scientists, sociologists, anthropologists, and economists) have contributed so much historical research. The indispensable reference work is Israel Beloch and Alzira Alves de Abreu, eds., *Dicionário Histórico-Biográfico Brasileiro: 1930–1983*, 4 vols. (Rio de Janeiro, 1984) which was published by the Centro de Pesquisa e Documentação de História Contemporânea do Brasil of the Fundação Getúlio Vargas. This Center is a principal archive and research center on post-1930 history. The dominant historical actor of the era is Getúlio Vargas, for whom we lack a first-class bibliography. Still useful is Karl Lowenstein, *Brazil Under Vargas* (New York, 1942), although it covers only up to 1943. A curiously emotionless primary source is Getúlio Vargas, *Diário*, 2 vols. (Rio de Janeiro, 1995). The context to the Vargas era is covered in Edgard Carone, *Revoluções do Brasil Contemporâneo* (São Paulo, 1965). An early biography by a non-Brazilian author is John W. F. Dulles, *Vargas of Brazil: A Political Biography* (Austin, 1967).

The post-1930 "emergency" government of Vargas provoked a full-scale military rebellion in São Paulo, as told in Stanley Hilton, *1932: A Guerra Civil Brasileira* (Rio de Janeiro, 1982). Those events produced a large memoir literature, which is cited in Hilton. There was also the later challenge posed by the Communist rebellion of 1935, which has produced varying interpretations, as in William Waack, *Camaradas* (São Paulo, 1993); Paulo Sérgio Pinheiro, *Estratégias da Ilusão* (São Paulo, 1991); and Marly Almeida and Gomes Vianna, *Revolucionários de 35* (São Paulo, 1992). The Communist Party has been much studied. Early attempts include Ronald H. Chilcote, *The Brazilian Communist Party* (Oxford, 1974) and John W. F. Dulles, *Anarchists and Communists in Brazil, 1900–1935* (Austin, 1973). The 1937 coup is analyzed in Aspásia Camargo, ed., *O Golpe Silencioso* (Rio de Janeiro, 1989). The São Paulo–based opposition is treated in John W. F. Dulles, *The São Paulo Law School and the Anti-Vargas Resistance* (Austin, 1986). One of the ugliest chapters of the Estado Nôvo is Vargas's delivering the wife of Luis Carlos Prestes to the Nazis. The story is told in Fernando Gomes, *Olga*, 4th ed. (São Paulo, 1985), which became a best seller. The Estado Nôvo also produced the corporatist labor policies that were to persist for sixty years. A key work of analysis is Angela Castro Gomes, *A Invenção do Trabalhismo* (Rio de Janeiro, 1988).

World War II led to much maneuvering by Brazil before it joined the allies in 1942. The background is given in Stanley E. Hilton, *Brazil and the Great Powers, 1930–1939* (Austin, 1975); and Ricardo Antonio Silva Seitenfus, *O Brasil de Getúlio Vargas e a Formação dos Blocos: 1930–1942* (São Paulo, 1985); while Frank D. McCann, Jr., *The Brazilian-American Alliance* (Princeton, 1973), is an excellent account of U.S.-Brazilian relations. See also Stanley E. Hilton, *Hitler's Secret War in South America, 1939–1945* (Baton Rouge, 1981).

The Vargas government of 1951–54 defined the direction of all subsequent Brazilian history. A key anti-Vargas figure who also played a central role in the demise of Jânio Quadros and João Goulart is profiled in John W. F. Dulles, *Carlos Lacerda, Brazilian Crusader*, 2 vols. (Austin, 1996). A de facto autobiography may be found in his marathon interview, Carlos Lacerda, *Depoimento* (Rio de Janeiro, 1977). For journalistic accounts of Vargas's suicide, see Hélio Silva, *1954: Um Tiro no Coração* (Rio de Janeiro, 1978); and Carlos Heitor Cony, *Quem Matou Vargas* (Rio de Janeiro, 1974). The political context is elucidated in Maria Vitoria de

Mesquita Benevides, *A UDN e o Udenismo* (Rio de Janeiro, 1981); Lucilia de Almeida Neves Delgado, *PTB: Do Getulismo ao Reformismo, 1945–1964* (São Paulo, 1989); Maria Vitoria Benevides, *O PTB e o Trabalhismo* (São Paulo, 1989), John D. French, *The Brazilian Workers' ABC* (Chapel Hill, 1992); and Salvador A. M. Sandoval, *Social Change and Labor Unrest in Brazil Since 1945* (Boulder, 1993).

One of the most important post-1945 presidencies was that of Juscelino Kubitschek (1956–61). The best analysis is Maria Victoria de Mesquita Benevides, *O Governo Kubitschek* (Rio de Janeiro, 1976). See also Francisco de Assis Barbosa, *Juscelino Kubitschek*, vol. 1 (Rio de Janeiro, 1960). Jânio Quadros (president, 1961) was one of postwar Brazil's most important politicians, yet he has been relatively unstudied. One exception is Vera Chaia, *A Liderança Política de Jânio Quadros, 1947–1990* (São Paulo, 1991). An overview that emphasizes the origins of the coup of 1964 is Thomas E. Skidmore, *Politics in Brazil* (Oxford, 1967); while Peter Flynn, *Brazil: a Political Analysis* (London, 1978), covers a similar period but is more sympathetic toward the Goulart government. For an account that argues for the existence of an extensive right-wing conspiracy in the early 1960s, see René Armand Dreifuss, *1964: A Conquista do Estado*, 3rd ed. (Rio de Janeiro, 1981). Important themes are treated in Michael L. Connif and Frank D. McCann, eds., *Modern Brazil: Elites and Masses in Historical Persoective* (Lincoln, 1989). Economic aspects are emphasized in John D. Wirth, *The Politics of Brazilian Development, 1930–1954* (Stanford, 1970). The indispensable source on the military is Alfred Stepan, *The Military in Politics* (Princeton, 1971). See also Nelson Werneck Sodré, *História Militar do Brasil* (Rio de Janeiro, 1965), for the interpretation by a former nationalist army officer.

The military government that ruled from 1964 to 1985 is recounted in Thomas Skidmore, *Politics of Military Rule in Brazil* (New York, 1988); and in Maria Helena Moreira Alves, *State and Opposition in Military Brazil* (Austin, 1985); Alfred Stepan, ed., *Authoritarian Brazil* (New Haven, 1973); and Lúcia Klein and Marcus Figueredo, *Legitimadade e Coerção no Brazil Pós '64* (Rio de Janeiro, 1978). For a detailed account of the armed opposition, see Marcelo Ridenti, *O Fantasma de Revolução Brasileira* (São Paulo, 1993). One of the most revealing memoirs of a guerilla survivor is Alfredo Syrkis, *Os Carbonários* (São Paulo, 1980). The reflections of a key figure on the left are given in Herbert de Souza (Betinho), *Revoluções da Minha Geração* (São Paulo, 1996). The uglier aspects of the regime are revealed in Joan Dassin, ed., *Torture in Brazil*, Jaime Wright, trans., (New York, 1986); and Lawrence Weschler, *A Miracle, a Universe* (New York, 1990). Evidence for U.S. involvement is given in A. J. Langguth, *Hidden Terrors* (New York, 1978).

Controversy over the extent of U.S. involvement in the 1964 coup, partially documented in Phyllis R. Parker, *Brazil and the Quiet Intervention, 1964* (Austin, 1979), has led to much writing on U.S.-Brazilian relations, as in Robert Wesson, *The United States and Brazil* (New York, 1981); W. Michael Weiss, *Cold Warriors and Coups D'état* (Albuquerque, 1993); Moniz Bandeira, *Presença dos Estados Unidos no Brasil* (Rio de Janeiro, 1973); and, by the same author, *Brasil–Estados Unidos: A Rivalidade Emergente (1950–1988)* (Rio de Janeiro, 1989). For a turn-of-the-century perspective, see E. Bradford Burns, *The Unwritten Alliance* (New York, 1966); and Steven C. Topik, *Trade and Gunboats* (Stanford, 1996).

The first military president is given a detailed two-volume biography in John W. F. Dulles, *President Castello Branco: Brazilian Reformer* (College Station, 1980) and *Castello Branco: The Making of a Brazilian President* (College Station, 1978). An "inside" picture of the second military government is furnished in Jayme Portella de Mello, *A Revolução e o Governo Costa e Silva* (Rio de Janeiro, 1979). The turning point of 1968 is colorfully described in Zuenir Aventura, *1968: O Ano Que Não Terminou* (Rio de Janeiro, 1988), which became a bestseller. The "transition to democracy" that began in the late 1970s is the subject of Alfred Stepan, ed., *Democratizing Brazil* (Oxford, 1989); Leigh A Payne, *Brazilian Industrialists and Democratic Change* (Baltimore, 1994); Fernando Henrique Cardoso, *O Modelo Político Brasileiro* (São Paulo, 1979); and Maria D'Alva Gil Kinzo, *Oposição e Autoritarismo* (São Paulo, 1988).

The economic policies imposed by the military government came in for both praise and attack. An excellent overall interpretation is Donald V. Coes, *Macroeconomic Crises, Policies, and Growth in Brazil, 1964–90* (Washington, D.C., 1995). An early favorable assessment was Donald E. Syvrud, *Foundations of Brazilian Economic Growth* (Stanford, 1974). A critical note was sounded by Sylvia Ann Hewlett, *The Cruel Dilemmas of Development* (New York, 1980); and by Edmar Bacha, *Os Mitos de uma Década* (Rio de Janeiro, 1976). The most widely read critic was Celso Furtado, who published a series of attacks on government policy, including *Análise do 'Modelo' Brasileiro* (Rio de Janeiro, 1972), *O Mito do Desenvolvimento Econômico* (Rio de Janeiro, 1974), and *O Brasil Pós-"Milagro"* (Rio de Janeiro, 1982). A defense of the heavy investment made in the public sector is given in Antônio Barros de Castro e Francisco Eduardo Pires de Sousa, *A Economia Brasileira em Marcha Forçada* (Rio de Janeiro, 1985). Failure to transform the agricultural sector is criticized in Francisco Graziano, *O Fracasso da Reforma Agrária no Brasil* (São Paulo, 1991). Peasant mobilization is studied in Biorn Maybury-Lewis, *The Politics of the Possible: The Brazilian Rural Workers' Trade Union Movement, 1964–1985* (Philadelphia, 1994); and Anthony W. Pereira, *The End of the Peasantry* (Pittsburgh, 1997).

Events since 1985 are less easy to put into historical perspective. Most accounts have been by political scientists, such as Bolívar Lamounier, ed., *De Geisel a Collor: O Balanço da Transição* (São Paulo, 1990); Alfred Stepan, *Rethinking Military Politics* (Princeton, 1988); Maria Victoria de Mesquita Benevides, *A Cidadania Ativa: Referendo, Plebiscito e Ini-*

ciativa Popular (São Paulo, 1991); and Wanderley Guilherme dos Santos, *Razões da Desordem* (Rio de Janeiro, 1993). Collective works include Fábio Wanderley Reis and Guilhermo O'Donnell, eds., *A Democracia no Brasil: Dilemmas e Perspectivas* (São Paulo, 1988); Antônio Lavareda, *A Democracia nas Urnas* (Rio de Janeiro, 1991); and Helio Jaguaribe, ed., *Sociedade, Estado e Partidos na Atualidade Brasileira* (São Paulo, 1992). For insight on the PT, which has done better than its critics predicted, see Margaret E. Keck, *The Worker's Party and Democratization in Brazil* (New Haven, 1992); Rachel Meneguello, *PT: A Formação de um Partido, 1979–1982* (Rio de Janeiro, 1989); and Jorge Bittar, ed., *O Modo Petista de Governar* (São Paulo, 1992). The brief presidency of Fernando Collor de Mello (1990–92) generated much polemical commentary. The most famous was the denunciation by his brother, Pedro Collor de Mello, *Passando a Limpo* (Rio de Janeiro, 1993).

The fate of the Amazon rain forest has been a growing concern in recent decades for both Brazilians and non-Brazilians. For a dire warning from two of the latter, see Suzanna Hecht and Alexander Cockburn, *The Fate of the Forest* (London, 1989). A careful analysis of Brazilian government policies is given in Anna Luiza Ozorio de Almeida, *Colonization of the Amazon* (Austin, 1992). The modern background to the current crisis can be found in John Hemming, *Amazon Frontier* (Cambridge, Mass., 1987); and in Warren Dean, *With Broadax and Firebrand* (Berkeley, 1995).

Post-1930 intellectual history, especially as it related to politics, is well-represented in such works as Lúcia Lippi Oliveira, ed., *Elite Intelectual e Debate Político nos Anos 30* (Rio de Janeiro, 1980); Jarbas Medeiros, *Ideologia Autoritária no Brasil: 1930–1945* (Rio de Janeiro, 1978); Sérgio Miceli, *Intelectuais e Clase Dirigente no Brasil: 1920–1945* (São Paulo, 1979); Carlos Guilherme Mota, *Ideologia da Cultura Brasileira: 1933–1974* (São Paulo, 1978); Antonio Candido, *Literatura e Sociedade* (São Paulo, 1985); Caio Navarro de Toledo, *ISEB: Fábrica de Ideologias* (São Paulo, 1977) and Daniel Pécaut, *Os Intelectuais e a Política no Brasil*, Maria Júlia Goldwasser, trans. (São Paulo, 1990).

Economic History

Economic history, long a neglected subject, has gained increased attention in recent years. The premier overall interpretation remains Celso Furtado, *The Economic Growth of Brazil*, Ricard W. de Aguiar and Eric Charles Drysdale, trans. (Berkeley, 1963). Brazil is examined within the Latin American context in the excellent general history by Victor Bulmer-Thomas, *The Economic History of Latin America Since Independence* (Cambridge, 1994). See also Werner Baer, *The Brazilian Economy*, 4th ed. (Westport, 1995); and Alberto Venancio Filho, *A Intervenção do Estado no*

Domínio Econômic (Rio de Janeiro, 1968). A highly useful overview is offered in Marcelo da Paiva Abreu, ed., *A Ordem do Progresso: Cem Anos de Política Econômica Republicana, 1889–1989* (Rio de Janeiro, 1990); and Paulo Neuhaus, ed., *Economia Brasileira: Uma Visão Histórica* (Rio de Janeiro, 1980). A highly useful set of data (some of which must have taken imagination to compile) is given in Raymond W. Goldsmith, *Brasil 1850–1984: Desenvolvimento Financeiro sob um Século de Inflaçao* (São Paulo, 1986). See also Carlos Manuel Peláez and Wilson Suzigan, *História Monetária do Brasil* (Rio de Janeiro, 1976); and Annibal Villanova Villela and Wilson Sugizan, *Política do Governo e Crescimento da Economia Brasileira: 1889–1945* (Rio de Janeiro, 1973). Despite the sketchy quality of the data, especially before 1945, good research has been done, as in Winston Fritsch, *External Constraints on Economic Policy in Brazil, 1889–1930* (Pittsburgh, 1988); and Warren Dean, *The Industrialization of São Paulo, 1880–1945* (Austin, 1969). The question of Brazil's "lag" in the nineteenth century is examined in Stephen Haber, ed., *How Latin America Fell Behind* (Stanford, 1997), with an explicit comparison to Mexico. Earlier work on the same theme is available in Nathaniel H. Leff, *Underdevelopment and Development in Brazil*, vol. 1 (London, 1982). The all-important demographic context is given in Thomas W. Merrick and Douglas H. Graham, *Population and Economic Development in Brazil* (Baltimore, 1979). The central figure in nineteenth-century attempts to diversify the economy is the subject of a detailed biography in Jorge Caldeira, *Mauá: Empresário do Império*, 3rd ed. (São Paulo, 1995). The story of Brazil's roller-coaster experience with the commercialization of rubber is told in Warren Dean, *Brazil and the Struggle for Rubber* (Cambridge, 1987); and Barbara Weinstein, *The Amazon Rubber Boom, 1850–1920* (Stanford, 1983).

The history of industrialization has been a favorite topic, although well-researched monographs are still relatively few. One of the earliest was Stanley J. Stein, *The Brazilian Cotton Manufacture* (Cambridge, Mass., 1957). Much of the early Brazilian scholarly concern focused on the quality of Brazilian entrepreneurs, as in Fernando Henrique Cardoso, *Empresário Industrial e Desenvolvimento Econômico* (São Paulo, 1964); and Ely Diniz, *Empresário, Estado e Capitalismo no Brasil: 1930–1945* (Rio de Janeiro, 1978). Subsequent literature includes Flavio Rabelo Versiani and José Roberto Mendonça de Barros, eds., *Formação Econômica do Brasil: A Experiência da Industrialização* (São Paulo, 1977); Wilson Cano, *Raízes da Concentração Industrial em São Paulo* (São Paulo, 1977); Carlos Manuel Peláez, *História da Industrialização Brasileira* (Rio de Janeiro, 1972); Wilson Suzigan, *Indústria Brasileira* (São Paulo, 1986); Helen Shapiro, *Engines of Growth* (Cambridge, 1994); and Marshall C. Eakin, *British Enterprise in Brazil* (Durham, 1989), on mining. The coffee sector has been the subject of much writing. For the nineteenth century, this work often overlaps with the literature on slavery cited earlier. Other representative publications include Pierre Monbeig, *Pionniers et Planteurs de São Paulo* (Paris,

1952); Thomas H. Holloway, *The Brazilian Coffee Valorization of 1906* (Madison, 1975); Verena Stoelke, *Coffee Planters, Workers and Wives* (London, 1988); and J. de Souza Martins, *O Cativeiro da Terra* (São Paulo, 1979).

The large literature on immigration is largely celebratory. An example of the more analytical approach is Jeffrey Lesser, *Welcoming the Undesirables* (Los Angeles, 1995). For an account of how the Italian immigrants fared in the west of São Paulo, see Thomas H. Holloway, *Immigrants on the Land* (Chapel Hill, 1980). The best account of German immigration is Frederick C. Luebke, *Germans in Brazil* (Baton Rouge, 1987). For works on urban history see Paulo Singer, *Desenvolvimento Econômico e Evolução Urbana* (São Paulo, 1968); Lucio Kowarick, ed., *Social Struggles and the City* (New York, 1994); James Holston, *The Modernist City: An Anthropological Critique of Brasília* (Chicago, 1989); Richard Morse, *From Community to Metropolis*, 2nd ed. (New York, 1974); and Boris Fausto, *Crime e Cotidiano* (São Paulo, 1984). *Favela* life is depicted in Nancy Scheper-Hughes, *Death Without Weeping: The Violence of Everyday Life in Brazil* (Los Angeles, 1982).

Race Relations

Race relations in post-abolition Brazil have slowly drawn scholarly attention, although the overall emphasis has remained on slavery. One of the first empirically based works was George Reid Andrews, *Blacks and Whites in São Paulo, Brazil, 1888–1988* (Madison, 1991). For an account of alleged prejudice in the Foreign Office, see M. Luiza Tucci Carneiro, *Preconceito Racial*, 2nd ed. (São Paulo, 1988). Intellectual controversies over race are analyzed in Thomas Skidmore, *Black Into White: Race and Nationality in Brazilian Thought* (New York, 1974); and Lilia Moritz Schwarcz, *O Espetáculo das Raças* (São Paulo, 1993). For a revealing survey of U.S. reactions to Brazilian race relations, see David J. Hellwig, ed., *African-American Reflections on Brazil's Racial Paradise* (Philadelphia, 1992). The basic facts about racial inequality in modern Brazil may be found in Peggy A. Lovell, ed., *Desigualdade Racial no Brasil Contemporâneo* (Belo Horizonte, 1991); and Nelson do Valle Silva and Carlos A. Hasenbalg, *Relações Raciais no Brasil Contemporaneo* (Rio de Janeiro, 1992). Afro-Brazilian culture, in its many dimensions, is a favorite subject for scholars in almost all disciplines. On religion, see Diana De G. Brown, *Umbanda, Religion and Politics in Urban Brazil*, 2nd ed. (New York, 1994); Ruth Landes, *The City of Women* (Albuquerque, 1994); and Roger Bastide, *The African Religions of Brazil*, Helen Sebba, trans. (Baltimore, 1978). On Afro-Brazilian-based social movements, see Michael George Hanchard, *Orpheus and Power* (Princeton, 1994).

Index